JOHN W. HOLMES
Editor

MAELSTROM

The United States,
Southern Europe, and the
Challenges of the Mediterranean

D0075345

THE WORLD PEACE FOUNDATION
Cambridge, Massachusetts

Library of Congress Cataloging-in-Publication data:
Maelstrom: the United States, Southern Europe, and the challenges of the
Mediterranean / John W. Holmes, editor.
  p.   cm.
Includes bibliographical references and index.
ISBN 0-8157-3718-1 (alk. paper). — ISBN 0-8157-3717-3 (pbk.: alk.
paper)
    1. Mediterranean—Foreign relations—1945–   . 2. United States—
Foreign relations—Europe, Southern. 3. Europe, Southern—Foreign
relations—United States. I. Holmes, John William, 1935–   .
II. World Peace Foundation.
JX1393.M43M34 1994
327′.09182′2—dc20   94-38862
                                                             CIP

9 8 7 6 5 4 3 2 1

The paper used in this publication meets the minimum requirements of the
American National Standard for Information Sciences—Permanence of Paper
for Printed Library Materials, ANSI Z39.48-1984

Foreword

ON OCTOBER 15–16, 1993, the Luso-American Development Foundation and the World Peace Foundation organized a conference in Lisbon on relations between the United States and Southern Europe. There were two basic reasons for this initiative. On the Portuguese side, there was a growing awareness of the importance of the development of the Maghreb for the security and development of Europe, particularly the countries on the "southern flank"; on the American side, there was the conviction that the process of seeking peace in the Middle East, and even stability in the Mediterranean, is only possible in the absence of serious political disturbances among the peoples of North Africa.

An analysis of questions of economic development and of demographic and migration policies—as well as of the reinforcement of democracy in Egypt, Libya, Algeria, Tunisia, and Morocco—reveals connections with even deeper questions of a sociocultural nature, including religion, the condition of Muslim women, and education. Political stability in the region cannot be attained unless there are better prospects for economic development and for the employment of youth.

International cooperation—such as that proposed by Spain, France, Italy, and Portugal at the Conference on Security and Cooperation in the Mediterranean organized in Malaga in June 1992 by the Interparliamentary Union—might be seen as premature. It would be difficult under the present circumstances to launch a new CSCE for Southern Europe and the Mediterranean. However, such a proposal nevertheless reflects the interest and concern of the Southern European countries.

What the Lisbon conference revealed were the relative tardiness of the concern over this matter and the urgent necessity to deepen our consideration of the various aspects of this complex question, which is crucial for the security of the region. It became clear that cooperation between Europeans and Americans in this area is essential, given that both have basically common concerns and interests.

From the standpoint of issues raised and doors opened, we can say that the goals of the conference were fully attained. But it represented only one small step; many others must be taken on this long and crucial trek.

Rui Chancerelle de Machete
President
Luso-American Development Foundation

Contents

Tables

Preface

THE WORLD Peace Foundation, as part of an effort to see how the international order had changed as a result of the end of the cold war, identified Southern Europe and the Mediterranean as an area of particular interest to the United States, where both old and new problems seemed to abound. We enlisted in our project a number of experts from government, foreign policy institutes, and the private sector. Our team of authors was made up mainly of Southern Europeans and Americans but also included an Algerian; the commentators invited to the principal conference of the project, held in Lisbon in October 1993, included Northern Europeans and an Egyptian as well. Participants, other than the authors, included Jeffrey J. Anderson, Michael I. Austrian, Salah Bassiouny, Richard J. Bloomfield, J. Calvet de Magalhães, John Chipman, Fernanda Faria, Kemal Kirisci, Remy Leveau, Robert J. Pranger, J. Ramos Silva, Dirk Vandewalle, and Pere Vilanova. This mix of participants contributed to making the project a voyage of discovery, uncovering new issues and fresh points of view.

The World Peace Foundation received a significant financial contribution from the Luso-American Foundation, whose hospitality in Lisbon was abounding. Special thanks go to Dr. Rui Machete, the chairman of the foundation, and to Charles Buchanan, its Administrator. NATO's Office of Information and Press also made a significant contribution to underwriting the costs of the project. Finally the Thomas Watson, Jr., Institute for International Studies at Brown University played host to the first of the project's meetings, in Providence, Rhode Island.

ix

ONE

Introduction

John W. Holmes

THE TENSIONS in the Mediterranean area have survived the end of the cold war and have if anything grown in seriousness in the last few years. In 1991 a major war was fought against Iraq; the balance of power in the Persian Gulf and the security of Israel remain of vital importance to the United States. Europe for its part is mesmerized by the prospect of the establishment of culturally (and possibly politically) inimical regimes on the south side of the Mediterranean.

This study began with the assumption that both the United States and Southern Europe have significant, perhaps vital, interests in the areas to the south and east of the Mediterranean. It also seemed clear that cooperation between them in pursuit of these interests is essential: for the United States because access to the Middle East would be difficult without Southern European help; for Southern Europe because the United States, at least for the moment, is the only power capable of effective involvement in the area.

Although the study confirmed these main points, it also brought to the surface other issues.

The end of the cold war has, in a sense, expanded the Mediterranean area: the largely Turkish-speaking republics of Central Asia are now to some extent part of an interacting Middle Eastern whole, and the Balkan states, forcibly tranquilized by Communist dominance, are once again turbulent neighbors.

Greece has been orphaned by the end of the cold war, which extinguished its old strategic significance for the United States, but it continues to matter because of its potential embroilment in the crisis in the Balkans. Turkey is still a strategic glacis, but facing the Islamic world, rather than the Soviet Union; the stability of its own Western allegiance is being undermined by European rejection.

1

Several factors, including the end of the cold war and fears generated by
the rise of Islamic fundamentalism, have created the promise of Israeli-
Palestinian peace. But as this promise develops into reality, the U.S.
government's willingness to turn a blind eye to the repressive practices of
the friendly but authoritarian regimes of the Arab world—first in importance among which is that of Egypt—will decline. These regimes, and that
of Algeria, are already near the tipping point.

Europe's concerns about developments to the south of the Mediterranean
have not been matched by action. Now it may be too late; accommodation
or containment may be the only options. The United States, in turn, has
tended to ignore developments in North Africa, despite the danger that they
could touch off a clash of civilizations from which the United States and its
global interests would not be exempt. (As the Algerian crisis worsened in
1994, the U.S. government gave signs of recognizing the problem; it became relatively active in urging an accommodation with the Islamic
fundamentalists in that country.)

Finally, whereas Southern Europeans continue to hope for the development of a common European foreign and security policy—renationalization
of defense is not for them an attractive option—for the moment their
security is tied to relations with the United States. Given the fading of old
institutions and the lack of vigorous new ones to deal with the problems in
this area, bilateral U.S.–Southern European relations seem more important
than ever.

For forty years U.S. policy toward Europe was dominated by the relationships with our principal adversary, the Soviet Union, and with our
principal allies, the European members of the North Atlantic Treaty Organization (NATO). The chosen means for dealing with Western Europe was
through NATO, and this approach was supplemented by bilateral links with
Western Europe's major military powers: Germany, the United Kingdom,
and France.

The end of the cold war has weakened the claim of these two relationships on American attention; on the other hand, in *relative* terms relations
with Southern Europe have grown in importance, assuming a relative
importance such as has not been seen since the years immediately following
World War II, when the United States went to the aid of Greece and Turkey
and created a permanent naval presence in the Mediterranean, well before
the launching of NATO.

Although the military relationship is central to U.S. interests in the
Mediterranean, U.S. relations with Southern Europe must have more than

one dimension. These countries are increasingly prosperous and mature democracies that steadily count for more in political terms. They have their own interests, to which the U.S. must attend if the relationship is to be healthy.

Maelstrom attempts to provide both information and analysis on the one hand and policy recommendations on the other, but the mix of these elements within each chapter is different.

Ian O. Lesser, in "Growth and Change in Southern Europe," argues that Southern Europe was peripheral during the cold war, but that in the new strategic environment problems and interests have shifted from central Europe to the south and east, making the countries of Southern Europe more important. They share the experience of transition from authoritarian to democratic rule and, with the partial exception of Turkey, have been integrated into the mainstream of European life. They have adopted a higher profile in European and international affairs.

However, some of these trends are vulnerable. Doubts about the adequacy of "European" security have grown; on the other hand, Southern Europe fears eternal relegation to a European second division as a result of its inability to meet the economic convergence requirements set by the European Union's Treaty of Maastricht. Turkey is a more acute, and dangerous, case of present and potential exclusion from full participation in Europe's institutions. Except in Portugal, Southern Europe's political systems have entered a stressful period.

After four decades of marginalization Southern Europe is on the front line of the new "arc of crisis." After years of sheltered prosperity, the countries of Southern Europe face a less secure future as a result of developments to their south and east. The current threat from the south is to the fabric of societies unused to mass immigration and fearful of spillover effects of Islamic radicalism; but a military threat could also emerge. Southern Europe is likely to become a less certain and optimistic but a more important place.

The second part of the book is made up of several chapters that examine the Mediterranean dimension.

Andrés Ortega comprehensively describes the political and economic situations in the countries of the Maghreb—Libya, Tunisia, Algeria, Morocco, and Mauritania—and the relations that the countries of Southern Europe have with them. Ortega notes the formidable problems posed by the failure of economic growth to keep up with population increases, by ragged progress toward democracy, and by the threat of Islamic fundamentalism. He argues strongly that Europe, particularly Southern Europe, cannot afford to ignore these neighbors and must try to help them over the hump to prosperity and democracy, although he acknowledges that events make it more difficult to act now than it would have been five years ago. Much, of course, depends on the countries of the Maghreb acting in their own interests. Ortega argues that the United States has a role to play in the region.

In chapter 4, "The Question of Migration," Nadji Safir corrects some misconceptions. Migration from the south of the Mediterranean is not a new phenomenon; regarding Islamic immigrants, new or established, as a challenge to European security and identity—as a sort of fifth column of radicalism and fundamentalism—ignores both their behavior and the possibility that they could be influences for modernism in their countries of origin. A population explosion is in progress in North Africa (not to speak of sub-Saharan Africa) that inevitably will lead to pressures for migration to the richer countries to the north of the Mediterranean. It is in Europe's interest, if it wishes to avoid mass immigration, to act more effectively to develop the economies on the other shore. Taking a broader view, Europe should see the North African population as a resource rather than a threat; with its own population static and aging, it should seek to benefit from the youthful labor force of its Mediterranean hinterland.

The Middle East, Graham E. Fuller writes in chapter 5, is in the process of change. Its very definition has changed: Central Asia now interacts with the more traditional Middle East. Countries like Turkey have new horizons. States like Iraq are under threat of schism. Russia's longer-term role remains to be clarified. The area's problems and movements are changing, too. Fuller challenges a mantra-like invocation of "oil" as a reason for outside involvement in the Middle East. The prospect of Arab-Israeli peace opens up new possibilities, among which is a diminished tolerance of the West for the regimes, friendly but authoritarian, that have been its allies. The rise of Islamism as a political force is virtually inevitable; the question is how, not whether. The challenge is to find ways gradually to allow fundamentalists to take part in the political system; the alternative, repression, is much more likely to lead to violence and radicalism.

Antonio Badini focuses on ways in which Southern Europe—and the United States—can and should bridge the Mediterranean gap. He recounts the failure of past efforts both to build regionalism within the Maghreb and to use the European Community as an agent for change there. He also

discusses the more far-reaching schemes for political and security cooperation around the Mediterranean, such as the Italo-Spanish proposal for a
Conference on Security and Cooperation in the Mediterranean, patterned on
the Conference on Security and Cooperation in Europe. He argues for an
approach using a name familiar to Americans: an Alliance for Progress.
This would attempt to encourage progress toward economic and political
liberalization while at the same time providing a catalyst for economic help
to the countries to the south of the Mediterranean.

The third section of the book looks at Southern Europe as a part of the
European Community (since Maastricht, the European Union).

How cohesive are the Southern European countries? Dimitri Constas, in
chapter 7, looks at the record. He finds that they have stuck together
effectively to influence Community policies relating to economic and social
cohesion (where they, as relatively poor members of the Community,
clearly have interests in common), and with regard to the Community's
neighbors around the Mediterranean. On the other hand, they have not
formed a cohesive bloc with regard to several important issues connected
with the future development of the Community, even though some of these,
such as enlargement, are materially important for them and for their relations with the Mediterranean. They seem caught between wanting the
benefits of Community membership and yet wanting (as much or more than
some of the bigger countries of Northern Europe) to preserve their sovereignty and freedom to make special bilateral arrangements, especially with
the United States.

Fernando Rodrigo, in chapter 8, looks in detail at one policy area,
defense. All of the Southern European countries have a background of
maintaining a strong and special relationship with the United States; as the
years passed, each experienced problems in its relationship with the United
States and with NATO, of which the United States was the leading member.
The common feeling of dissatisfaction with cold war–vintage security
arrangements was not enough, however, to produce a sense of shared
identity. When, at the end of the cold war and in connection with the Gulf
War, the European Community began to discuss a potential security capacity of its own, the Southern European countries, like their northern neighbors, divided along Europeanist versus Atlanticist lines. Changed
circumstances have in recent years led Portugal, Spain, and Italy both to
limit defense spending and to redirect their national defense efforts to
develop a capability for action in the Mediterranean context. Southern
Europe remains divided even in this regard, for Greece and Turkey continue

to spend formidable shares of their national income on defense and perceive quite different threats—including each other.

The next two chapters examine how the Southern European countries might relate in the future to the United States—still, as for the last forty years, a vital point of reference.

Roberto Aliboni, in chapter 9, examines the prospective relevance of the Community, which already has played a strong role in the economic and political development of Southern Europe, for transatlantic relations. Southern Europe has been both marginal and central to both NATO and the Community; it has in fact used its participation in one grouping to improve its bargaining power within the other. In the post–cold war era, Southern Europe finds itself more clearly central, at the meeting point of the two arcs of crisis, to the east and to the south, that surround Western Europe. By itself Southern Europe is not able to cope with these challenges; if its countries avoid a futile return to nationalism, they are left with the traditional Euro-Atlantic options. In principle a European Community that had an effective Common Foreign and Security Policy would be an optimal means for Southern Europe to respond to challenges from the Mediterranean and the Balkans. Prospects for such a growth in the Community's role and competence are currently not bright. Yet the United States is now much less antagonistic to the development of a European security and defense identity. If the United States pursues a multilateralist policy, a Community approach could contribute to a better U.S.-European division of labor. However, should the United States move to a policy akin to strategic unilateralism, there could be a conflict: it might find a strong Community orientation on the part of Southern Europe to be a hindrance to U.S. operations in the Mediterranean area. Given Southern Europe's need of both the United States and the Community, and the dangers of making a choice between the two, Southern Europe will continue to try to reconcile Europeanism with Atlanticism.

Jaime Gama comes at the same problem from a somewhat different angle. He argues that although great powers, like the United States, may view Southern Europe or the Mediterranean as a unit, in fact national (or at least subregional) differences are the reality. A variety of multinational organizations are extending their influence to elements of the life of the area; these include NATO, which has been undergoing a rejuvenation and redirection. Gama examines in some depth developments in his own country, Portugal, the most Atlanticist nation in Southern Europe but one that is evolving from its old very special and dependent relationship with the

United States. Yet these developments do not eclipse the importance of bilateral relations: whereas in other policy areas multilateral relations may grow in importance, in defense and security policy bilateral relations will prevail.

In the last chapter John Holmes looks at the problem of the cooperation between Southern Europe and the United States in confronting the problems around the Mediterranean from an American perspective. The United States is, he thinks, pursuing a strategy of selective disengagement from the world; this is not a peculiarity of the Clinton administration, but rather a fundamental and lasting change. This change does not preclude U.S. involvement abroad, but in the future such involvement will be based neither on extended ideas of interest based on alliances nor on humanitarian grounds, but on national interest, rather narrowly conceived. The oil resources of the Persian Gulf and the U.S. commitment to Israel make the eastern Mediterranean one of the few parts of the world that continues to be vital to the United States. Access to that area requires that the United States extend its interest to the entire Mediterranean. For the foreseeable future neither NATO nor a division of labor with the European Union nor new forms of Mediterranean cooperation will suffice to protect American interests. U.S. policy will have to be made effective by a combination of unilateral and bilateral means. This approach, given the evolution of Southern Europe, will require more, not less, attention by Washington to its allies. The United States may at some time weary of its burden even in this important area. Southern Europe should therefore push for the development of a European Union competent in security matters with which the U.S. *could* divide responsibility.

Several themes crossed the boundaries of the chapters of this book and also received extended discussion at the two conferences held in the course of the study.

—First and foremost, is there a Mediterranean in more than a geographic sense? The answer seems to us to be that for many purposes the Mediterranean area should be seen as a series of subregions, but that there are linkages between them. Ironically, radical Islam, one of the area's chief problems, is a linkage of growing importance.

—Akin to that question, is there a Southern Europe, and if so what is it? Again the group of countries that most of us considered to form Southern Europe exhibited strong individual characteristics. Yet the core group of countries that we wound up examining most closely possess a number of traits in common. Portugal, Spain, Italy, and Greece are countries that have, over the last generation or two, emerged from a common background of economic underdevelopment and authoritarian government. France, although highly relevant to Mediterranean issues—its role is considered in several chapters—has a different political-economic background, an identity as a former great power that still plays a dominant role in European affairs, and a vision of the world and its place in it that goes far beyond the Mediterranean. Turkey, for quite different reasons—a member of NATO, it has been excluded from the European Union—also seems to be a special case, in but not entirely of Southern Europe.

—As in almost every foreign policy discussion, there was a clash between realism and idealism or humanitarianism. In this case it mainly took the form of laments from some Europeans about the seeming unwillingness of the United States to involve itself except when its own national interests are engaged. At least one American participant, however, thought that among the developments of the post–cold war era would be not only a new stress on action for humanitarian reasons but also a growth in the power of the United Nations.

—There was, however, considerable agreement that although the U.S. commitment to involvement in Europe as a whole had diminished and might dwindle further, the U.S. interest in the Mediterranean remained strong. A substantial U.S. air and naval presence in the Mediterranean might survive virtual withdrawal of U.S. forces from the continent. (The fact that such a commitment would be founded on problems outside Southern Europe is a sore point with some Southern Europeans and makes careful handling of U.S. bilateral relations all the more important.)

—The troubles in the former Yugoslavia, and especially the war in Bosnia, were a constant source of concern, both in and of themselves and because of their obvious relevance for this study. The agonies of Yugoslavia would have overwhelmed this book had they become part of it; although there are a number of references to the problem and its implications, we chose not to make it one of the topics for formal discussion. The Yugoslav situation remains what it has been throughout our work: a *potential* danger to the already fragile stability of the Mediterranean, a danger particularly to the perennially problematic relationship between two Southern European nations, Greece and Turkey.

—Turkey was a recurrent subject of discussion. Here there was initially an American-European split: the Americans were persuaded both of the importance of Turkey, in and of itself and as an example, and of the need for its inclusion in "Europe." Some of the European participants started out with a view that sharply excluded Turkey from being considered "European"; but by the end of the project Turkey played an important role in some of their thinking, even if the rejectionist view survived.

—On one issue there was no disagreement: the potential for real cultural-political trouble in the Maghreb and also in Egypt. Islamic fundamentalism, generally seen as a reaction to the failures of various forms of modernism, is, most participants agreed, inexorably spreading. For a variety of reasons, the regimes in place have lost legitimacy and no longer have such unconditional support from their Western patrons. The group divided, however, on the prospects for a relatively painless transition to a new order of things on the southern shore of the Mediterranean. Although there was some agreement that rigid repression was an inferior strategy compared to gradually opening up to fundamentalist political forces, there was division as to the possibility, at this time, of the West's contributing to the development of these countries in such a way and at such a rate as to improve the chances of their future being a relatively liberal one, both economically and politically. To generalize, those currently actively involved in government were the most inclined to say that difficult though the task is, it must be attempted. Others felt that it is already too late, at least in the case of Algeria, where the world simply will have to cope with an explosion that is by now inevitable.

TWO

Growth and Change in Southern Europe

Ian O. Lesser

WITH THE recent sweeping changes in international affairs, old assumptions about the relationship of the United States to Europe and Europe's regions are changing rapidly. Under cold war conditions, Southern Europe—for the purposes of this analysis, Portugal, Spain, Italy, Greece, and Turkey—was relegated to the periphery by policymakers and observers on both sides of the Atlantic. What little treatment the region did receive was generally couched in terms of security within the "Southern Region" of the North Atlantic Treaty Organization (NATO), itself an increasingly irrelevant framework in the post–cold war world. Developments in Europe and farther afield have fundamentally altered not only the character but also the locus of political, economic, and security concerns. In the new strategic environment, problems and interests have shifted decisively from the center of Europe to the periphery, both south and east. As a result the countries of Southern Europe are emerging as more important actors in the evolution of European and transatlantic institutions, influencing the prospects for stability on the European periphery and as far afield as the greater Middle East.

The debate over the character of the new international order has focused above all on issues of societal change and political and economic development. In this context the evolution of Southern Europe since World War II provides a useful reference point for the discussion of transitions (domestic and external) elsewhere, not least in Eastern Europe and the territories of the former Soviet Union. The question of transitions also provides much of

The views expressed in this chapter are the author's own and should not be interpreted as representing the views of RAND or its research sponsors.

the rationale for including Turkey in the discussion of Southern Europe. As the European Union (EU) and NATO consider the wisdom and implications of extending their membership and reach eastward, Turkey's future role in relation to Europe remains ambiguous. Unquestionably a member of the European "system," Turkey is less clearly a part of Europe in cultural and political terms. Yet its role in the Southern European environment and its prominence in transatlantic strategic perceptions cannot be ignored.

The following discussion emphasizes trends important to the internal and geopolitical evolution of Southern Europe as a whole, with secondary attention to specific national circumstances. What have been the key points of evolution across Southern Europe? How has the region's relationship to Europe and the Atlantic community changed? What are the current challenges, and why does the region merit new attention in a transatlantic context?

A Historical Perspective

For much of modern European history, Southern Europe and the Mediterranean world as a whole were at the very center of cultural, political, and economic affairs. Europe's southern borderlands were the leading theater in the thousand-year confrontation with Islam around the Mediterranean and its hinterlands. This extended confrontation, a dominant factor in the evolution of Southern Europe from the eighth through the eighteenth centuries, has not unreasonably been described as the "first Cold War."[1] Beyond political and military confrontation, the Mediterranean has, albeit with periods of greater and lesser intensity, been a center of cultural and economic exchange between civilizations influencing the development of Europe as a whole. This experience has contributed to the contemporary interest in the theme of Mediterranean unity, whether lost, actual, or potential. It has also given rise to a substantial school of historiography exploring the role of Southern Europe as both a bridge and a barrier in geopolitical terms.[2] Echoes of this history and the theme of Mediterranean unity can be found in the increasingly active foreign and security policies of the Southern European states, most notably Spain and Italy. They are most pronounced in proposals such as that for a Conference on Security and Cooperation in the Mediterranean (CSCM) and are not absent from narrower regional initiatives in the western Mediterranean. In both cases, Southern European countries (along with France, whose southern vocation is pronounced but accompanied by more global interests) and institutions are understood to have a special role in addressing problems on the European periphery.

The European discovery of America, the opening of the Atlantic system, and the European penetration into Asia and Africa were largely the result of Portuguese and Spanish exploration. It is a striking geopolitical irony that these Southern European initiatives ultimately led to a marked decline in the political and economic importance of the Mediterranean basin. From the North American perspective, it is equally noteworthy that the American involvement in European security also had its start along an Atlantic-Mediterranean axis, with a naval presence in the western Mediterranean.[3] The parallel expansion of the "Turkey trade" and support for national movements in the Balkans gave additional political and economic weight to American interests in the Mediterranean and Southern Europe.[4]

The essential point is that Southern Europe has had a pivotal role in the geopolitical evolution of the European, Mediterranean, and Atlantic systems. But the pattern since the seventeenth century has on the whole been one of decline when measured in global terms, with the evolution of the region overwhelmingly tied to developments and decisions made elsewhere. In this sense the political marginalization of the region during the cold war was hardly a departure from modern historical patterns.

Growth and Change Since 1945

The postwar evolution of Southern Europe has been characterized by three broad themes: democratization, Europeanization, and the adjustment of external policies. To a significant degree these have been interactive and open-ended processes. From a policy perspective, the net result has been a broad convergence in terms of prosperity and political development, both across the region and in relation to Western Europe as a whole.

Political and Economic Transformation

First, although the pace and style of political change have varied, the countries of Southern Europe share the experience of transition from authoritarian to democratic rule. This has not been an uninterrupted process, as the era of the Colonels in Greece demonstrates, and in the case of Turkey the movement toward democratization and transparency remains incomplete. However, the process of democratization and occasional anxiety about its durability have been overwhelmingly important factors in shaping internal and external policies from Lisbon to Ankara. With the death of Franco and the rapid consolidation of democratic rule, Spain has moved from a position of diplomatic isolation to one of considerable activism on the international scene.[5] For Portugal, Spain, and Greece, membership in the European Community and NATO has had enormous symbolic as well as practical value as proof of membership in the Western democratic "club" and as a legitimate, external outlet for military establishments.[6] In a somewhat different context, Italy's central role in both institutions was understood as serving the cold war purpose of reinforcing the country's Western vocation in the face of substantial communist strength. In reality Italian communists and socialists also had a substantial stake in Western institutions. Indeed a position on the margins of cold war Europe arguably fostered the growth of Eurocommunism across Southern Europe. Lacking full membership in Europe, membership in NATO (and to a more limited extent in the Council of Europe) has served a critical political function in Turkey, offering tangible proof of the country's Western credentials. In the view of many Turkish observers, participation in NATO has also had a positive influence on the character of civilian-military relations and made the possibility of a conscious return to authoritarianism more remote.[7]

The potential relevance of the Portuguese, Spanish, and Greek transitions to democracy and experience of European integration to the process of reform under way in the East has emerged as a common theme among Southern European observers. To the extent that the countries of Eastern Europe and the former Soviet Union are eager to return to the European cultural, political, and economic fold, and to join established Western security institutions as a hedge against regional risks, the Southern European experience may well provide a variety of useful models.

Second, and with the partial exception of Turkey, the countries of Southern Europe have become progressively more European in character and outlook. As noted earlier, this evolution has been most pronounced in political terms and was given considerable impetus by Spanish, Greek, and Portuguese membership in the EC. Relatively high rates of economic growth and continuing integration into the European economic mainstream have brought Portugal, Spain, and Greece levels of prosperity approaching the European norm, despite some notable examples or regional underdevelopment within states (such as the Mezzogiorno and Andalusia). The economic development of Italy since the 1970s is the most striking example, with the Spanish economic success of the 1980s not far behind. Structural problems have persisted, not the least of which are the relative weight of the public sector and the extent of public debt when judged against EC standards, and the related problem of capturing revenue from the robust "black" and "gray" economies. However, the general trend has clearly been rapid movement toward the European mainstream in standards of living. At the same time Southern European societies have come to resemble their Western European partners in broader cultural terms to an extent that would have been unthinkable in the immediate postwar years (and this includes the spread of urban ills associated with advanced industrial societies elsewhere). Traditionally net exporters of labor to northern Europe and North America, with increasing prosperity Portugal, Spain, Italy, and Greece have become destinations as well as conduits for economic migrants and refugees from North Africa and Eastern Europe. Turkey has been a leading exporter of labor to Northern Europe, with a Turkish community of some 1.5 million in Germany alone.

Frustrated in its ability to pursue the European option, Turkish society has nonetheless been strongly influenced by the process of European integration affecting its Southern European partners. The desire to "join" Europe in the institutional sense has shaped the views of the political class as well as large portions of the public. At the same time Turkey has also experienced very high rates of economic growth, especially through the Ozal era, accompanied by the challenges of inflation and inadequate distribution of wealth. Although outside Europe in a formal sense—and in the perception of most Europeans—Turks in general have also become more European in terms of their economic and political expectations. The tension between these expectations and Europe's reluctance to envision EC membership for an Islamic country of sixty million people (with a per capita income that remains half the EC average) raises important questions for Turkey's future orientation.[8]

Foreign and Security Policy Adjustments

The progressive Europeanization of Southern Europe has encouraged a third and parallel transformation in the region's approach to external policy. As elsewhere Portuguese, Spanish, Italian, and Greek attitudes toward foreign and security policy throughout the cold war were shaped by the imperatives of containment and the structure of defense cooperation with the United States. In the case of Portugal the process of colonial withdrawal was an additional and important factor. Under classical cold war conditions NATO's southern allies were marginalized as a result of their limited military potential (Turkey was and continues to be an exception in this regard) and remoteness from the principal points of East-West confrontation in central Europe. Italy was indeed a player in NATO Central Region as well as Southern Region affairs, but this involvement made little difference to the perception of strategic marginalization in Rome.

The problem of strategic "coupling"—a central dilemma for European strategists throughout the cold war—was particularly complex from the Southern European perspective. For the southern allies the problem was not only to assure the credibility of extended deterrence across the Atlantic, but also to maintain the linkage between security in central and Southern Europe. As the unifying perception of a Soviet threat to Europe has evaporated, these linkages have been exposed to new debate. Traditionally the American presence on the continent and in the Mediterranean has been the leading factor in coupling security in Europe's regions. Over the next decade, and in the wake of the East-West competition, it is not inconceivable that the U.S. military presence on the continent will shrink to quite modest levels (or even disappear), while a substantial air and naval presence in the Mediterranean will almost certainly remain. Such a development would obviously cause the Southern European countries to be viewed in a new light on both sides of the Atlantic.

The cold war position of Southern Europe was unique in other ways. Notwithstanding the existence of a Warsaw Pact threat to northeastern Italy, Thrace, and eastern Turkey, the strategic environment in the Southern Region was characterized by the absence of a focus of vulnerability comparable to that on NATO's central front. The remoteness of the Soviet threat and the existence of diverse strategic traditions and local security concerns encouraged distinct and often assertive national policies toward the Atlantic Alliance.[9] Greece's turbulent relations within NATO, now normalized, provided a leading example of this phenomenon.[10] Even the nuclear guarantee to Europe, while embracing the Southern allies, was focused overwhelmingly on deterring the Soviet threat to centers of political and economic importance in central rather than Southern Europe. The defense of Frankfurt and that of Athens were never really equivalent in NATO strategy.

In the aftermath of the revolutions in Eastern Europe and the waning of the cold war there was considerable concern across Southern Europe that requirements for development and investment in the East would result in a diversion of resources and political attention that might otherwise have flowed southward to the Mediterranean. In economic terms these fears have not yet been realized. In fact Italian, Greek, and Turkish enterprises have themselves been among the most active in exploring new opportunities in Eastern Europe, the Balkans, and the territories of the former Soviet Union. Over the longer term, however, there can be little doubt that demands for EC development assistance and investment in the East will compete with perceived requirements in the less-developed areas of Southern Europe as well as North Africa, where Southern Europeans believe they have a special stake.

Above all the end of the cold war highlighted the extent to which decisionmakers from Lisbon to Athens increasingly looked to Brussels in framing their external policies. With the important exception of Italy, whose commitment to the European idea was long-standing, the Southern European countries had not been in the vanguard of the movement for a common European foreign and security policy or "European pillar." By the time of the Gulf War, however, the situation had evolved considerably, with the progressive Europeanization of Southern Europe making itself felt in this as in other areas. In the case of the Gulf, the existence of a European consensus on cooperation with the United States was an essential factor behind the very extensive Southern European contribution to the coalition operations. In the case of Spain and Greece, this included granting the United States access to facilities, in some instances for mounting offensive operations against Iraq, which would have been difficult or even impossible to arrange on a strictly bilateral basis.[11] Beyond the question of security cooperation with the United States, decisions about defense budgets, the structure of forces, and the character of operations in which Southern European countries are willing to participate can no longer be divorced from their European context. Turkey, as a full participant in neither the EC nor the Western European Union (WEU) and a nation whose prospects for full membership in both organizations remain poor, has been increasingly isolated from this process of Europeanization affecting the region's foreign and security policy.

East-West disengagement and the apparent demilitarization of relations on the continent worked to the advantage of Southern Europe by opening the way for diplomatic initiatives in which military power figured only slightly if at all. The Southern European countries have emerged as leading advocates for a variety of regional initiatives and have adopted a far higher profile in European and international affairs. This activism has not been limited to governments. The past decade has seen greatly increased interest in foreign affairs in the private sector and academic settings, with the establishment of new international policy institutes and the emergence of a

network of Southern European analysts devoted to the study of Mediterranean and broader questions. In the Italian case, and possibly elsewhere, the
broadening of the debate on foreign affairs can be traced to deliberations
over the deployment of theater nuclear forces in Europe in the early 1980s
and the growing public interest in previously arcane questions of strategy.[12]

Prominent Southern European initiatives include the Portuguese, Span-
ish, French, and Italian dialogue with the members of the Arab Maghreb
Union plus Malta (the "Five plus Five"), the Italian-led Central European
Initiative focused on (but not limited to) regional development in the
Danube Basin, Greek and Turkish initiatives in the Balkans, and Turkey's
Black Sea Economic Cooperation Zone. A more ambitious proposal for a
Conference on Security and Cooperation in the Mediterranean, reaching
from Mauritania to Pakistan in its "global" variant, has at times taken up a
great deal of diplomatic energy in Rome and Madrid. Active pursuit of the
CSCM concept has been deferred pending the outcome of the Middle East
peace talks in Washington. With movement toward a comprehensive settlement in this area, the CSCM could reemerge as a vehicle for Southern
European activism.[13]

Post–Cold War Challenges

The end of the cold war has swept away much of the basis for European
and North American perceptions of Southern Europe. It is also changing the
way in which Southern Europeans see themselves and their international
role. Above all new concerns about instability on the European periphery
and problems of North-South relations place the region in the geopolitical
front rank.[14] On the domestic scene the political and economic optimism of
the past decade is also coming under increasing pressure.

Will the Trend toward Europeanization Continue?

Southern Europeans have been among the most active supporters of
deeper European integration. With the post-Maastricht, post-Yugoslavia
crisis of confidence in European institutions, the trend toward Europeanization faces some formidable countervailing pressures. These have been
strengthened by the exposure of previously buoyant economies—Spain is
the leading example—to recession and mounting unemployment. Although
the notion of a European defense identity continues to find support across
the region, political and strategic concerns have encouraged a careful ap-

proach. Portugal continues to search for a Euro-Atlantic balance, which in practice produces a marked Atlanticism.[15] Italy remains wary of European defense initiatives that give too much weight to Germany or encourage a Franco-German condominium. Greece, highly sensitive to the potential consequences of developments in the Balkans, has pursued policies at variance with mainstream European opinion on the former Yugoslavia and Yugoslav Macedonia. Even Turkey's European aspirations have been affected by the perceived abandonment of Bosnia's Muslims by the Community, with many Western-oriented Turks openly questioning the value of European institutions as a context for Turkish foreign and security policy.

To a greater or lesser degree each of the Southern European countries is experiencing a period of reassessment with regard to Europe and, in some cases, a renationalization of outlook and policy. On balance the attachment to Europe and the desire for multilateral approaches to security and security-related problems remain strong. Yet the potential for a renationalization or regionalization of policy has grown, especially on such highly politicized issues as immigration. Moreover, even those Southern Europeans who remain firm supporters of European integration will continue to be concerned about their ability to meet the economic "convergence" requirements of the Maastricht Treaty. Failure to meet these requirements could result in a two- or even three-speed Community in which some of the southern members may find themselves relegated to the institutional periphery.

Whither Turkey?

Turkey's geopolitical importance has grown, but the country remains outside the process of Europeanization in a full, institutional sense and is unlikely to join Europe in the way that most Turks have wished. Moreover, it is unclear that Turkey itself will continue to pursue its European vocation with the same vigor as in the past. The death of President Turgut Ozal and the depth of Turkish disillusionment over the fate of Bosnia have combined with political turmoil in Ankara and instability in southeastern Anatolia to lower the general level of enthusiasm and energy for pursuing deeper relations with Europe. Nonetheless, Ankara is preparing for the establishment of a full customs union with the EC in 1995, an important step toward the revitalization of the country's associate status within the Community. After a period of more moderate growth, the Turkish economy is once again growing at a rate of roughly 10 percent a year, the highest in the Organization for Economic Cooperation and Development. (Attempts to reduce inflation and the size of the public sector have been much less impressive.) Ultimately, however, the prospects for Turkish integration into Europe will have more to do with culture and politics than with economics, a fact that is likely to become more apparent as the Turkish economy continues to grow by the conventional measures of gross national product and gross domestic production per capita.

The emergence of Tansu Ciller as prime minister might have helped to give Turkey the Western "look" important to deepening ties with the West (and indeed this was the view of many politically centrist Turks). The reality, however, has proved to be more complex, largely as a result of an increasingly hard-line, military approach to the Kurdish insurgency in southeastern Anatolia. This, together with the failure to move rapidly on broader questions of human rights and political reform, has only served to deepen European reservations about Turkey.

Prior to the Gulf War it was fashionable to speculate on the prospects for radical Islam in Turkey. The failure of Islamists to move beyond a stable but politically marginal base of support, together with new Turkish activism in the Balkans, the Caucasus, and Central Asia, has encouraged a more recent focus on Turkish nationalism and its regional consequences. As the enthusiasm of the political class for political initiatives in the Black Sea and Central Asia has waned (the interest in economic opportunities remains strong), the question of Islam has once again come to the fore. As the Ataturkist tradition has come under strain, the secular, Western, noninterventionist character of Turkish foreign policy also faces an uncertain future. Turkey has been described as a society "torn" between its Western and Islamic roles.[16] Without positing any fundamental change in the role of Islam in Turkish politics, it is possible to envision the progressive development of a more "Islamic" foreign and security policy in Ankara. To some extent this may already be observed in the overt linkage between Turkish cooperation in the containment of Iraq and Western policy toward Bosnia.

The evolution of relations between Europe and Turkey will have important implications for stability in southeastern Europe and could influence relations between Islam and the West in ways that would affect the security of Southern Europe as a whole. In this context it is not surprising that a growing number of observers in Greece have begun to note the importance of "anchoring" Turkey in post–cold war European institutions. The European desire for movement toward a common foreign and security policy, although somewhat deflated at the moment, makes this a more difficult proposition. Although Turks are fond of describing their geopolitical role as that of a *bridge* between east and west, north and south, Europeans are more inclined to view Turkey as a *barrier,* a strategic glacis separating Europe from the instability of the Middle East. Few Europeans would be enthusiastic about the additional and direct exposure that full Turkish membership in the EC and the WEU—and borders with Iran, Iraq, and Syria—would imply.

A Second Political Revolution?

The countries of Southern Europe share a varied tradition of political transition. Recent developments across the region suggest that the political evolution of these countries is hardly complete and that it has entered a new and stressful period. The political upheaval in Italy—with the expansion of regional movements such as the Lega Lombarda, the revival of domestic terrorism, and the virtual collapse of the established political class—is the leading example. The results of Italy's most recent elections, in which the right wing showed impressive strength, reinforce the impression of rapid change in the political landscape after decades of essential immobility.

Long-standing political arrangements are also under pressure elsewhere, although in less revolutionary fashion. Evidence of this may be seen in the return of Andreas Papandreou's Panhellenic Socialist Movement party to power in Athens and in continuing political turmoil in Ankara. In the latter case right-wing Turkish nationalists as well as Islamists are showing considerable strength against a background of increasing violence in the Kurdish region of southeastern Anatolia. Even in Spain the narrow victory of the ruling Socialist Party in the 1993 elections suggests that the political assumptions of the last decade can no longer be taken for granted. Only in Portugal does the political scene appear essentially stable and evolutionary. Overall Southern Europe is perhaps experiencing a more turbulent variant of the pressure on established politicians and institutions that is evident on both sides of the Atlantic.

In some cases political change is being driven by the desire for more complete, more transparent democracy. In other instances developments are being fueled by economic stagnation and mounting pessimism about the efficacy of "business as usual." Regionalism and ethnicity are potent political forces in much of Southern Europe—from their more moderate expressions in the Azores or Catalonia; through more pressing movements in the Basque country, the southern Tirol, and northern Italy; to the violent insurgency in the Kurdish region of Turkey. The current climate of political change is to a considerable degree a product of the regional and ethnic cleavages to which Southern Europe is exposed. The role of the "Macedonian" question in Greek domestic politics provides a striking example of this phenomenon. Finally it is interesting to speculate on the extent to which criticism of established institutions and patterns of governance also represents a revolt against more specifically Mediterranean traditions of clientalism and political "arrangement."[17]

It may be argued that chaotic politics have hardly prevented Southern European countries from playing an active, predictable role in international affairs in the past, as witness Italy's steady foreign policy despite decades of perceived political instability. But the hypothesis may not hold. As many observers have noted, Italy's hectic party politics masked an essential stability within the political class and the foreign and security policy establishment. In Portugal and Spain the stabilization of democratic politics has been a prerequisite for the conduct of a credible foreign and security policy. To some extent the point holds for Greece and Turkey as well, although here external activism has also served at times as a prop to authoritarianism. What would be the external policy implications of a period of prolonged political instability in Southern Europe? One consequence might be less energy for the pursuit of regional initiatives launched over the last few years, including frameworks for north-south, pan-Mediterranean, and Black Sea cooperation. The absence of self-confident and secure leaderships on both sides of the Aegean would almost certainly harm the prospects for deeper Greek-Turkish détente and perhaps increase the risk of destabilizing involvement in the Balkans and the Caucasus. Above all domestic uncertainty could make it more difficult for Southern European leaderships to play an effective role in multilateral diplomacy at a time when the Mediterranean region is emerging as a center of political and security challenges.

From the Periphery to the Center?

After four decades of relative marginalization, Southern Europe finds itself on the front line along what many observers have begun to describe as a new "arc of crisis." After a long period of growing affluence and security, the countries of Southern Europe are facing a less certain and less secure future as a result of developments across the Mediterranean, in the Balkans, and on the southern periphery of Russia. At the same time Southern Europe is poised to play a potentially critical role in the political and economic development of the southern Mediterranean, as well as new security arrangements within and outside NATO.

As noted earlier, Southern Europe—especially Italy, Greece, and Turkey—is fully exposed to the effects of ethnic conflict in the Balkans and the Caucasus. These effects include potentially massive refugee flows, economic dislocations, and pressures for direct intervention.[18] The conflict in the former Yugoslavia has transformed security perceptions in Athens and Ankara, with the prospects for stability in the Aegean now heavily dependent on the outlook for escalation in the Balkans.[19] Ankara has resisted domestic pressure to intervene in some fashion on behalf of Bosnia's Muslims. Yet the potential for a more active Turkish policy as security guarantor for the roughly nine million Muslims in the Balkans cannot be ruled out. At a minimum the crisis has badly shaken Turkish confidence in the efficacy of NATO and the Western security guarantee at a time when both are subjects of intense debate in Turkey. Turkish unease about the conflict between Armenia and Azerbaijan is, if anything, even more pronounced, bringing with it the specter of a confrontation with Russia. From the Greek perspective the conflict and the possibility of a wider conflagration involving Albania, Bulgaria, and Turkey has given rise to a pronounced sense of insecurity. Politically the crisis has done nothing to improve the climate of relations with the EC, already strained by financial issues. Although less direct, Italy's exposure in the Balkans is substantial. The memory of the large-scale exodus of Albanian refugees in 1991 is still very much alive, and the potential spillover of ethnic violence onto Italian territory in the form of terrorist incidents cannot be discounted.[20] In the broadest sense Italy would find it difficult to insulate itself from the effects of continuing violence and instability across the Adriatic.[21]

To the extent that cleavages between north and south or Islam and the West become a more prominent feature of the post–cold war landscape, Southern Europe as a whole will face more difficult political and security dilemmas.[22] The character of security in the western and eastern basins of the Mediterranean remains distinctive, with a preponderance of "harder" military issues in the east. North-south problems in the western Mediterranean remain largely political and economic. Yet both areas will be affected by the expansion of the security canvas to include a range of nontraditional issues—political and economic development, migration, economic and environmental security—as well as more clearly military concerns such as the proliferation of conventional and unconventional weapons in North Africa and the Levant.

Observers in the European countries of the western and central Mediterranean often refer to an emerging "threat from the south," a notion largely unrelated to the security of territory in the traditional sense.[23] Rather it is the perceived threat to the fabric of societies unaccustomed to large-scale immigration, and, more broadly, fear of the spillover or milieu effects of Islamic radicalism and conflict in the Muslim south. The dramatic demographic imbalance between Southern Europe and the Mediterranean lands to the south and east is a leading factor in both concerns.[24] The growing demographic weight of Europe's Islamic periphery suggests that relations across the Mediterranean are likely to become more central to European foreign policy, and perhaps by extension more important to transatlantic relations. As self-described borderland states, the countries of Southern Europe will be exposed to the risks as well as the benefits of increased attention.

These concerns are given more extreme expression in the notion of a post–cold war "clash of civilizations."[25] From a Southern European perspective, the civilizational cleavages and dilemmas imposed by geography are hardly new (Turks are equally familiar with the civilizational tensions possible within societies). At the same time Southern Europeans are aware of the opportunities for accommodation between civilizations and the special role of borderland states in this regard. North Africans already perceive the development of a new strategic confrontation between "haves" and "have nots" and fear the emergence of a new Berlin Wall along north-south rather than east-west lines. The foreign and security policy views of a new generation of political elites as well as Islamic opposition leaders in the South will inevitably be affected by these perceptions, to the detriment of Southern European security.

Pace Samuel Huntington, the leading military risks around the Mediterranean remain south-south rather than north-south. The strategic environment facing Southern Europe will nonetheless be strongly influenced by the character of regional rivalries and the quest for post–cold war geopolitical weight across the Mediterranean. Above all the growing balance of conventional military capability between north and south, and the acquisition of weapons of mass destruction and the means for their delivery at longer range, will impose new requirements for deterrence and reassurance in Southern Europe. The nature if not necessarily the outcome of Southern European deliberations regarding Western interventions outside Europe would certainly be affected by the vulnerability of northern Mediterranean population centers to ballistic missile attack. An expansion of the European security space southward and eastward (that is, what used to be termed "out-of-area" involvement) would make the Southern European countries more obvious consumers of security within NATO, the WEU, or any other European security organizations that may emerge.[26]

Finally, Southern Europe is poised to play a more central role in the economic life of Europe, not least in the areas of transport and energy flows. As the countries of Eastern Europe are reintegrated into the international economy, links to the Mediterranean sea lanes will almost certainly acquire greater significance for access to oil and nonfuel resources.[27] If the necessary conditions of stability can be fulfilled, the fortunes of Adriatic ports such as Trieste, as well as Thessaloniki, could revive. In the western Mediterranean, new pipeline projects linking Algeria to Europe via Morocco and Spain, and the expansion of existing capacity across the central Mediterranean via Italy, will create new and potentially beneficial interdependencies. In the east, the expansion of Caucasian and Central Asian energy exports will require new pipelines through Turkey, reinforcing that country's long-standing role as a conduit for oil from the Persian Gulf. More broadly, a reversal of the post-1945 shift of Europe's economic center of gravity westward could bring new opportunities for Italy, Greece, and Turkey.

Conclusions: Southern Europe toward the Twenty-First Century

Southern Europe has experienced extraordinary growth and change since 1945, with trends in political and economic development steadily moving the region as a whole into the European mainstream. Over the last decade, and particularly since the political revolutions in Eastern Europe and the disintegration of the Soviet Union, Southern European capitals have emerged as centers of activism focused on, but not limited to, Mediterranean affairs. As the character of the political, economic, and military challenges facing Europe in the post–cold war world has changed, the region's position on the margins of European and international affairs is also changing rapidly. Above all the shift of the leading strategic dilemmas facing Europe from the center to the periphery, both southern and eastern, has placed the Southern European countries, including Turkey, in positions of increased opportunity and risk. By virtue of their history and location, and the apparent direction of post–cold war international affairs, Southern Europeans now have a more important role to play as models for political and economic development and as interlocutors between north and south,

Islam and the West. As a result the evolution of Southern Europe has become more important to the evolution of Europe as a whole and, by extension, more central to a relevant North American involvement in Europe.

In seeking to adjust their internal and external policies to diverse post–cold war challenges—from economic recession and refugee flows to arms proliferation and terrorism—the countries of Southern Europe will also confront pressures for regionalization and renationalization capable of interrupting established patterns of evolution. As Southern Europe moves toward the twenty-first century it is likely to become a less certain, less optimistic, but considerably more important place.

Notes

1. See Ada Bozeman's discussion on this and the role of *marca* or borderland states in the European system in *Strategic Intelligence and Statecraft: Selected Essays* (Washington: Brassey's, 1992).

2. These themes are pursued in Fernand Braudel, *The Mediterranean and the Mediterranean World in the Age of Philip II* (New York: Harper & Row, 1972, first published 1949); and Henri Pirenne, *Mohammed and Charlemagne* (London: Unwin, 1974, first published 1939).

3. Southern Europeans as well as Americans, accustomed to viewing the American military presence in the Mediterranean as a cold war phenomenon, often overlook the fact that this presence is almost two hundred years old.

4. See James A. Field, *America and the Mediterranean World, 1776–1882* (Princeton University Press, 1969).

5. On the democratization and modernization of Spanish society and its consequences for external policy, see Carlos Alonso Zaldivar and Manuel Castells, *Spain Beyond Myths* (Madrid: Alianza Editorial, 1992); and Joyce Laqsky Shub and Raymond Carr, eds., *Spain: Studies in Political Security* (Praeger, 1985).

6. On the role of civil-military relations in democratic transitions, see Lawrence S. Graham, *The Portuguese Military and the State: Rethinking Transitions in Europe and Latin America* (Boulder, Colo.: Westview, 1993).

7. See Ronald Chilcote and others, *Transitions from Dictatorship to Democracy: Comparative Studies of Spain, Portugal and Greece* (New York: Crane Russak, 1990); and Howard Wiarda, *The Transition to Democracy in Spain and Portugal* (Washington: American Enterprise Institute for Public Policy Research, 1989).

8. See Graham E. Fuller and others, *Turkey's New Geopolitics: From the Balkans to Western China* (Boulder, Colo.: Westview/RAND, 1993); and Morton Abramowitz, "Dateline Ankara", *Foreign Policy*, no. 91 (Summer 1993), pp. 164–81.

9. See, for example, John Chipman, ed., *NATO's Southern Allies: Internal and External Challenges* (London: Routledge, 1988); Diego A. Ruiz Palmer and

A. Grant Whitley, "The Balance of Forces in Southern Europe: Between Uncertainty and Opportunity", *International Spectator,* vol. 23, no. 1 (January-March 1988), pp. 28–42; and Ian O. Lesser, *Mediterranean Security: New Perspectives and Implications for U.S. Policy* (Santa Monica, Calif.: RAND, 1992).

10. See Thanos Veremis, "Greece and Southeastern Europe," in F. Stephen Larrabee, ed., *Political Change and Security in the Balkans: Old Problems and New Challenges* (Lanham, Md.: American University Press, forthcoming); and Theodore C. Kariotis, *The Greek Socialist Experiment: Papandreou's Greece, 1981–1989* (New York: Pella, 1992).

11. See Fernando Rodrigo, "The End of the Reluctant Partner: Spain and Western Security in the 1990s," and Herminio Santos, "The Portuguese National Security Policy," in Roberto Aliboni, ed., *Southern European Security in the 1990s* (London: Pinter, 1992), pp. 99–116 and 86–98.

12. This phenomenon is similar to that described by Peter Haas as the rise of "epistemic communities" in relation to environmental policy in the Mediterranean. See Peter M. Haass, *Saving the Mediterranean: The Politics of International Environmental Cooperation* (Columbia University Press, 1990).

13. See the "Joint Document on CSCM by France, Italy, Portugal, and Spain," in *The Mediterranean and the Middle East After the Gulf War: The CSCM* (Rome: Italian Ministry of Foreign Affairs, March 1991), pp. 89–93.

14. On post–cold war strategic perceptions, see Aliboni, *Southern European Security in the 1990s.*

15. See José Calvet de Magalhaes, Alvaro de Vasconcelos, and Joaquim Ramos Silva, *Portugal: An Atlantic Paradox* (Lisbon: Institute for Strategic and International Studies, 1990).

16. Samuel P. Huntington, "The Clash of Civilizations?" *Foreign Affairs,* vol. 72, no. 3 (Summer 1993), p. 42.

17. See, for example, Robert Fox, *The Inner Sea: The Mediterranean and Its People* (Knopf, 1993).

18. The disruption of the land route through the former Yugoslavia to central and Western Europe has imposed notable economic hardship on both Greece and Turkey.

19. See Nicholas X. Rizopoulos, "A Third Balkan War?" *World Policy Journal,* vol. 10, no. 2 (Summer 1993), pp. 1–5.

20. Some 10,000 Albanians arrived at Italian ports within a period of days during August 1991; roughly 24,000 had arrived in earlier migrations. Greece has absorbed far larger numbers of Albanians (perhaps 100,000) and Romanians. Over 320,000 Bulgarian Turks sought refuge in Turkey in 1989; over half have since returned to Bulgaria.

21. On the effects of the Yugoslav crisis and other developments on Italian and Greek security perceptions, see Ettore Greco and Laura Guazzone, "Continuity and Change in Italy's Security Policy," and Yannis G. Valinakis, "Southern Europe Between Détente and New Threats: The View from Greece," in Aliboni, *Southern European Security in the 1990s.*

22. Edward Mortimer, "New Fault Lines: Is a North-South Confrontation Inevitable in Security Terms?" in *New Dimensions in International Security,* Adelphi Paper 266 (London: International Institute for Strategic Studies, Winter 1991–92).

23. With some exceptions: the insecurity of the Spanish enclaves of Ceuta and Melilla on the Moroccan coast is one, and the air and ballistic missile risk to Southern Europe is another.

24. It is estimated that the populations of Turkey and Egypt in the year 2025 will reach 100 million each, and that of the five states of the Arab Maghreb Union will total some 127 million. The population of these seven countries combined will roughly equal that of the EC.

25. See Huntington, "The Clash of Civilizations?"

26. On the shift of security problems to the European periphery and the issue of NATO expansion, see Ronald D. Asmus, Richard L. Kugler, and F. Stephen Larrabee, "Building A New NATO," *Foreign Affairs,* vol. 72, no. 4 (September-October 1993), pp. 28–40.

27. *Europe's Maritime Interests: Conference Report and Proceedings* (Ebenhausen, Germany: Stiftung Wissenschaft und Politik, 1991).

Part One

THE MEDITERRANEAN
DIMENSION

THREE

Relations with the Maghreb

Andrés Ortega

THE MEDITERRANEAN is a meeting point between North and South, between rich and poor, between Islam and the Christian West. Nowhere is this situation more acute than in the western part of this sea, where only fourteen kilometers, but all sorts of issues, separate Southern Europe from the Maghreb (which originally meant Morocco, Algeria, and Tunisia but has since been extended to include Libya and Mauritania).[1] The challenge for Europe and for the Maghreb is to manage and if possible to overcome this division.

The end of the cold war presents new opportunities for political and social change in these North African countries, but also new concerns. Although the Maghreb countries can no longer count on playing the East-West competition to their own benefit, a return to old forms of competition and power politics among European states, and the emergence of a new kind of confrontation between South and South and between North and South, are not excluded. The Maghreb is a test case. Regional prospects depend to a large extent on the determination and capability of the Maghreb countries to integrate into the world economy and to share, or at least coexist with, different values—an attitude that the North should also adopt. The positive evolution of the Middle Eastern situation can also bring benefits to the Maghreb.

Does It Matter?

Why is the Maghreb important to Southern Europe (and even to the United States)? There are a number of reasons that range from geopolitics to ecology, economics, society, and culture. Basically, the Maghreb matters

I am grateful for their comments on earlier versions of this chapter to Dimitri Constas, John Holmes, Alvaro Iranzo, Alejandro Lorca, Katlyun Sabá, and Dirk Vandewalle.

because the stability, prosperity, and security of the Maghreb countries, and of the Mediterranean in general, represent stability, prosperity, and security for Southern Europe. Two transitions are taking place at the same time, and they interact in positive and negative ways: the European transition and the Maghreb's transition. The latter has at least three dimensions: demography, society, and politics.

European Concerns

From a mid- and long-term perspective, Europe needs to develop a good neighbor policy aimed at creating stability and prosperity to its east *and* to its south, although these two simultaneous objectives can conflict. Europe cannot be a fortress of prosperity surrounded by poverty and backwardness, first of all, because the Southern European countries would become an inhospitable frontier instead of a bridge. This change in turn would make of the Mediterranean a vulnerable frontier of Europe. Second, poverty is a strategic enemy for everyone.[2] The prospect of 300 million poor people just across the sea, in countries in which problems of economic growth, political development, and cultural roots are deeply interwoven, creates a potential for mass migration, an issue of great concern for all Europeans, not just Southern Europeans. Some five million people of Maghreb origin (about 10 percent of the Maghreb population) currently live in Europe. This situation can obviously have repercussions on the way Europe thinks of itself and lives, a problem that is more intense in some areas than in others. The Maghreb is thus not "alien" to Europe, and in particular to the Southern Europeans. Immigration, sometimes massive in local terms, coupled with the crises of values and economy in the North, is already having major political effects, from xenophobic and racist reactions to the upsurge of extreme right-wing movements. This situation is pressing a number of countries to reform their traditional concept of nationhood through changes in immigration and nationality laws, as is happening in Germany or France. Mass immigration could jeopardize the stability of the European democracies. The need to regulate the flow of inmigration makes itself felt at the European Union level.

The Maghreb, according to the conclusions of the European Council in Lisbon in June 1992, "constitutes the Southern border of the [European] Union. Its stability presents a common important interest for the Union." Thus, "priority should be given to the following actions: promoting a constructive dialogue aimed at creating an area of peace, security and prosperity in which fundamental principles of international law would be applied . . . and building a framework for cooperation in every domain."[3]

The Maghreb is also important for Africa as a whole. A successful transition in South Africa and in the Maghreb could bring about a framework for better development of the whole of the black continent.

Demography and Economy: A Difficult Couple

The demographic issue in the Maghreb is a time bomb. Its population has more than doubled in the last thirty years. If this trend is not reversed, with a cumulative annual growth rate of around 3 percent it will double again, from the current 59 million to 144 million in 2025, according to World Bank projections. This issue currently seems to be taken less seriously than in the past. Nonetheless there are some signs that population growth could ease. In Tunisia, for example, despite some setbacks, the rate of population growth forecast for the period 1991–2000 is 1.9 percent, compared to 3 percent in 1966.[4] Yet even if this projection is confirmed, the real positive effects of this trend will not be felt for at least a generation.

We are thus faced with an essentially young population, with bleak prospects, life expectancies of sixty-two to sixty-six years, deficient education, and low indexes of human development (0.6 for Tunisia; 0.528 for Algeria; 0.433 for Morocco).[5] These countries are far ahead of most of the African countries, yet they do not look southward. Their reference point is the North, where gross national product (GNP) per capita is at least ten times higher. For the population, migration and television have broadened the gap between expectations and capabilities and thus which produced an intense sense of frustration.

There has been economic growth in the area, but it has been uneven and outflanked by the demographic explosion. Agricultural production, particularly in Algeria, has not matched population growth, and low levels of food self-sufficiency (40% in Algeria) have resulted. Morocco's GNP grew over the period 1986–88 at an annual rate of 5 percent, but per capita income fell about 1 percent. Furthermore, the economic recession in the West is heavily burdening these economies. In 1993, for instance, Morocco's financial planning for the year assumed 6.5 percent growth, but actual growth was probably much lower. In Algeria the policy of not rescheduling the debt led to stagnation and to a decrease in imports of about 3 percent, since most of the foreign aid received by Algeria has been allocated to the payment of debt. Algeria's economy grew at a annual rate of 5 percent between 1980 and 1985, but growth fell to less than 1 percent and even to negative numbers in 1990, before stabilizing in 1991. The reforms approved by the International Monetary Fund (IMF) seem to have run out of steam. Algeria's government, however, expects that in four or five years the situation will improve as gas and oil exports grow from $10–11 billion to $16–17 billion. On the other hand Tunisia and Morocco have accepted the discipline of the IMF, with promising results. Tunisia, which started a privatization process ahead of the other countries, has enjoyed an annual GNP growth rate of 6.6 percent over the last few years (8.6 percent in 1992), coinciding with exceptional harvests.

Unemployment has been on the rise; it now affects between 15 and 30 percent of the working population, mostly people under thirty. During the late 1980s and early 1990s, Algeria created only 100,000 jobs, less than half the planned number. Tunisia, despite its growth, created only 45,000 instead of the projected 75,000. These high rates have led to mass emigration to France and other member countries of the European Union (EU). Youth unemployment is a huge problem and acts as an incubator for radical Islamism, leading to the rejection of corruption, but also to confrontations between generations, higher unemployment, and greater despair. Inflation runs high at an annual rate of 15 to 40 percent.

Economic liberalization—fiscal, monetary, and commercial, affecting markets, privatization, and foreign investments—has evolved at different paces and with different results. It may produce a real "revolution of the economic apparatus and instruments,"[6] but it has also raised the risks of political and social instability. One of the results of this process of radical change has been a split between generations (possession of a secondary school diploma is no longer enough), between social strata, and between regions. The EU is providing aid to ease the effects of this transformation, but if the "social dimension" of the adjustment process is neglected, the liberalization process itself could be put at risk.

The reforms have had some important positive results. In Morocco the public deficit has been lowered and foreign investment grew by 58 percent in 1992. But the attempts at modernization, coupled with a high degree of mismanagement, have brought about a huge increase in Maghreb countries' foreign debt, the service of which accounts for 30 percent of exports of goods and services in the case of Morocco (reduced from 60 percent only a few years ago), 25 percent in Tunisia, and 71 percent (up from 35 percent in 1980) in Algeria. Furthermore, the high level of military expenditures by these countries only serves to aggravate their economic situation.

Table 3-1. *The Maghreb: Socioeconomic Overview*

Parameter	Algeria	Morocco	Tunisia	Libya	Mauritania
Surface area (thousands of square kilometers)	2,382	450	164	1,760	1,031
Population (millions, 1991)	25.6	25.7	8.2	4.4	2.1
Year in which population will next double	2017	2020	2025	2050	2015
Population forecast for year 2025 (millions)	52	48	14	14	5
Life expectancy at birth (1990)	65.1	62.0	66.7	62	47.0
Unemployment rate (percent of working population)	25	18	20	...	...
Schooling index	0.20	0.22	0.16	...	0.02
Illiteracy rate	46	64	41	25	69
Per capita income (millions of U.S. dollars, 1990)	2,230	880	1,260	...	...
Real per capita gross domestic production (adjusted $ purchasing power parity, 1990)	3,011	2,348	3,579	...	1,057
Percent of external trade with EC	71	61.3	73.6	79.7	51.4
Television sets per 1,000 inhabitants	74	74	80	91	23
Human development index, 1990	0.528	0.433	0.600	0.658	0.140

Sources: UNDP (1992, 1993), Banco Mundial, European Commission, World Bank, *El Estado del Mundo 1993*.

The Maghreb is also important for Europe as a trade partner. The Mediterranean countries constitute the third largest trade partner of the EU, ahead of Japan. The volume of trade represents a total of $65 billion, with a surplus of $5 billion to $7 billion a year in favor of the EU, although the volume has dropped in real terms. Even if these countries represent less than 4 percent of the EU's external trade, the importance and potential of the region is greater than that figure suggests. Energy imports, for instance, will grow. In this regard, Algeria's exports of natural gas to Spain are due to increase from 2,500 cubic meters in 1985 to 7,000 cubic meters in 1995, when the Maghreb-Europe gas pipeline that will join Algeria and Spain (and the rest of Europe) through Morocco should enter service. Italy and Algeria agreed in 1991 to double the capacity of the gas pipeline built between them in 1983 to 40,000 cubic meters by the year 2000. There has also been an upsurge in the activities of those European companies that view the Maghreb countries as a "European Mexico." They have relocated manufacturing activity to take advantage of the Maghreb's low-wage labor.

For the Maghreb this trade is of paramount importance, as the EU represents 70 percent of total exports and 60 percent of total imports for the region (two-thirds of this total is made up of trade with the Southern

European countries). This pattern of commercial exchange with the EU contrasts with the lack of intraregional trade among the Maghreb countries themselves; intraregional trade accounts for less than 4 percent of their total trade.

Table 3-1 presents a socioeconomic overview of the region.

Political Evolution

The stabilization of North Africa, coupled with the democratization of Southern Africa, could bring some hope for the rest of the continent, but the opposite is also true. Developments in the Maghreb were viewed, overall, with optimism some years ago. Yet the crisis in Algeria, the Gulf War, and the international economic crisis—North as well as the South—have all led to greater pessimism about the future of the region. The Maghreb is no longer a model for modernization in the rest of the Arab world.

Periodic crises seem to shake these countries, like the bread revolts in Tunisia or the effects of the Gulf War, which alienated people from those governments, like that of Morocco, that took an anti-Saddam stance. In the current context, however, one has to differentiate even more carefully than before among the different countries and actors in the area. The political evolution of each country has been unique. In Algeria and Tunisia there has been a certain political liberalization in parallel to the economic one. This liberalization, directed by those in power, took the form of a change from a one- to a multiparty system. The move enjoyed some success in Tunisia but was aborted in Algeria, whereas Morocco's evolution proceeds at its own pace.

Europe, lacking significant degree of any control over the political evolution of these countries, feels some vulnerability. The Maghreb countries seem to have a bifurcated political and economic evolution, attempting to combine a Smithian path to economic reform with a Hobbesian way of ruling.

In Algeria, the interruption of the electoral process in December 1991 intended to prevent the Islamic Salvation Front (FIS) from coming to power, and the accompanying coup, have led to a dynamic of repression and terrorism, and to a certain radicalization of the moderate wing within the fundamentalist movement. The assassination in June 1992 of Mohamed Boudiaf, president of the High State Council, reflected the resurgence of a terrorist movement, and a reaction to it, that now count their victims in the thousands. This trend underwent a qualitative change in the fall of 1993 when foreigners began being murdered by Islamic radical terrorists. The army, which plays a crucial role in Algeria, seems to remain united. Prime Minister Redha Malek seemed, in the fall of 1993, to combine toughness and dialogue, stick and carrot, in trying to deal with a situation in which economic problems were intensifying. The offer of dialogue in December 1993 by the High Council to some political forces did not include any representatives of the FIS or other radical Islamist movements. Nonetheless in the summer of 1994 the government made a new series of gestures to the FIS that could herald the beginning of a new kind of dialogue. This approach, although difficult and likely to be lengthy, and despite important resistance within the regime and probable continuing terrorist activity, could lead to a transition and general elections.

In Tunisia, where a "medical coup" in November 1987 brought Zine al-Abidine Ben Ali to the presidency, ending the long Bourguiba era, the cycle of repression and violence that was triggered by radical Islamism could be coming to an end, an evolution that, coupled with a positive economic performance, could facilitate a process of democratization. Yet there are still many clouds on the horizon.

Morocco, for the time being, may be seen as a pole of stability. In spite of their shortcomings, recent constitutional reforms and the elections held in June 1993 could indicate some change in direction, although probably not enough of a change to eliminate completely the "democratic deficit." Furthermore, Morocco has still to come to grips with its critical social deficit.

As for Libya, even though there may be some signs of possible political change, the reform process that started in 1987 has not yet succeeded in solving one of the key problems for this country: the succession to Colonel Muammar Qadaffi. Libya's attitude regarding the Lockerbie affair has not contributed to a positive evolution, as witness the Security Council's imposition of sanctions on Libya in the areas of arms sales and air traffic (but not on maritime trade) in April 1993, and their intensification in December 1993.

Mauritania lives in a situation of "controlled democracy" and, despite formally being an "Islamic republic," does not seem to face an Islamic challenge, although it is confronted by very serious racial and tribal conflicts and a critical economic situation.

Several other problems threaten prospects for the region. First among these is the struggle for regional hegemony over the "Maghreb puzzle."[7] In this struggle, the Western Sahara conflict is the most serious one since it involves a confrontation between the two regional powers: Morocco and

Algeria. In fact the issue is a legacy of the French and Spanish decoloniza-tions of the Maghreb, and it holds one of the major keys to peace in the region. Although Morocco claims sovereignty over the Western Sahara, Algeria has traditionally supported the Polisario Front in its struggle for independence from Morocco. For Spain, the former colonial power, the Sahara issue represents a poisoned legacy of Francoist foreign policy. Indeed one of the major foreign policy priorities of the new democratic regime was to redefine Spain's stand regarding the Western Sahara's de-colonization process. The Madrid Declaration, under which Spain aban-doned its responsibility for the Western Sahara, was signed in November 1975 and amended shortly afterward. The Spanish government officially declared that the decolonization process would not be concluded until the Saharan people had freely expressed their will. After years of dispute, the Western Sahara issue remains on the UN agenda. Efforts to reconcile the views of Morocco and the Polisario Front have not yet progressed to the point at which a referendum can be held.

The Radical Islamic Challenge

The rise of Islamic radicalism (or "fundamentalism," although this is a word of Western Protestant origin) in the Maghreb is usually seen as part of a larger movement extending from Asia to the Atlantic. It can be seen as "measles" (an inevitable but nonfatal and nonrecurring illness), as a threat deriving from what Samuel Huntington has called a "clash of civiliza-tions,"[8] or as a normal result of participation by Islamists in the workings of the state. We tend to see this issue much more in terms of challenge or risk than as a threat. To treat it as a threat could give rise to a self-fulfilling prophecy, as was partly the case in the confrontation with the Soviet Union.[9] The challenge need not always be seen as a threat to regional stability or Western interests. Islamic fundamentalists do not want to change our life.

So-called Islamic fundamentalism is not a single movement, not even in a country like Algeria. Diverse in its Shia (as in Iran) and Sunni (as in the Maghreb) configurations, it is polycentric, although over the years the degree of coordination between various factions has grown. The rise of fundamentalism has been uneven within the Maghreb countries and has had different causes. These include a reaction against the lack of economic prospects; the gap between classes; the economic and technological revolu-tion, which has changed or broken secular traditions, affecting youth in particular; and a sense of revolt against corruption. In the Maghreb, fundamentalists are usually urban people with a technical and scientific education, who, in a generational split, look for a model of society which is not that of their fathers (which made independence the primary value), nor the Western model, nor the failed Soviet communist experiment. They are left with Islam, looked at in a different way. In a sense, they can be seen as an emerging civil society.[10]

Fundamentalism questions the definition of the relationship between the ideals of Islam and the modern world, a relationship that in most instances, including Morocco, has still to be renewed. It also has a dimension that combines Islam and Arabism: in the Arab state, power must be legitimized by Islam. A clear example is Morocco, with the king as temporal power, legitimized as religious leader and descendant of the Prophet. A problem is posed by the fact that radical Islamism often attacks the established power if it is a "Europeanizing" power. It is difficult to say what would happen in a society with radical Islamists in power. Jordan is a good example of how they could lose influence if subsumed within a coalition government. Other examples, such as Iran and the Sudan, point in less positive directions.

In political terms, paradoxically, as in the Algerian and Tunisian cases, it has been the process of political change that has opened the way for the arrival in power of radical Islamism (although only 22 percent of the electorate voted for the FIS in Algeria). The interruption of the democratic process to prevent those movements from coming to power has made matters worse. Fundamentalist elements were very seriously repressed in Tunisia after their alleged participation in an aborted coup. They have also been repressed in Libya. In Morocco, the different (and easier) situation as far as radical Islamism is concerned can be explained by a lesser degree of secularization of the regime (the king being not only the political but also the religious head of the country), a larger rural population, a more cohesive identity, and a process of political reform that has avoided a single-party system. In Algeria, President Chadli Benjedid's idea of a "cohabitation" with the FIS could not be put into practice. Nevertheless, despite this failure, it appears increasingly certain that any solution in Algeria must ultimately reckon with the FIS and the Islamic movement in general.

Why do we fear an Islamic Maghreb, or even merely an Islamic Algeria? Not because it would undermine Western economic (and in particular energy) interests, since the country would still need to strengthen economic ties with its Northern neighbors (although this has not been the outcome in the Middle East, despite the economic rationale). Not because it would halt modernization, since the fundamentalists' goal seems to be to Islamize

modernity instead of modernizing Islam; they even promise greater economic liberalization. Not because the country would be nondemocratic,
since the West has frequently dealt with nondemocratic regimes. Nor because of the threat of a nuclear Algeria, which would be a threat in and of
itself independent of any other consideration, and even more so if it responded to radical Arab nationalism.

Fundamentalism even has some positive aspects, such as a new emphasis on morality, a strong opposition to corruption, and a search for cultural
roots.[11] Taking the "measles" rather than the threat approach to the problem,
King Hassan II of Morocco stated to *Acharq Al Awsat* at the beginning of
1993: "I would have liked to see the [integralist] experience carried out.
Algeria would have constituted a laboratory which would have revealed
how the religious extremism can overcome its contradictions." He later
changed his position, and one may doubt whether neighboring countries
could resist such a contagion.

The main reasons for our fear of an Islamic Algeria are as follows. It
could trigger a civil war, or a war of attrition, within its own borders and in
neighboring countries, and even armed conflict among Maghreb states. (In
Algeria some Islamic radicals have already turned to terrorism in response
to violent repression by the state.) The advent of Islamic rule would also
trigger a mass emigration, especially by the middle class, and would undermine the prospects for economic growth in the entire area, widening (even
if only psychologically) the gap between Europe and the Maghreb, contributing to the "frontierization" of Southern Europe. This is one of the main
reasons why the Europeans look for an interlocutor in the area, and in
particular why they turn to Morocco. Finally there is the problem of
what would happen if the Islamic populations within Europe became
"fundamentalized."

As for violent Islamic fundamentalism, its rise is a problem not only for
the Maghreb but also for other major countries like Egypt and Turkey. The
Gulf War clarified some realities and changed others—like the financing of
Islamic fundamentalist movements by Saudi Arabia, which cut off the FIS
when it supported Saddam Hussein (although the Islamic fundamentalists
may look to other financial sources). Nowadays there is a growing danger
of closer links between Sudan and Iran, and of Sudan trying to export the
Islamic revolution. However, the main factors in the rise of fundamentalism
seem to be internal rather than external.

The rise of fundamentalism tends to lead gradually to the equation in the
Western public's perception of these political-religious movements with

Islam in general—a dangerous misperception. As an Iranian proverb says, Islam is a sea in which one can find almost any fish.

There are reasons to believe that Islamic fundamentalism will spread. But we must avoid a North-South confrontation that replaces the old East-West confrontation. Fundamentalism should not be "diabolized." The problem is not merely one of confrontation between North and South, or between rich and poor, but between Christians and Muslims, a confrontation with roots that date very far back. To prevent this conflict, there must be a dialogue between cultures. Yet even though goverments may try to implement such a dialogue, there may still be a problem at the "street" level, with growing separatist, racist, or anti-Western positions being adopted among the citizenry in the North as well as the South.

Security Problems

If we define security in broad terms as the preservation of a way of life, the Maghreb holds major security importance for the Southern European countries, posing a number of risks, either direct or indirect (through emigration), with economic, social, religious, ecological, or military causes. For instance, the Mediterranean is a vital route for energy supplies, and the Maghreb will be even more important once the Maghreb-Europe gas pipeline is operational in 1995. But there is no threat in the traditional sense of the word. Instead these countries perceive several threats from the North.

In military terms the Mediterranean, and in particular the Maghreb, have a strategic significance that may have changed in military terms, and that will probably change again, but which remains of the utmost importance for the Southern European countries. For instance, in the mid-1970s, the countries of North Africa did not have submarines. By 1989 there were already thirteen. These countries have also recently acquired antiship missiles, which could technically enable them to limit by military means freedom of movement in the western Mediterranean.

Military expenditures grew markedly from 1982 to 1986, reaching levels of 5 percent of GNP in some cases. Algeria, Libya, and Morocco have land and air warfare equipment superior in numerical terms to the armament of the countries of the Northern shore. Moreover, this superiority could be enhanced with the arms that have become available as a consequence of the demise of the Soviet Union and of the limitations imposed on Europe by the Conventional Forces in Europe Treaty. However, the Maghreb countries rely heavily on the outside world for their arms supplies, and their training and technical knowledge are significantly below the European level. (One of the main challenges for the future is for the West to retain this technological superiority which proved decisive in the Gulf.) Thus Libya may have two thousand tanks, but only 20 percent or so of them are operational. The Maghreb countries do not have the capability to project conventional forces in Europe. But they see that Europe has the capacity to project force outside its territory, which explains Maghreb suspicions regarding the development of a European defense identity.

Nevertheless the search for "strategic weight" by some of those countries, especially Algeria or Libya, might bring new risks now, and even threats in the future, of proliferation of conventional and unconventional weapons. A particular problem is the proliferation of weapons of mass destruction (chemical or nuclear) and the systems to deliver them. By the year 2000 it is possible that every Southern European capital will be within range of ballistic missiles fired from Algeria or Libya, or in any case from airplanes.[12] In this context, the U.S. plan for Global Protection Against Limited Strikes proposed by the Bush administration may become more important for the Europeans.

As for nuclear armaments, King Hassan of Morocco, a country that is party to the Treaty on the Non-Proliferation of Nuclear Weapons (NPT) and that openly supported the anti-Iraq coalition, said in the midst of the Iraqi invasion of Kuwait,

> India and Pakistan have their own bomb. Yet does anybody challenge them? The Israelis have their bomb, too, and they have not yet signed the NPT. . . . So everything is allowed to a few but forbidden to others. . . . If some have the atomic bomb, why leave the others unarmed? If Iraq wants to build its own nuclear weapon, while it faces someone that has 200 nuclear warheads, in my opinion it has the right to do it. Either it is allowed for everyone or it is forbidden for all. It is not possible to have double standards. I would even say it is an outrage to our pride as Arabs. Everyone can have his bomb except the Arabs.[13]

Following the much heralded start-up of a nuclear reactor 250 kilometers from its capital, Algeria announced at the end of 1993 that it would become a party to the NPT (which Mauritania has not signed). As for chemical weapons, the Maghreb countries are parties to the Geneva Conventions on chemical and biological weapons, with the exception of Libya, a potential violator.

As has already been noted, potential South-South conflicts in which the North might get involved seem to be more worrisome than possible North-

South conflicts. Last but not least there is the problem of terrorism, both internal and external.

The Middle Eastern Connection

The Middle East and the Maghreb may be geographically far apart, but they are closely connected in other respects, and what happens in one area has repercussions in the other. Events in the Middle East during the Gulf War shook confidence and sometimes divided government and society in the Maghreb. The Palestinian issue and the lack of progress in the peace process in the Middle East also had repercussions in the Maghreb. Maghreb attitudes have also positively influenced events in the Middle East. For example, the moderate position of King Hassan of Morocco and that nation's attitude toward Israel have helped the peace process. The new prospects of a general peace settlement opened up by the Israeli-Palestinian agreements, which have been compared to the fall of the Berlin Wall in Europe, could benefit the Maghreb politically and dissipate some of its tensions. A unique opportunity presents itself for economic, security, and environmental cooperation between Europe and all of the Southern Mediterranean, even if the priority of European aid to the Occupied Territories (500 million ECU for five years) may reduce the amounts available for the Maghreb. For King Hassan what is at stake is not only peace between Israel and the Palestinians, but also the beginning of a new era between the West and the Orient.

Europeans and the Maghreb

National interests shape different approaches to the Maghreb. There is no single Western, nor European, nor even Southern European vision of the Mediterranean and the Maghreb. Furthermore, the Mediterranean is increasingly becoming a space in which the Northern countries feel they can act to some degree autonomously. Within the general framework of cooperation and assistance, there can be some competition between France and Spain. Not so between Italy and Portugal. All Southern European nations, with the possible exception of Portugal, share common concerns regarding immigration.

France has historical, economical, political, and social interests, including important investments to defend, in the Maghreb, especially in Algeria and Morocco. We should also recall that France has the largest immigrant population of Maghreb origin. In a way France, with the burden of its colonial past, is a regional superpower. Faced with the crisis in Algeria, it has had changing attitudes. These in turn reflected a relative loss of influence in the region owing to its attitude during the Gulf War. France has greatly contributed to the creation of multilateral frameworks to deal with the Maghreb, although there are renewed signs of a more traditional national approach.

Spain is the only European country that shares a border with Morocco, because of the Spanish North African enclaves of Ceuta and Melilla, and it is separated from Morocco by only fourteen kilometers at the Strait of Gibraltar. Spain therefore has a vested interest in not becoming an inhospitable frontier, a circumstance that could push it toward a peripheral situation in Europe. Competition in agricultural products, fear of mass immigration, a colonial past in the Sahara, and cooperation and competition with other European powers are additional factors that shape the Spanish position. Democratic Spain has modified its previous foreign policy approach of playing Algeria against Morocco instead of fostering cooperation in the region. With Spanish entry into the European Community (EC) the relationship between Spain and Morocco has changed deeply. Many problems that used to be bilateral now have a European Union dimension. Spanish companies are increasingly investing in Morocco and Algeria. Spain has also been the major supporter of the pipeline that should bring Algerian gas through Morocco and across the strait to Europe. In its approach to the Maghreb, Spain needs the European Union as a force and means multiplier. It also needs, in some respects, the support of the United States.

Italy, for geopolitical reasons, looks more toward the Middle East than toward the Maghreb, but the evolution of the Maghreb has major importance for Italy's interests because of the immigration dimension, ecological problems, security concerns aggravated by geographic proximity, and important energy, commercial, and investment links that must be defended, in particular after the spectacular growth of Italian foreign aid in the last decade. Geography and history should make it natural for Italy to have a special relationship with Libya, similar to the one that France has with Algeria, but these relations are limited because of the behavior of Libya itself. The internal crisis in Italy can also help to explain its lack of activism in Mediterranean affairs over the last two years.

Portugal (which sold Ceuta to Spain) has recently "discovered" the Maghreb. Attaching great interest to Southern European initiatives, Portugal has become increasingly involved in the Maghreb from an investment and trade point of view as well. This new interest is reflected, for instance, in the opening of a Portuguese embassy in Algiers two years ago and in the visit of Hassan II to Portugal in September 1993, in the signing of a

Luso-Moroccan financial and partnership protocol a year before, and in the bilateral defense agreement between Portugal and Morocco. Portugal has been active in the "Five plus Five" talks and recently joined the Maghreb-Europe gas pipeline project. Morocco was the first Arab or African country that recognized the new Portuguese regime born of the 1974 "Carnation Revolution." Portugal is also important for Morocco as a European Union country without a "Mediterranean" agriculture.

Although perhaps not with the required intensity, other European countries have also started focusing on the Maghreb. Germany pursues economic interests in the area, including a significant degree of trade, and also keeps the region in mind in the context of the growing immigration problem of the last few years. Germany's defense minister has said that the Maghreb and the Middle East are of considerable importance for Europe's security.[14] Other Northern and Nordic European countries have also recently devoted greater attention to this region.

As far as the European Union as such is concerned, the development of a Mediterranean policy in general and a policy toward the Maghreb in particular is important both in itself and as a component of a Common Foreign and Security Policy.

In 1972 the EC put into practice the so-called Global Mediterranean Policy, which dealt essentially, in its first phase, with trade and aid. It covered not only the Maghreb, but all of the Mediterranean except Albania, Libya (for political reasons), and Mauritania (which is part of the Lome Convention). As far as cooperation and aid are concerned, the amounts involved were very limited. In the period 1977–91, only 3 percent of the total foreign economic and financial assistance that the countries of the southern Mediterranean received came from the EC (as against 14 percent from the EC member states, 28 percent from the Organization of Petroleum Exporting Countries, and 31 percent, mostly for Egypt and Israel, from the United States). Algeria, for instance, in 1977–91 received 504 million ECU (and even that sum was not totally used).

The entry of Spain into the EC in 1986 made it necessary to change the Mediterranean Policy, and thus in 1990 the Twelve launched the Renewed Mediterranean Policy with new content and increased financial assistance: 4.4 billion ECU for the whole of the Mediterranean, of which 1.07 billion was earmarked for the Maghreb. A similar amount was granted for "horizontal cooperation," for financing programs like the Maghreb-Europe gas pipeline or environmental protection actions, apart from the bilateral aid provided by individual European countries (which is sometimes difficult to

Table 3-2. *EC Technical and Financial Assistance to the Maghreb*

Country	EC Budget	EIB loans (million ECU)	Total
Morocco			
1971–1991	356	297	653
(Protocol I–III)			
1992–1996	218	220	438
(Protocol IV)			
Algeria			
1971–1991	144	360	504
(Protocol I–III)			
1992–1996	70	280	350
(Protocol IV)			
Tunisia			
1971–1991	208	250	458
(Protocol I–III)			
1992–1996	116	168	284
(Protocol IV)			
Total Maghreb			
1971–1991	708	907	1,615
(Protocol I–III)			
1992–1996	404	668	1,072
(Protocol IV)			

Source: European Commission.

quantify with precision). In spite of the increase, these figures may still look small. Yet they should not be judged in isolation, since the Mediterranean Policy extends beyond aid: since the launching of the policy, the industrial exports of the Maghreb have increased by 500 percent.

EC technical and financial assistance to the Maghreb is summarized in table 3-2.

Who Does What?

"A marginalized Maghreb would become, sooner or later, an unstable Maghreb," according to a Spanish view.[15] Europe has to contribute to the stability of this region, offering these countries the prospect of a permanent connection to Europe. However, their expectations cannot be the same as the ones held by the Eastern European countries. There is a fundamental difference: the Eastern European societies want to integrate as soon as possible into the Western system. The societies of the Maghreb share this goal in terms of levels of consumption, but are much more negative toward other aspects of Western modernity.[16] In any case relations between Europe and the Maghreb countries must start from the premise of reciprocity.

What to Do?

A broad dialogue should be established with these countries, on the understanding that we have to defuse the possibility of an emerging threat, not approach problems in terms of threats. The worst way of acting would be a Southern revival of containment—with a purely negative content—or even of deterrence. Some are in favor of such a defensive policy toward the Maghreb, which differs sharply from a neighborly relationship. The best way to proceed is to try to incorporate, to anchor, these countries into Europe. Most of their problems are not of a military nature and so cannot be solved militarily. Europe must go to the roots of the problems, but the Maghreb countries must as well. Nonetheless there is still a gap between what the EU and its member states say they must do in the Maghreb and what they actually do.

Is it too late? No doubt it will be more difficult to act now than it would have been five years ago. But it is not too late. In political terms it can never be too late to deal with a neighbor. We should not underestimate the challenges, but neither should we underestimate the opportunities.

A variety of issues have to be tackled with different countries, and a "variable geometry" or "multispeed" approach will probably be more viable, more likely to succeed, and even to lead eventually to a single geometry. But this selective incorporation has to go hand in hand with an equal-opportunity approach.

POLITICAL DIALOGUE AND ISLAMIC RADICALISM. Southern Europeans do not fully agree on what to do in terms of political change and Islamic fundamentalism in the Maghreb. But the vicious circle between political liberalization and the arrival in power of fundamentalism, which leads to repression and the lack of a political solution, must be broken. The choice between mosque and barracks has to be avoided. Is it possible to do so? France has had differing attitudes toward the events in Algeria, turning from open criticism of the coup to open cooperation with the Algerian regime. Although in August 1993 the French foreign minister said that the status quo in Algeria could not be defended, and later on President Mitterrand seemed to defend the road of political dialogue with radical Islamism (but not with terrorist Islamism), the staunch attitude taken by Interior Minister

Charles Pasqua and the murders of French citizens have tilted France toward a more rigid approach to Algerian radical Islamism. This approach contrasts with the line taken by Italy, Spain, and the United States, which have opted for a constructive approach that might open the door to full political dialogue, democratization, and economic cooperation.

Is dialogue possible with and within fundamentalist groups? In Algeria's case it should develop within a framework of pluralism and respect for human rights. The West should not approach it with a sense of superiority, since the object is not so much to modernize Islam, as to Islamize modernity in those countries.

Islamic radicalism must and can be tamed. The example of Jordan, already mentioned, is a good one, pointing in the right direction of making Islamic radicalism a normal part of the political spectrum and of life.

Fundamentalism is not monolithic, and within these movements there are moderate elements with which Europeans should establish better relations. Islamic radicalism may even be losing strength, according to some observers.[17] This loss of strength would allow a more balanced approach to the integration of Islamism and democracy. Internal and external dialogue must be the first step toward democracy. But this internal dialogue, and the external one as well, must go beyond the problem of fundamentalism to tackle the development of civil societies in these countries, the promotion of and respect for human rights, and the carrying out of democratic elections.[18]

The EU's Renewed Mediterranean Policy gives new importance to respect for human rights and to the promotion of democratic values in those countries. This evolution requires greater pressure from the United States and the European Parliament. With the Maastricht Treaty in force, the European Parliament has veto power over treaties with third countries. Respect for human rights is a principle included in the latest bilateral treaties, such as the Treaty of Friendship and Cooperation signed by Spain and Morocco, and in agreements under negotiation with the EU.

To carry on this dialogue, the West has also to contribute by continuing its own struggle against xenophobia and racism, in order to overcome the perception in the South that "the West hates Islam," just as Islamism is seen in the North as anti-Western (which to some considerable degree it is, especially since the Gulf War).

Political dialogue is not enough. Problems must be tackled at their roots: political, economic, social, and cultural. The West should continue to push for reforms in all these areas, but given the attitudes and risks that have arisen it would be sensible to suggest prudence and moderation in the pace of the reforms.[19]

IMMIGRATION COOPERATION. To control immigration police measures by themselves will not bring about a solution, and could in fact lead to the emergence of a new Wall, this time in the Mediterranean. But no police force or *cordon sanitaire* will be able to stop people who lack expectations in their own countries. The best way to bridle immigration is to develop credible expectations in those countries.

Apart from that approach, the cooperation of the other side—the control of emigration—is necessary. The example provided by Morocco when, at the request of Spain, it decided in 1992–93 to control illegal emigration is a good precedent. The action taken by the Moroccan authorities put a brake on the illegal passage of immigrants in dangerous boats. The best way to control immigration, and to treat immigrants with the respect and decency they deserve, is to set quotas, according to the needs of the market and society, although this approach has not yet been taken by the EU as such. Tunisian president Ben Ali, speaking to the European Parliament in June 1993, proposed setting up a Euro-Maghreb Charter that would define the rights and duties of the immigrants from the Maghreb in the EC.

The immigration dialogue should be complemented by a cultural dialogue. To ensure good relations between the Maghreb and Southern Europe, it is essential not to trample on the dignity of either party. Understanding, coexistence, interaction, and tolerance have to be developed. The role of television (through what some fundamentalists call "para-diabolics," a play on the French phrase for television satellite antennas, *disques paraboliques*) and other instruments and channels of communication has to be enhanced. Europe can also exert a cultural influence on the Maghreb through the immigrant population and its policies toward immigration, and vice versa.

ECONOMIC PARTNERSHIP. To have the possibility of overcoming their major problems, the Maghreb countries need to be part of the world economy and world networks. For this purpose the Maghreb needs Europe. It can be said that if Europe stagnates, the Maghreb's situation will worsen, in turn making problems more acute for Europe. If Europe returns to a path of growth, with lower interest rates, the Maghreb *could* benefit if it seizes the opportunity. Economic cooperation is the most important instrument.

Western economic aid has been conditioned more on economic than on political reforms, although with the hope that aid could open the way for democracy. Thus in spite of the political situation, economic reforms, backed by the IMF, helped Algeria to obtain credits from the World Bank, France, Italy, Spain, and the EU.

Although Europe might need the help of the United States and even Japan (leading creditor of private debt in Algeria) in this effort to help the South, it is unlikely to get it.

Aid is not the only answer. Trade and investments can be more important. Private European investments in the Maghreb countries have grown over the last few years (from $46.5 million in 1983 to $165 million in 1990, although this is not much if we take account of inflation) and have permitted the development of important sectors like textiles, agriculture, and the chemical and electronics industries. The pace of investment should increase even more in the future, despite the economic crisis in Europe and the scant understanding of public opinion. Trade barriers, despite the same kind of obstacles, also also have to come down, and if they do technology flow will be facilitated. The European Council stressed in June 1992 the new importance of horizontal cooperation, mentioned previously. There is within the EU a new movement toward the creation of a free trade area between Europe and the Maghreb (starting with Morocco and Tunisia).[20]

A general problem is that in some countries (Spain, for instance) one can find differing points of view in the foreign affairs ministry and in the agriculture ministry. Faced with such conflicting visions, there is the need in the Mediterranean countries of the North to reconcile the geopolitical vision and the economic and trade vision.

A further problem with the development of the Maghreb is that it has to come about mainly through private investment—a bottom-up approach—although aid from and other actions by the EU can act as a catalyst. As far as investments are concerned, however, the states of the Maghreb, in particular Algeria, are high-risk countries, with poorly trained work forces. That is, they are the opposite of the central and Eastern European countries and may also be less attractive than Mexico or Southeast Asia.

Finally the differing political evolution of these countries can bring about different foreign investment patterns. Thus, for instance, there is a renewed interest by Spanish investors in Morocco (in sectors like textiles, banking, and agriculture) while interest in Algeria is declining.

SECURITY DIALOGUE. As with the issue of radical Islamism, in terms of military security we run the risk of creating a threat where there is now only a risk, of generating a self-fulfilling prophecy. A main risk is that of South-South conflicts involving the North. The Maghreb is obsessed with horizontal security. The problems of frontiers are important. A security dialogue has to be reinforced with these countries to help deactivate those risks.

No doubt Europe is more interested than the Maghreb countries in a security dialogue, which for the North African states should probably be accompanied by economic concessions. Mention has already been made of the sense of a "threat from the north" felt in the Maghreb.

A new atmosphere in the Middle East—especially if it encourages agreements on confidence-building measures and arms control and proliferation in the area—could help the security dialogue in the western Mediterranean (indeed it would be a unique opportunity), as could a peaceful solution to the Western Sahara conflict.

Europe, through the Western European Union (WEU), is opening a security dialogue separately with the Maghreb countries and with Egypt, a proposal that is backed by the WEU Parliamentary Assembly. A similar kind of opening should also be explored at the NATO level, following up on the statement made at the January 1994 NATO summit. In addition, the interest of the Maghreb countries in participating in the Conference on Security and Cooperation in Europe process has been indicated by Morocco.

This dialogue must also aim at the establishment of more transparency, greater cooperation in the field of armaments, and the establishment of confidence-building measures. The revision conference for the Treaty on the Non-Proliferation of Nuclear Weapons (NPT) to be held in 1995 should also be an occasion to make parties to the Treaty the countries of the area that have not already accepted it, especially after France's accession. The control and transparency mechanisms of the NPT should be reinforced, granting greater powers to the International Atomic Energy Agency (such as intrusive inspection capabilities) and considering United Nations sanctions against violators. Similar steps should be taken as far as chemical weapons are concerned.

Bilaterally the Southern European countries should proceed with their military cooperation and arms sales policy toward the Maghreb countries, while they continue their own triangular dialogue among Italy, France, and Spain on western Mediterranean security. The commitment not to use force in solving disputes should be generalized.

THE MAGHREB'S OWN OBSTACLES. A number of positive initiatives toward this region could fail because of obstacles deriving from the Maghreb countries themselves. The lack of economic unity and the disparities among them are important obstacles to regional development and cooperation. It is up to the Maghreb countries to open the way for European investment. All of these countries are making serious efforts at economic reform, as we have already mentioned. In all of them recent laws allow foreign investors to purchase up to 50 or 51 percent of the shares of companies. Nonetheless, in the short term, the effects of these reforms have been limited. They have not made those countries attractive enough to generate foreign investment, and the situation is even further clouded by the murders of and threats against foreigners in Algeria.

As far as political reforms are concerned, there has been some misuse by the state of its own power, as in Algeria. Morocco is the country that has gone farthest in its political reforms (and that has developed the closest ties with the EC). A major problem, as we have seen in the case of Algeria, is that changes have opened or could open the way for Islamists to reach power, provoking an authoritarian reaction that can make matters worse.

Attempts since 1964 to construct a Great Maghreb have failed. Political and economic tensions among these countries—like the Sahara conflict, the Achilles heel of the contruction of a Great Maghreb, according to Balta[21]— are preventing development of the Arab Maghreb Union (AMU), which also includes Libya and Mauritania. Nonetheless the AMU has always been viewed not as the *result* of an understanding, but as a way of solving common problems and *creating* this understanding.[22] Furthermore, the economies of the Maghreb countries do not complement each other, and their different political situations could aggravate these differences by making some countries (like Morocco) more attractive than others (like Algeria) to foreign investments.

The Maghreb's own problems are paralyzing multilateral cooperation— be it the "Five plus Five" process, the "five plus twelve" conversations, or the Euro-Arab dialogue—thus undercutting these countries' prospects. Thus there is a need for a bottom-up approach by the South: the internal transformation of the South could become an engine for change and improvement not only internally or regionally but also in the relations between the Maghreb and Europe.

The Structures

We should, however, recognize that even in the most optimistic scenario, the problem of competition with the East for EC attention and funds remains. The volume of EC financial aid for the East and the novel features of some of its instruments (such as PHARE, EBRD, and TEMPUS) have fostered a sense of frustration in the Maghreb countries, which feel marginalized. This feeling has been reinforced by other events, such as the temporary nonapproval by the European Parliament of the EC-Morocco IV financial protocol. EU aid (not including that of the member states) to the Maghreb has been 2.5 ECU per inhabitant per year, as against 7 ECU for the Eastern and central European countries (and even 4.5 ECU for the countries of the Lome Convention).[23] Nonetheless by 1996, with the Renewed Mediterranean Policy, EU funds for these countries will have increased by 370 percent (compared to 72 percent for Asia and Latin America and 41 percent for the Lome Convention countries).

The concept of a "Euro-Maghreb partnership," a new kind of association, moving away from the traditional logic of assistance toward of "coresponsibility" in development, was proposed by the European Council held in Lisbon in June 1992. New instruments and new areas are being considered in this respect by the European Commission, like the creation of a Euro-Maghreb Development Bank, following the model of the European Bank for Reconstruction and Development (although this idea has already been opposed by some member states). Common action in social and cultural affairs is also under consideration. The EU is introducing a major new element into its approach: the intensification of relations between private investors and operators in Europe and public and private operators in the Maghreb, aimed at promoting investments and joint ventures.

Because of the situation in Algeria, as we have mentioned, a "single-speed" approach would not get the train moving. The EU is thus negotiating an association treaty with Morocco and has started to negotiate another one with Tunisia, aimed at setting up a free trade area. The need to proceed at a reasonable and prudent pace, however, limits this endeavor in its first stage to the granting of important trade concessions, with special attention to sensitive products on both sides as well as to Morocco's new industries. Nonetheless this situation will be reviewed by the year 2000. A full free trade area might not exist either today or tomorrow, but it is becoming an important incentive for future developments. Although it is inevitable, this differentiation among the countries of the region has drawbacks, preventing as it does regional integration, at least in the short or medium term.

Yet the EU initiatives on their own are not enough. Bilateral relations between the Maghreb and the Southern European countries are even more important. To have a greater effect, however, these bilateral relations would have to be better coordinated on both sides. It is doubtful that this will happen on either side. Bilateral and multilateral (EU) aid policies must be coordinated, but the EU countries are reluctant to lose sovereignty in this field. The EU should also encourage programs of cooperation among the Maghreb countries themselves, and thus relaunch a "twelve plus five" dialogue.

The "Five plus Five" dialogue points in the right direction. It brings together Italy, France, Spain, Portugal, and lately Malta with Libya, Algeria, Morocco, Tunisia, and Mauritania. After the first ministerial meeting, held in Rome in 1990, the Algiers Declaration in 1991 institutionalized the process. It has, however, been paralyzed since then by the attitude of Libya in the Lockerbie affair. Perhaps other more limited venues could help restore momentum to this track.

A renewed effort at multilateralization should be made, in particular through two new processes, the Corfu Conference and the Mediterranean Forum. The Corfu Conference, stemming from the European Council of June 1994 and due to begin functioning in 1995, should launch renewed dialogue and cooperation between the EU and its member states and their Mediterranean partners, particularly regarding economic cooperation. The Mediterranean Forum proposed in 1994 by Egypt could thus be used mainly to foster political cooperation. The other pillar of cooperation could be the peace process in the Middle East. The two could be connected by the kind of Conference on Security and Cooperation in the Mediterranean proposed earlier by Spain and Italy.

The United States and Southern Europe in the Maghreb

So far we have not talked much about the United States. Is the Maghreb a "new" issue in transatlantic relations? It can become one, and thus become another area of common interest and cooperation.

U.S. Interests

The U.S. perception of the Maghreb has throughout recent decades been greatly influenced by its vision of the Middle East, and by the cold war, although its interest in the Mediterranean goes much further back. The United States is now facing changing perspectives and new aproaches. It seeks less involvement in South-South conflicts. Conversely in some ways the Maghreb countries may look at the United States as a counterbalance to an independent European defense identity in the area, a prospect that they fear.

Morocco still remains a high priority. It may have lost some of its military interest, but it has regained importance with the role of King

Hassan II in the Middle East peace process. U.S. diplomacy has strongly pressed Morocco to settle the Sahara issue. However, U.S. interest and attention seem to focus on Algeria.

The United States also gives increased importance to human rights and carefully follows the rise of Islamic fundamentalism, which, as it evolves toward terrorist activities, affects U.S. interests. Fundamentalism's effect on the Maghreb and the effect of the Maghreb on fundamentalism are probably the main issues of concern for the United States, which has particular concerns about Egypt and Turkey. Even though its interests in the area are limited, if a cultural war broke out between Islam and the West in this part of the world, U.S. interests would suffer. The United States also seems more interested in the CSCM and similar projects.

Prospects for European-U.S. Cooperation

At least for certain member countries, like Spain and Italy, the U.S. presence in the area is welcome, and there is room for cooperation, although there is no guarantee that this cooperation will take place. The Maghreb could become a topic for the United States–EU dialogue instituted by the Transatlantic Declaration. This cooperation should start from joint analysis of the situations and political processes in the area.

There are differing interests in the area between the United States and Southern Europe: trade competition, political vision (Libya), military bases and their use, the United States' selective engagement approach, and its view of the region primarily in terms of oil and the problems of Israel. In particular, the evolution of Algeria, and the policy to be adopted toward it, could produce growing strains between France and the United States. But there are also coinciding interests, for example those regarding the Middle East and the furtherance of democratization in those countries. It could also be said that the United States looks at its relations with Southern Europe as part of its relations with Europe. Southern Europe would thus be a subframe within the general EU framework.

There are three main issues as far as the area is concerned: order and disorder in the Maghreb, European integration and disintegration (or paralysis), and U.S.-European cooperation and competition. We can describe three scenarios, which complement each other.

In the first disorder in the Maghreb would probably enhance U.S.-European cooperation (bilateral and multilateral) in the area and grant a greater role to NATO. Conversely a state of order in the Maghreb would not feed U.S.-European cooperation.

In the second the furtherance of European integration, and in particular the development of the Common Foreign and Security Policy, could focus on the Maghreb as a test case for European action. A process of stagnation, or retrogression, in European integration would possibly make cooperation with the United States a priority for the individual Southern European states.

In the third the question of whether relations between the United States and Europe evolve in a cooperative or a competitive direction could be decisive for the Maghreb. A competitive relationship would not bring stronger cooperation on Maghreb issues.

Concluding Remarks

Europe cannot ignore the problems of the Maghreb, as its own future, especially the Southern European future, is closely linked to it. The Maghreb is not alien to Southern Europe, which cannot turn its back on this region.

Europe and the Europeans should try to prevent existing ideological and cultural gaps from evolving into major issues that could spill over into other fields and lead to a renewal of containment, aimed at the South. The positive evolution of the Middle Eastern situation creates an opportunity for the Maghreb. Much depends on whether a conflictual or a cooperative approach is chosen. Cooperation and dialogue seem to be the route the Europeans should follow, and they should bring the United States with them in this endeavor.

Notes

1. From a geographic point of view, it is more exact to limit the Maghreb to Morocco, Algeria, and Tunisia. But the vision of the "Great Maghreb," which underlies the creation of the Arab Maghreb Union, adds Libya and Mauritania. Libya is a land of transition toward the Middle East, Mauritania is a land of transition toward black Africa. The Maghreb is not homogeneous in resources, nor in political and economic systems—thus the difficulty of discussing a concept that exists mainly in geography. See Alejandro Lorca, *Las Fronteras de la Unión Europea* (Madrid: Instituto Internacional Carlos Quinto–Taller de Estudios Internacionales del Mediterraneao, 1993).

2. Commissariat Général du Plan, *Monde Europe: Repères et Orientations pour les Français 1993–1997* (Paris: Dunod–La Documentation Française, 1993).

3. "Rapport au Conseil Européen de Lisbonne sur l'évolution probable de la Politique Etrangère et de Sécurité Commune visant à cerner les domaines se prêtant à une action commune vis-à-vis de pays ou de groupe de pays particuliers," Press

communiqué, Lisbon, 1992. Quoted in Yves Boyer, "Europe's Future Strategic Orientation," *Washington Quarterly,* vol. 16, no. 4 (Autumn 1993), p. 151.

4. Programma de las Naciones Unidas para el Desarrollo, *Informe sobre el Desarrollo Humano 1993* (Madrid: CIDEAL, 1993).

5. *Desarrollo Humano 1993.*

6. Alberto Navarro, *La Comunidad Europea, el Magreb y España* (Madrid: INCIPE, 1993).

7. Paul Balta, *Le Grand Maghreb* (Paris: La Découverte, 1990).

8. Samuel P. Huntington, "The Clash of Civilizations?" *Foreign Affairs,* vol. 72, no. 3 (Summer 1993), pp. 22–49.

9. John L. Esposito, *The Islamic Threat: Myth or Reality* (Oxford University Press, 1993).

10. Michel Camau, in Bernabé Lopez, ed., *España-Magreb, Siglo XXI* (Madrid: Mapfre, 1992), p. 105.

11. Jorge Dezcallar, "El Fundamentalismo Islámico en el Mundo Árabe: Las Razones de su Éxito," *Política Exterior,* vol. 5, no. 24 (Winter 1992), pp. 131–42.

12. Ian O. Lesser, *Security in North Africa: Internal and External Challenges* (Santa Monica, Calif.: RAND, 1993).

13. Jacques Amalrik, "Un Entretien avec le Roi Hassan II du Maroc," *Le Monde,* August 16, 1990, p. 1.

14. Volker Rühe, "Redefining the Security Interests in Europe," *Wall Street Journal* (European Edition), September 9, 1993.

15. Navarro, *Comunidad Europea.*

16. Commissariat Général du Plan, *Monde Europe.*

17. Claire Spencer, *The Maghreb in the 1990s,* Adelphi Paper 274 (London: International Institute for Strategic Studies, 1993).

18. Judith Miller, "The Challenge of Radical Islam," *Foreign Affairs,* vol. 72, no. 2 (Spring 1993), pp. 43–56.

19. Navarro, *Comunidad Europea.*

20. Lorca, "Las Fronteras de la Unión Europea."

21. Balta, *Le Grand Maghreb.*

22. Michele Brondino, in Bernabé Lopez, ed., *España-Maghreb, Siglo XXI* (Madrid: Mapfre, 1992), p. 114.

23. Navarro, *Comunidad Europea.*

FOUR

The Question of Migration

Nadji Safir

AT A TIME when the question of migration is asserting itself as one of the essential structural dimensions of the world situation, Southern Europe, on more grounds than one, finds itself directly affected.[1] Furthermore, Southern Europe, being a frontier area bordering the Mediterranean, beyond which an "other world" begins, is in fact a region where all the essential questions of our times come together.

Indeed, if one looks at it from an economic perspective, the Mediterranean clearly marks the boundary between the North and the South of our world, at a time when the disparities between the two groupings—in favor of the North as all analyses attest—are becoming more strongly accentuated.

If one looks at it from a geopolitical perspective, Southern Europe functions as a component of the European pole in relation to the two other poles, North America and Japan, with which it is in competition.

If one looks at it from a strategic perspective, with the end of the East-West confrontation, the definition of a grouping going from "Vancouver to Vladivostok" necessarily makes Southern Europe into a frontier in a new context in which, one way or another, the enemy that has "disappeared" in the East, probably mistakenly, is replaced by one seen as possibly lying to the south.

If one looks at it from a cultural perspective, in a world where, no matter what area of civilization is in question, the dynamic of identification is strengthening (or rather being exacerbated), once again Southern Europe seems to be a frontier since the Mediterranean represents the divide between East and West, or between Islam and Christianity.

It is, therefore, clear that two groupings are facing each other across the Mediterranean that are separated by many characteristics. However, other characteristics unite them. Indeed, the notion of the Mediterranean as a space common to the two shores—like a shared inheritance in terms not only of basic economic, ecological, social, and cultural facts, but also of norms and values—is an undeniable reality that offers the necessary basis for cordial relations in many fields.

All the more so because movements of population throughout history, and especially in the contemporary period, have indisputably contributed to the birth of powerful links, which currently take the form of the communities on the north side which have their origin to the south of the Mediterranean.

The migratory flows that have been the basis for the establishment of these communities, after having for a long time been taken for granted by the partners of the region, are more and more perceived by them—and particularly by those in the North—as disturbing phenomena.

In any case it appears that the Mediterranean problem must in the future more and more be structured, other than by the four perspectives to which we have already referred, according to the demographic perspective, which appears to be, as the editors of the *Le Plan Bleu* write, "the most serious factor."[2]

Demographic Characteristics

The demographic characteristics of the region are summarized in table 4-1. The data give a clear picture of the growing population imbalance that characterizes the region.

Yet more than the current data, it is the prospects for the future that best illustrate the extent of the imbalance. "Of the 170 million additional people living on the shores of the Mediterranean in 2025, 68 percent will have been born in an Arab country, 22 percent in Turkey, and only 10 percent in Europe."[3]

At the same point in time, Morocco will have a larger population than Spain, while Algeria and Tunisia, taken together, will have a larger population than France.

The situation within the region is all the more noteworthy because it displays some significant differences compared to other parts of the world. Consider that essential indicator, the fertility rate. In 1991 in the United States and Mexico (which have their own migration connection) it was 2.0 and 3.3, respectively. In the Mediterranean region it is at the same time higher in the South (ranging from 3.6 to 6.5) and lower in the North (ranging from 1.3 to 1.8).

Table 4-1. *Demographic Characteristics of the Mediterranean Region*

Country	Population (millions)				Annual rate of population growth		Fertility rate (1991)
	1960	*1991*	*2000*	*2025*	*1960-91*	*1991-2000*	
Portugal	8.8	9.9	9.9	10.1	0.4	0.1	1.5
Spain	30.5	39.0	39.6	60.8	0.8	0.2	1.4
France	45.7	57.0	58.8	40.6	0.7	0.4	1.8
Italy	50.2	57.7	58.1	56.2	0.5	0.1	1.3
Greece	8.3	10.2	10.3	10.1	0.6	0.2	1.5
Total northern shore	143.5	173.8	176.7	177.8			
Morocco	11.6	25.7	31.7	47.5	2.6	2.3	4.5
Algeria	10.8	25.6	32.7	51.8	2.8	2.7	5.4
Tunisia	4.2	8.2	9.8	13.4	2.2	1.9	3.6
Libya	1.3	4.7	6.4	12.9	4.0	3.4	6.5
Egypt	25.9	53.6	64.8	93.5	2.3	2.1	4.2
Turkey	27.5	57.2	68.2	92.9	2.4	2.0	3.6
Total southern shore	81.3	175.0	213.6	312.0			
Southern shore as percent of northern shore	56%	100%	120%	175%			

Sources: UNDP, *Human Development Report 1993* (Oxford University Press, 1993); FNUAP, *Etat de la Population Mondiale 1993* (New York, 1993); Eurostat, *Demographic Statistics 1992* (Luxembourg, 1992); Leon Tabah, "Demographic Imbalance Between the Countries of the Mediterranean Basin," report presented to the Council of Europe, 1991; Commission of the European Communities, Cellule de Prospective, *L'Europe dans le Mouvement Demographique* (Brussels, 1990).

One additional characteristic of these populations should be emphasized, one that points out another very clear imbalance in their structure. In the North the proportion of persons over 60, already high, is destined to grow and reach 26 percent in 2020, with a median age of 43.9 years (in 1970 it was 32.0), while at the same time in the South it will be only 12 percent, with a heavy proportion of young people. On the basis of the demographic data alone, it clearly appears that, to use the words of a French demographer, "because of the empty spaces that it creates, the demographic depression in the North constitutes a factor of attraction."[4]

If one integrates into this analysis the economic prospects for the region, this hypothesis takes on still more significance.

Economic Prospects

The principal economic and social indicators for the region are summarized in table 4-2. Once more the difference between the two shores of the Mediterranean is clear.

Both shores are suffering from the current economic downturn. The prospect for the future, however, is that current trends will only be strength-

Table 4-2. *Social and Economic Indicators for the Mediterranean Region*

Country	Human development index		Per capita GNP (dollars)		Share of agriculture in GNP (percent)	Secondary school enrollment ratio
	Rank	Value	1991	Growth rate, 1989–90		
France	8	0.971	20,600	1.8	3	97
Italy	22	0.924	18,580	2.1	3	78
Spain	23	0.923	12,460	2.9	5	100
Greece	25	0.902	6,230	1.2	17	97
Portugal	41	0.853	5,620	2.7	...	53
Turkey	73	0.717	1,820	2.9	18	51
Libya	87	0.658	...	...	...	...
Tunisia	93	0.600	1,510	1.2	18	44
Algeria	107	0.528	2,020	–0.8	13	61
Morocco	119	0.433	1,030	1.6	19	36
Egypt	124	0.389	620	2.0	18	81

Sources: UNDP, *Human Development Report 1993* (Oxford University Press, 1993); World Bank, *Rapport Annuel 1992* (Washington); *World Bank Atlas 1992* (Washington, 1992).

ened since, whatever difficulties the north shore will confront, it is the southern shore that will be burdened by the most serious constraints, notably by the growing burden of unemployment. The following analysis underlines this point:

> Unemployment is a serious economic, social, and political phenomenon throughout the region. More than 15 percent of the active population is unemployed in the countries of the Maghreb, in Egypt, and in Iran, while in Jordan and in Yemen the unemployment rates exceed 25 percent. The consequences of past demographic growth will continue to show up as extraordinary increases in the working age population during the next 20 years. If the region is to find social stability thanks to the productive employment of those currently unemployed and of the work force that will enter the labor market in the future, the rhythm and the nature of economic growth must develop considerably compared to what they have been in the recent past.[5]

Thus in the case of Algeria the number of new job seekers is estimated at 250,000 a year in the period 1990–95, whereas annual job creation between 1990 and 1992 scarcely exceeded 90,000: a considerable deficit.

Consequently the region is destined to suffer from a significant migration problem: given the constraints upon the southern shore, the positive results that can be expected from the processes of adjustment that are underway will make themselves felt only in the long term, and they will certainly not absorb the labor supply destined to enter the market.

As is emphasized by the *Human Development Report* of 1992, "the pressures of immigation will continue unless there is development in the South. Economic opportunities—better access to global markets and foreign direct investment—have to migrate towards people if people cannot migrate towards economic opportunities."[6]

This analysis is valid for the Mediterranean more than for any other region of the world, especially because of the intensity of the relations that have so long existed there, and that have created situations that are irreversible.

Contemporary Mediterranean Migration: Former Realities

South-to-North migration has been going on for many years, particularly since the beginning of this century, and especially within the framework of the former colonial relationship.[7]

In fact, of all the countries of Southern Europe, only France was really a country of immigration, which came especially from this region. The other countries of the region were all countries of emigration, including emigration in the direction of France.

Starting in the 1960s, the region witnessed a new migration, deriving from the southern shore of the Mediterranean but moving in the direction of a country of Northern Europe: the migration from Turkey to Germany.

At present, to differing degrees, the countries on the north shore of the Mediterranean all play host to communities deriving from the south shore, although the only one for which they represent a statistically important reality is France. In France the community of Maghrebian origin is on the order of 1.5 million people, of whom 500,000 are workers. In Spain and Italy communities with origins on the south shore of the Mediterranean (mainly the Maghreb and Egypt) are beginning to take on meaningful size: on the order of 200,000 persons in each country. The Turkish community, numbering on the order of 2 million in Europe as a whole, is concentrated mainly in Northern Europe, in Germany, where 1,700,000 Turks live.

Although it is difficult to estimate the size of the migratory flows from the southern shore in the most recent period, it is clear that since the beginning of the 1990s, faced with the restrictive measures taken by the European governments as well as the difficult economic and social situation that prevails there, they have considerably diminished. Indeed at the present time the migration problem in the region has less and less to do with significant new flows, and more and more to do with the integration into the societies of the North of the immigrants already resident there.

From this point of view the situation is not identical for the three countries of the northern shore most affected—Spain, Italy, and France. Developments in the first two countries—new destinations for immigrants, particularly from Morocco, Tunisia, and Egypt—might give the impression that they are playing host to the bulk of the recent migrants.

The countries of Southern Europe are not affected solely by flows coming from the countries bordering on the Mediterranean; it is necessary to mention as well the flows coming from sub-Saharan Africa (especially into France, on the order of 150,000; Italy, around 50,000; and Portugal, around 30,000).

Finally, aside from the number of foreign nationals originating on the southern shore, for obvious historical reasons a significant number (one that is unfortunately hard to quantify) of European citizens, French especially, trace their origins to the southern shore of the Mediterranean, with which they maintain connections, especially cultural ones, that are often complex. Therefore for at least one country—France—immigrant communities deriving from the southern shore of the Mediterranean are not a new phenomenon but, very much to the contrary, well established social realities. This fact raises the following question: Why, for several years now but with a sharpness that grows as time passes, have the phenomena connected to the migration problem become essential elements in the debates going on both within the affected societies and in the relations between the states that are involved?

Contemporary Mediterranean Migration: Some New Issues

Three major issues form the structure of the new migration problem in the region.

—The first relates to the perception of the economic crisis, which, especially since the beginning of the 1980s, has been seen as a durable phenomenon from which the region will not emerge for a long time. It is noteworthy that this perception of the crisis is held by the most diverse groups, and as much in the North as in the South. That is because in the North—where an overall withdrawal reflex is reinforced by the conviction that in the South the necessary conditions for economic growth are not yet all in existence and that, therefore, migratory flows are destined to continue and even to grow—it is no longer a question, as a French official said, of taking in all the misery in the world.

—The second issue concerns the change in the nature of migration. Long tolerated as a transitory phenomenon, it is more and more perceived as a permanent phenomenon that straightforwardly poses the question of the integration of the populations concerned. In the South the dominant perception of migration is of a departure that, if not definitive, is at least likely to be long lasting. All that has been said, as much in the North as in the South, regarding voluntary return or reinsertion is today clearly perceived to be applicable only to a very restricted number of individual cases.

That is why, in the North, there is a progressive change in attitude. Once an "invited worker" (a *Gastarbeiter,* to use the eloquent German term), the immigrant has now become the person with whom one is destined to live.

Furthermore, the picture gets more complicated because cohabitation is necessary not just with the worker himself, but also with his family, given that the family reunification policies give him the right to have them come to join him in his adopted land.

—The third issue regards the redefinition of the relations prevailing in the region. Like all other regions, the Mediterranean is affected by the new world situation, dominated by the end of the East-West confrontation. Looked at this way, the question of migration is directly relevant, especially to the new European situation, which makes central and Eastern Europe, one way or another, a "natural extension" of the structure that is being built in the West. Long the principal reservoir of potential migration, the southern shore of the Mediterranean is now squarely confronted by the "competition" from Eastern Europe, which benefits in addition from a "cultural proximity premium."

These new considerations all contribute to redefining very clearly the problem of migration in the region as a new phase in its history. The events that we are experiencing today are analyzable in terms of a transition dominated by three major themes: those of identity, security, and cooperation.

Migration and Identity

The debate in the North about the question of migration is also, one way or another, a debate regarding the relations that Europe ought to maintain with Islam. It is clearly perceived that the extra-European flows of immigrants, whether they come from the southern shore of the Mediterranean or from sub-Saharan Africa, come from Muslim societies. They therefore pose the question of relations with the culture of the host countries.

The presence of Muslim communities on European soil, which has long been a fact, makes European Islam a tangible reality: currently it ranks as the second most widespread religion in three important countries of the European Community: France, Germany, and the United Kingdom. The number of Muslims in all of the countries of the European Union (EU) combined is currently estimated at around 7 million. An important proportion of these are citizens of the member states, and therefore, on the basis of the Maastricht Treaty, of the EU.

Given the worldwide context of growing emphasis on identity, it is evident that Europe cannot help being concerned, as is shown by the more and more open manifestations of xenophobia and racism. The social strata affected by the economic recession constitute an especially favorable environment for the incubation and development of these feelings, for which immigrants in general, and Muslim immigrants in particular, constitute preferred targets.

In such a context migratory flows deriving from the southern shore of the Mediterranean are obviously very much at risk because they run into active resistance in the societies concerned. The resistance is all the stronger because it is manipulated by political forces that often have extremist agendas and for which immigration is an "easy" issue that can be exploited to yield immediate results.

The new European situation created by the Maastricht Treaty poses the question of European identity. This, at least judging by the texts of the treaty, has never been envisaged as being of a religious nature, for example "Christian." If the Maastricht Treaty makes reference to "common values" (notably in title V, article J.1, point 2, regarding the objectives of the common foreign and security policy), the concept appears to be sufficiently broad that the followers of a spiritual doctrine like Islam can quite fully accept it.

That said, the dominant perception of Islam in Europe is often of an essentialist and static nature. It does not sufficiently take into account the dynamics of Islam as a spiritual message and the sum of individual and collective practices—nor, especially, does it take into account the Muslim communities. These communities in Europe are inserted into a new context of developed industrial societies, which cannot help but directly influence all their perceptions and attitudes.

In this regard it is worth noting how very poorly understood at present are both the developments within the Muslim communities established in

Europe and the influence that these developments can have on their countries of origin. Quite obviously the "model" functioning in Europe and dominated (whatever its various national particulars) by two major facts, religious pluralism and secularism, will in the end necessarily influence the societies on the southern shore. Going in the opposite direction, developments within the societies on the southern shore also spread within the communities established in Europe; however, all available evidence leads one to think that here, as in other domains, the relations between the two shores will in the end, one way or another, bear the stamp of the dynamic at work in the North, as the dominant cultural model.

In any case, if the question of identity is important in and of itself, it is also important from another perspective, that of security. This issue is frequently brought up, often in an implicit but more and more in an explicit way, in connection with the question of migration.

Migration and Security

Over the course of the last few years, the question of migration has progressively become part of a new field of discussion, that related to security. First there were the problems of internal security as seen by the host countries. Then—and this was an essential turning point—emphasis shifted to the problems of security in a broader sense, implying a set of problems in terms of international relations. This evolution, extremely important for its consequences, direct and indirect, immediate and distant, derives fundamentally from a new understanding of the concept of security, which broadens its meaning in two directions:

—It can no longer be limited to the military field alone and now necessarily involves such other fields such as the economy, ecology, and culture, to mention only the most important.

—It can no longer be limited to the state alone as principal and often sole operator, since civil society more and more considers itself as the party that has to pay the bill.

As a result of this new double connotation, migration immediately becomes an issue, first of all because it is seen as involved in the problem of identity.

In this regard, voices are raised on the northern shore of the Mediterranean denouncing immigration as an "invasion" especially because the actual or potential flows come from Muslim countries, and thus raise the issue of the nation's identity, both in and of itself and as component of the general perception of security.

There is also another perception on the northern shore of immigration in terms of security, one that proceeds from a more restricted and traditional meaning of the concept, and that makes immigration at worst a source of threats, at best a source of risks. In that perception, immigration functions as a "fifth column," putting itself at the service of foreign interests—in this case, of Islam.

In reality the links between the communities originating on the southern shore and their countries of origin are far from being as strong and open to exploitation as such perceptions suggest. In fact it increasingly appears that the migratory processes are escaping the control of the sending countries, particularly in the context of political crisis and of the growing strength of the informal economy, whose dominant principles are also at work in the migratory process. Under such conditions it is difficult to imagine that, as a rule, the migrant could be transformed into an agent. He would be operating for the account of a state with which he has less and less connection, and from whose policies, plainly, he has often fled.[8]

That said, it is clear that in the end the communities originating on the southern shore and living in Europe can constitute pressure groups acting to defend their specific interests, especially in the areas of religion and culture. In so doing they would not diverge very much from the practice of other communities that are particularly active from this point of view. Each of them, in its own fashion, exercises its democratic rights, particularly in a context in which the principles of identity are gaining ground. The emphasis on identity reinforces the legitimacy of such practices, which are not the work of immigrants alone, whatever their origins.

Nevertheless, reductive perceptions of the immigrant exist, and it is thus that, in an analysis that may be marginal but which has the merit of frankness, it is written that "the twenty-first century could once again find Islam at the gates of Vienna, *as immigrants or terrorists if not as armies.* Indeed, *massive Islamic immigration* into France may already have reversed Charles Martel's victory in 732 at the Battle of Tours."[9] The hierarchy introduced by the author is highly significant because it postulates a neat gradation from the immigrant to the terrorist to the soldier of an enemy army.

Such attitudes exist in certain milieus on the northern shore, even if often they are not made explicit with the same clarity. They too contribute to the emergence of tensions in the region. Fundamentally they stem from analyses of a more general character. These, in their turn, have their origin in new evaluations of the world strategic situation in the aftermath of the end of the East-West confrontation. These evaluations make the South into the new enemy—at least potentially.

The fact is that the new strategic space ranging from Vancouver to Vladivostok is, with the exception of its American portion, flanked to the south, for the most part, by the Islamic civilization. Many of that area's tendencies are perceived as disturbing, particularly since the change of regime in Iran and the recovery of dynamism by the Islamist movements.[10]

Aside from factors of a purely political and security nature, social and economic factors—especially the enormous and inverted differences in demographic and economic potential—are involved in the perception of the area of Islamic civilization. In fact the real problems on the southern shore of the Mediterranean lie at this level of economic and social conditions, as the Communiqué of the Atlantic Council held in Rome in November 1991 recognized. In its analysis they are the sources of Islamic radicalism. That is why the problems of security are always closely connected to those of cooperation in all the approaches being made at the regional level and, above all, the proposal for a Conference on Security and Cooperation in the Mediterranean, as well the so-called "Five plus Five" framework, both still in an embryonic stage.

It appears that hereafter in these approaches to cooperation the migratory phenomenon will constitute an essential dimension, in a way a *passage obligé*.

Migration and Cooperation

Aside from events at the regional level, it is by now agreed at the world level that only policies that get to the root of the problem are capable of coping with the migratory logic that is expressed in the formula of the French demographer Alfred Sauvy that if the wealth does not go where men are, men will go where the wealth is.

This key idea is very widely shared within the region, in the North as much as in the South, but without so far having produced particularly tangible results in terms of cooperation.[11] This situation has led to the Maghreb being described, in a Spanish official document, as a "time bomb." Indeed, the gaps in development and in living standards between the two sides of the Mediterranean—which in the opinion of all experts are still growing—by now are clearly perceived, in the North and the South, as no longer susceptible to "routine management," which would certainly lead to serious tensions.[12]

Thus, among other illustrations of this new awareness at the European level, the Renewed Mediterranean Policy has been developed. It has as its starting point a perception expressed repeatedly in significant language:

> The pressure of migration will be all the more massive and uncontrollable if the European Community does not establish *new and more equitable* trade relations with Mediterranean third parties, and does not institute *cooperation that is quantitatively and qualitatively different from that of the past* in order to contribute to the development and growth of these countries.[13]

In addition the theme of migration is, at the highest level, assuming a growing importance in the European institutional vision, as these extracts from a document that is particularly valuable in this regard illustrate. Among them is a point entitled, "to act on the migratory pressure: to take migration into account in the foreign policy of the Community," which includes the following recommendation: "That is why the Community should make explicit in its future cooperation agreements where it is clearly necessary, the dimension of migration, dealing with aspects such as: . . . The examination in each of the countries involved of the questions relating to the maintenance in its zone of origin of the population that might potentially emigrate."[14]

It appears, therefore, that on the European side at the level of positions of principle, an overall vision is in the process of being born, of emerging progressively, despite difficulties inherent in the process of European construction and especially those deriving from the Maastricht Treaty.

As for the South, taken as a whole, it is clear that there is no common perception of the problems connected with migration, whether in general or in connection with the prospects for cooperation between the two sides. It is as if only national interests were involved, despite efforts—often purely formal—to develop common positions.

From this point of view the serious crisis that the Arab Maghreb Union is experiencing has obvious repercussions for the question of migration, even though it should be a priority theme as regards both cooperation between the member states and that to be promoted with Europe.[15]

That is why, at the multilateral level, no notable action deserves to be singled out. The rare actions actually undertaken are only in their beginning stages, with no real prospects for cooperation taking shape.[16] This is true even though all the countries on the southern shore are experiencing serious economic difficulties in a context constrained by structural adjustment programs, with social consequences that are difficult to cope with, much less manage, because they involve a growing number of persons who are left out and who are therefore tempted by any adventure, even the most destabilizing. In this situation, in concrete economic reality the only forces operating are the harsh demands of the market, whose logic prevails; the principal index is the flow of direct investments.

From this point of view the performances of the countries on the southern shore of the Mediterranean are, in comparison with those of the rest of the world, exceedingly modest. For example, over the four years 1987–90, Egypt, with investments amounting to $4.375 billion, attracted less capital than Portugal ($4.795 billion), Argentina ($4.792 billion), Malaysia ($5.972 billion), and Thailand ($5.389 billion). A European source sums up the situation well in the following words: "I draw your attention to the miraculous performance of tiny Asian countries like Singapore and even Malaysia, which in the past ten years have been able to attract *more private investment than all the Mediterranean countries combined.*[17]

By now the figures speak for themselves. It is clear that without an overall, long-term vision, necessarily involving a sharpened awareness on the part of all the partners of their real common interests, the risks of regional disaster are great. However important the processes of the world economy, it is not sufficient to submit passively to them. The result might be negative. An overall and coherent approach to the problems of the region, especially the economic and social problems, is indispensable.

Migration and Regional Prospects

Migration is now an active issue in the Mediterranean. It has already been established that it will continue to be one for a long time to come, thus becoming a structural dimension of the regional problem.

In the North, four key ideas are destined to influence the prospects of the countries involved:

—The difficulties connected with the necessary adaptations to the worldwide changes that their economies will experience, with all their consequences for society. Although these adaptations will cause difficulties in the short and medium terms, it is possible that in the long run a recovery will take place, resulting especially from the beneficial effects expected of the process of integration. It is, however, appropriate to note—and this is a new and important fact—that a resumption of growth does not necessarily imply a sharp reduction in the rate of unemployment.[18] Therefore tensions will persist because of trends in the labor market. These will continue to have a negative impact on the view held in the North of migratory flows, whether actual or potential.

—The pursuit of the process of European construction initiated by the Maastricht Treaty. In this regard it is appropriate to ask oneself what real significance to attach to the concept of Southern Europe, inasmuch as important issues, and the question of migration in particular, are more and more being raised at the EU level.[19]

Making the Southern European countries the designated interlocutors with the southern shore may be an approach subject to debate given the current primacy of a common European vision in which the countries of Northern Europe also have their piece to speak.[20]

It is nevertheless clear, however, that the countries of Southern Europe will continue to enjoy considerable autonomy, permitting them to define their own positions with regard to the relations they intend to maintain with their neighbors on the southern shore. It is just as clear that this autonomy must necessarily be redefined within the European institutional framework, which will progressively assert itself despite its current stammering.

—The growing emergence of Europe as a worldwide pole, in competition with the two other poles (American and Asiatic), forming what is now called "the Triad."

The political as well as economic prospects opened up by the Treaty on European Union should produce a general dynamic that will benefit Europe but that might turn sour in a context in which internationalization imposes its norms and the two other competing poles are very energetic.[21]

The policies that these two poles follow with regard to their immediate neighbors constitute for Europe an index of their will to deal in a dynamic manner with constraints that are just as complex as those that confront Europe.[22]

As for the countries of Southern Europe, despite the strong solidarity that ties them to the other European countries within the framework of the European Union, they nonetheless remain subject to the rigors of European and worldwide competition, in which they are not always the strongest performers.

—The persistence of European demographic decline with acute problems especially in matters of social welfare, given the growing aging of the population. The demographic projections, which show clearly the aging as well as the very weak growth of the population, do not automatically lead to the conclusion that it will be necessary to draw on the population sources outside Europe. However, it is generally agreed that for particular segments of the population, especially skilled labor, Europe will have need of external resources. In this field, as in others, it will be in competition with the other worldwide poles, as is underlined by the following analysis:

> Due to the demographic process in Europe and due to the urgent need for human resources in the next century, the EC will have *to compete worldwide* for mobile professionals, highly qualified workers, and specialists. Racism and xenophobia are definitely self-defeating, because they repulse the kind of (complementary) human resources *Europe will desperately need!*[23]

The problem in the South has three key components:

—The economic difficulties being encountered in one form or another by all of the countries will persist and probably be aggravated. The most disturbing problem will be that of unemployment. In no significant case will the unemployment rate be held to levels compatible with managing society without major dysfunction. The structural adjustment programs that are being implemented, leading to the spread of the market economy, imply changes that will be difficult to effect, particularly in the context of a reduction in available financial resources.

—Demographic growth will continue at relatively elevated rates, despite the discernible downward trend. The fundamental process of demographic transition, generally begun on the southern shore in different degrees depending on the country, does not eliminate the extremely severe constraints that already exist. Thus the annual rate of growth of the active population should be in the neighborhood of 4 percent. This would require a rate of economic growth so high as to be inconceivable, given existing structural constraints, if unemployment is to be held to current levels. Under these circumstances, there is every reason to believe that the migratory potential of the southern shore will continue to be very high and directed toward the nearest rich countries, that is, those of Southern Europe.

—A context of political crisis with serious risks of instability could trigger explosions in certain countries. This is a direct consequence of the two series of phenomena already cited, of an economic and a demographic nature, as well as other political factors tied in a more specific manner to the histories of the different countries. The profound crisis of legitimacy that the political elites are experiencing, especially as a result of the clear failures of the development policies they have followed, is leading in certain cases to a true crisis of the state, which is incapable of accepting the need for a new division of economic and political powers after a long period in which nothing changed. Under such conditions the answers offered by Islamism more and more appear—especially for the disenfranchised—to be an acceptable bet, given the impossibility of moving in other directions.

If one combines all of the key ideas that form the structure of the regional problem, it is quite obvious that the migration issue pervades all of them. Aside from all the potential economic migrants (and they are numerous) the prevalent instability on the southern shore can lead to migration in response to other motivations, but a migration whose effect will be the same: to reinforce the pressure on Europe.

In this regard, it is best not to exaggerate excessively the possible impact, in terms of massive migration, of the political changes that could take place in certain countries of the southern shore. In reality it is as if the process of migration had already begun and was taking place drop by drop, especially in the milieus that consider that a political explosion, for example, of the "Islamic Republic" type, would damage their interests or lead to practices contrary to their principles.[24]

In any case, it seems difficult to imagine massive migrations from the southern to the northern shore because they would pose extremely complex, if not insurmountable, problems in the context of the European societies.

A less concentrated and more continuous increase of the pressure of migration on Europe seems more plausible. In fact such an increase would pose a serious problem for the southern shore, for it might be made up of the most dynamic elements in its societies, those who often have a combination of skills, a spirit of enterprise, and capital. This loss of resources would be extremely prejudicial for the southern shore. It would aggravate the crisis, generating new migratory pressures. The South might find itself in a true vicious circle, with dramatic consequences.

Another important migration problem must be pointed out, for it will more and more directly affect both shores of the region: migration from sub-Saharan Africa. The extraordinary migratory potential of Africa is directed more and more at Europe, and the migrant wave necessarily encounters North Africa along the way, whether as a transit area, an inter-mediate stop, or even, often against the will of the traveler as a final destination. A trend that has existed for some years will intensify in the future: the countries of the Maghreb will find themselves faced with a problem of migratory flows from sub-Saharan Africa, involving not only economic migrants but also those driven by ecological and political motives.

This complex situation challenges the two shores of the Mediterranean. Yet this cause of concern should be turned into an opportunity for trilateral cooperation among the northern shore, the southern shore, and sub-Saharan Africa. Now is a good time to work out the outline of such future cooperation. Without such a vision, the situation runs the risk of quickly getting out of control and of complicating still further the problems of all kinds that affect North Africa, and whose consequences, in terms of migration toward Europe, are evident.

Since the question of migration is destined to remain, for a very long time, one of the fundamental elements of the Mediterranean problem, it is appropriate to understand its new significance.

New Significance of the Question of Migration

The region around the Mediterranean is, for several reasons, important for and typical of the world order toward which we are heading. Proof of this declaration is the fact that it includes all of the aspects of North-South relations as stated by Francis Fukuyama:

> In many respects, the historical and post-historical worlds will maintain parallel but separate existences, with relatively little interaction between them. There will, however, be several axes along which these worlds will collide. The first is *oil* which was the background cause of the crisis caused by the Iraqi invasion of Kuwait. . . . The second axis of interaction is less visible than oil presently but *in the long run perhaps more troublesome: migration.* . . . The final axis of interaction between the two worlds will be over certain *"world order* questions."[25]

Indeed, whether it is a question of immigration (the subject of this chapter), a question of energy, or questions relative to the world order (such as sensitive weapons, the example used by Fukuyama in his book), the Mediterranean is on the agenda. Its prominence in this respect reflects the degree to which it is a sensitive area, and the fact that, in a world in which cultural factors are more and more pertinent, it is the meeting place for two great areas of civilization.

How then can so sensitive an area, one that has almost a symbolic value, transform itself into a place for intercourse rather than confrontation?

Seen in the light of the problem of migration, the answer lies in four major propositions:

—There must be a new, completely transformed vision of cooperation in the region.

It is clear that the approaches utilized heretofore have been ineffective and have produced only mediocre results, falling short of both expectations and objectives. First of all, an overall vision in terms of common interests, which takes into account the imperatives of the internationalization of the economy, must prevail. From this point of view the southern shore should be treated as an opportunity for Europe, as a necessary condition for its functioning as one of the world's "poles." The southern shore and most especially the Maghreb must no longer be seen as a brake on the functioning of the European pole but, quite the contrary, as an integral part of its basic mechanisms.

It is paradoxical to hear Europe complaining about competition from the Asiatic pole when perversely, by its direct investments as part of the process of globalization, it itself nourishes that pole and contributes to the support of the very crisis from which it is suffering.[26]

If the logic of the market must remain the prevailing logic, it should not, in any case, be the only one. It must necessarily be part of an overall vision based on the balances to be maintained in the region.

The institutionalized process of bilateral and multilateral cooperation, just like the economic exchanges between private operators, must be directed by arbitration and incentive mechanisms of a macro- and microeconomic character, taking account of the effects, in terms of reducing migratory pressures, expected from any investment.

At this point it must be noted that it is difficult to establish a clear, direct relationship between economic growth and migratory pressure inasmuch as, at least in the short and medium term, an increase in the rate of economic growth is not necessarily accompanied by a reduction in the pressure of migration. In fact, in certain cases, economic growth and migratory pressure have grown at the same time. However, such observations cannot lead to inaction, for it is clear that in the long term only economic growth, and therefore the development of the reservoirs of migration under discussion, can significantly reduce the migratory pressure aimed at the northern shore.

—The migration issue must be made explicit in regional relations, making it an official, fully accepted dimension thereof.

The objective should be to arrive progressively at first control of, then management of, the migratory flows and of all the questions to which they are connected.

In this regard, just as in the North the migration issue is more and more becoming an element in foreign policy, it should in the South become a dimension giving structure to actions to be taken in the region, both bilaterally and multilaterally.

In numerous instances throughout the world there is increasing support for the idea of a controlled regulation of migratory flows that would not simply be left to the laws of the market.[27] Taking a similar approach, the French president of the European Commission, Jacques Delors, answering a question about the opposing, more laissez faire, theses, declared, "No, economics are secondary compared to politics. Certainly the enterprise has a very great role to play but it cannot regulate political and social life. To let the market regulate the great human movements that migrations are would be *ineffective and catastrophic.*"[28]

This point of view is widely shared. Thus two authors to whom we have already referred advance the proposition of a General Agreement on Migration Policy (GAMP). In their opinion it would have a double objective, which they present in the following manner, making explicit reference to the Mediterranean: "Ideally a GAMP should seek (i) to reduce income differences through increased economic growth in the potential emigration countries, (ii) to create new additional employment opportunities in the home countries of potential migrants."[29]

What about mmigration quotas negotiated by the countries concerned on the two sides of the Mediterranean on the basis of their shared interests? This idea assumes, first of all, that a consensus about the formula would emerge both within the European countries involved and between them within the framework of the European Union. This outcome, quite clearly, is difficult to envisage under the present circumstances. On the contrary the objective everywhere is to put a stop to immigration, especially that coming from the southern shore of the Mediterranean.

However, in the medium and long term, within the framework of the functioning of the European pole, the necessary assumption of responsibility for the migration problem may yet bring back to life the subject of quotas as a possible means of regulation.

However, the formulation of the problem of migration remains inadequate if it does not go on to treat the problem in all its aspects. Only such a comprehensive treatment will permit an assumption of responsibility that is equal to the requirements of the future.

—A regional approach must be formulated to human resource problems, ranging from population to education and training employment. In fact immigration comes into the picture only at the end of the chain. It represents a negative "way out" since it results from the failure to manage the three links of the chain.

That is why, at least at the regional level, the objective should be to arrive at a General Agreement on Human Resources Policy (GAHRP) as indispensible complement to the GAMP.[30] The question of human resources is important for several reasons, especially because it determines the capacity of the southern shore to become a particularly effective partner in worldwide competition.

The central link at this level is the system of education and training. The crisis through which it is passing in the countries on the southern shore of the Mediterranean is the most evident index of the more general crisis that they are undergoing, which leaves them few positive prospects for economic growth.

The attraction for European investors of the Asian countries is in part explained by the quality of their labor force and therefore by their system of education and training. At present the rigors of the structural adjustment programs on the southern shore are striking hard at their education and training systems, which were already quite perturbed, and are reducing them to institutions that increasingly have a formal mission that is distant from the most elementary requirements of international standards. That is why only the reinstatement of those systems at the very center of the problem of regional cooperation can restore the rhythm necessary for them to match the economic dynamics to be put into place.

—The migrants from the southern shore must be integrated into the societies of the North.

This is also an important dimension of regional cooperation since, one way or another, the countries of the southern shore have a role to play in ensuring the best possible integration of new immigrant communities on the northern shore. As previously noted, the return to their countries of origin of migrants from the southern shore can involve only individuals and groups of limited size and thus can no longer appear to be a realistic proposition.

Behind the different and very complex questions that integrating communities originating on the southern shore into their host societies raises, there lies great anxiety regarding Islam. If European Islam is by now a reality, it is also evident that it is far from being fully integrated into the societies in which it exists and that it continues to stimulate questions and, in certain cases, fears. These feelings often arise from misunderstanding, if not ignorance. The Muslim communities in Europe, as well as their communities of origin, the "sending countries," are just as often in the same situation vis-à-vis European cultures. Therefore the importance of the cultural dimension in the process of regional cooperation on the migration question cannot be overemphasized. It is the sine qua non for any dialogue between the two sides.

In this regard the notion of confidence-building measures in the Mediterranean—put forward in the common document of the Northern countries that proposed a Conference on Security and Cooperation in the Mediterranean, and inspired by the notion of confidence-building measures born in the context of East-West relations—should certainly, if it is to be retained as a working hypothesis, be reviewed and adapted both to the conditions prevailing in the region and to this new stage of history.

In this sense it is clear that the notion of confidence presumes, as a necessary and difficult preliminary, real mutual knowledge, and also concrete measures addressing the problems that exist in the region.

The sequelae of the Gulf War in the collective consciousness of the South; the negative perception of the European "management" of the crisis in the former Yugoslavia, which has gravely damaged the interests of the Muslim population of Bosnia-Herzegovina; and the throbbing Palestinian problem, the true original fracture, at least in the contemporary period, of relations between the two shores—all these demonstrate that the maintenance of satisfactory relations between the two sides depends on an overall approach that takes into account the real challenges that exist. In the final analysis, beyond the problems connected to the question of migration—and they are numerous and complex—it is the stability of the entire region that is at stake.

An essential phenomenon of the end of this century, and one certainly destined to affect civilization in the century to come, international migration has no intrinsic significance but rather serves as an indicator, a magnifying glass that permits us to follow better the realities that are involved. In the Mediterranean it teaches us that the existing imbalances are often too great and the perceptions of the problem too remote to endure, unless the two sides are led to thorough reassessments. These will certainly be costly and painful—indeed they must in the end leave open the possibility of a divorce.

That is why the strategic wager for all the partners involved consists in adopting, starting now, the changes that are necessary, and not having them imposed later under conditions that will be more and more difficult—or even impossible. This necessary solidarity between the partners on the two shores is not based on simple wishful thinking but instead proceeds from their basic interests, given the process of globalization that is moving ahead. The twenty-first century is already being proclaimed, urbi et orbi, the century of the Pacific—as was emphasized by the recent Seattle summit of the heads of state and government of the Asia-Pacific Economic Coooperation group. At this time the rest of the world, including the Mediterranean, meaning the area that includes both shores, northern and southern, must wonder about its own prospects. From this point of view the migration question—on the condition that it is seen in a broader context, in terms of the optimal use of human resources—is not necessarily a handicap for the Mediterranean and for Southern Europe. What is more, if seen clearly and addressed properly, it can in the end be an important trump card in the intense global competition that lies ahead.

Notes

1. The problem of the definition of Southern Europe demands some clarification. Without entering into a fundamental debate on the position and the vocation of certain countries (notably France, which for some analysts may be a country of Northern Europe), we opt in this chapter for an empirical approach to the question. Thus from our point of view the countries bordering the Mediterranean (Spain, France, and Italy) will be considered as the countries of Southern Europe (understood to mean the South of Western Europe); for various reasons Portugal will be added to this group.

2. Michel Greno and Michel Batisse, eds., *Le Plan Bleu: Avenir du Bassin Mediterranéen* (Paris: Economica, 1988), p. 71.

3. Rafic Boustani and Philippe Fargues, *Atlas du Monde Arabe: Geopolitique et Societé* (Paris: Bordas, 1990), p. 39.

4. Jean Claude Chesnais, "L'evolution demographique, facteur de déséquilibre international: La fracture méditerranéenne," communication presented to the conference on "Securité collective en Mediterranée et au Moyen Orient," held in Brussels, November 5–6, 1991, by the Centre d'Etudes de Defense), p. 7.

5. World Bank, *Annual Report 1992* (Washington, 1992), p. 163.

6. UNDP, *Human Development Report 1992* (New York: Oxford University Press, 1992), p. 58.

7. For the data regarding immigration in Europe several sources have been used: Eurostat, *A Social Portrait of Europe* (Luxembourg: Office for Official Publications of the European Communities, 1991); International Organization for Migration, *Tenth IOM Seminar on Migration, 15–17 September 1992* (Geneva, 1992); European Community, *Le Courrier ACP* 129 (September-October 1991); several internal documents of the Commission of the European Communities in Brussels.

8. An illustration of the real distance between the communities with origins in the Arab and Muslim countries established in Europe and the governments of their countries of origin was very clearly furnished during the crisis and then the war in the Gulf. These communities displayed considerable circumspection with regard to Iraqi policy.

9. William S. Lind, "Defending Western Culture," *Foreign Policy,* no. 84 (Fall 1991), p. 45; my emphasis. On the same argument see Samuel P. Huntington, "The Clash of Civilizations?" *Foreign Affairs,* vol. 72, no. 3 (Summer 1993), pp. 22–49.

10. It is worth recalling in this regard the notion of a "new arc of crisis" applied to the zone running from North Africa to Central Asia. For relatively early use of the term, see George Joffe, "European Security and the New Arc of Crisis: Paper I," and Curt Gasteyger, "European Security and the New Arc of Crisis: Paper II," in *New Dimensions in International Security,* Adelphi Paper 265 (London: International Institute for Strategic Studies), pp. 53–81, especially p. 69.

11. Indeed by now it is among the most generally accepted ideas on the handling of the migration question, as is demonstrated by our earlier quotation from the 1992 *Human Development Report* (see note 6).

12. The "time bomb" reference is from Ministry of Foreign Affairs (Spain), "L'Europe et le Maghreb: Rapport," Madrid, February 26, 1992. The document goes on to emphasize the increasing desparities in development and living standards by pointing out, with regard to the Western Mediterranean, that "Whether one likes it or not, this geographical contiguity produces a strong interdependence between the North and South shores of the Western Mediterranean, which contrasts with the *growing* economic imbalances between the two"; my emphasis.

13. European Parliament, "Resolution A3-121/91 on a Renewed Mediterranean Policy (Consideration 1)"; my emphasis.

14. Commission of the European Communities, "Communication de la Commission au Conseil et au Parlement Européen sur l'Immigration," SEC (91) 1855 final, Brusssels, October 11, 1991, p. 18.

15. The Union remains a formal framework, without real content. In the framework of the Arab Maghreb Union the ministers responsible for migration problems have met and have adopted a resolution, but this has not led to any coordination of national policies.

16. In April 1993 a workshop was held in Turin, organized by the International Labour Organization and bringing together, aside from three Maghreb countries (Morocco, Algeria, and Tunisia) and five "fund-granting" European countries (Germany, Belgium, Italy, Spain, and France), several multilateral organizations (the European Economic Community, World Bank, and United Nations Development Programme).

17. The performance figures are drawn from the *Bulletin du Club Financier Méditerranéen* 6 (April 1993). The quotation is from an internal document of the staff of the Commission of the European Communities; my emphasis.

18. Thus the editors of the *Human Development Report 1993* write: "We are witnessing a new and disturbing phenomenon: *jobless growth.* And policy-makers the world over are searching for development strategies that combine economic growth with more job opportunities"; UNDP, *Human Development Report 1993* (Oxford University Press, 1993), p. 3; emphasis in original. In the same vein, the President of the French Senate declared, "To make believe that it's the recovery that

will reduce unemployment is to contribute to keeping alive a hope which, when it's not fulfilled, will wind up producing a *social explosion*"; Alain Frachon, "M. Monory ne croit pas à 'la relance' de la croissance dans les années à venir," *Le Monde,* July 24, 1993, p. 24; my emphasis.

19. The Treaty on European Union, the so-called Maastricht Treaty, places migration among the subjects of "common interest" in article K.1, points 1–3.

20. In this regard a Bundestag resolution dated December 2, 1992, "Bases for German Policy with Regard to the States of the Maghreb," is worth quoting: "to activate the plans for a Conference on Security and Cooperation in the Mediterranean, while, however, guaranteeing that active collaboration within the CSCM is not limited solely to the Southern member states of the European Community while the Federal Republic of Germany looks after Eastern Europe. These two problem areas, the East and the South of Europe, require a common European policy which includes the bilateral measures of *all* the member states"; my emphasis.

21. It is appropriate in this regard to take note of the increasingly military language used to describe worldwide economic competition as well as the hypotheses formulated regarding growing rivalries taking the form of "economic warfare," at least within the Triad. Very representative of these theses are such works as, to name but two, *The Coming War with Japan* by George Friedman and Meredith Lebard and *Head to Head: The Coming Economic Battle Among Japan, Europe, and America* by Lester Thurow.

22. Representative of U.S. policy is the North American Free Trade Agreement (NAFTA), concluded with Canada and Mexico; Japan's is a dynamic overall policy that has reshaped all of Asia. NAFTA is clearly not going to solve by itself the numerous and complex problems that have long affected Mexican society, as has been demonstrated by recent events, especially those in the state of Chiapas. However, it certainly represents a step in the right direction, that of the ultimate integration of Mexico into the dominant processes of the world economy.

23. K. F. Zimmermann and T. Straubhaar, "Immigration and the European Community," in *Human Resources in Europe at the Dawn of the 21st Century* (Luxembourg: Eurostat, 1992), p. 431; my emphasis.

24. In comparison to the historical reference that the "Cuban model" represents everything is happening as if one were, on the southern shore of the Mediterranean, already seeing a repeat, but with its own specific ways and means. It is, however, also possible that in a given country an acceleration of the rhythm of migration may take place, if a brutal breakup occurs.

25. Francis Fukuyama, *The End of History and the Last Man* (New York: Free Press, 1992), pp. 277–78; my emphasis.

26. Thus, according to a report by the French Senate, "the trade deficit alone— 16 billion francs—of France with the two Chinas, mainland and Taiwan, is equal to the surplus achieved with all of its partners in the European Community put together"; Pierre-Angel Gay and Caroline Monnot, "Les délocalisations sont destructrices d'emplois," *Le Monde,* June 4, 1993, p. 17.

27. This certainly does not exclude diametrically opposed approaches, such as that of the American Nobel laureate in economics, Gary Becker, according to whom, in essence, the movement of people, being a good, should be free.

28. "Vaincre les douze peurs de l'an 2000: Les réponses de 24 penseurs et experts," *Le Nouvel Observateur,* Collection Dossiers 14, p. 16; my emphasis.

29. Zimmerman and Straubhaar, "Immigration and the European Community, p. 431.

30. It goes without saying that the formulas used—GAMP and GAMRP—cannot in any case, from our point of view, represent precise institutional frameworks. Instead they are indicators of areas of common planning and cooperation to be put into place to address the problems common to the countries on the two shores, which in the past often have been neglected in an economics-based approach giving priority to "hardware." This approach has brought with it a number of the dysfunctional developments that we observe today.

FIVE

Interests in the Middle East

Graham E. Fuller

THE END of the cold war, the Maastricht Treaty, and uncertainty over the future role of NATO all raise questions about the character of the new Europe and its relations with the world beyond. The Middle East increasingly has become a factor in the broader evolution of a new European identity, its interests, and the determination of U.S. interests in the region as well. Even as Europe is undergoing a state of rapid geopolitical evolution, so too is the Middle East, perhaps even more so. One of the major challenges to Western policy will be to elaborate a new set of relationships with the Muslim world.

The Middle East in the Changing World Order

The very concept of how the Middle East itself is defined is undergoing change. The term is now expanding to embrace newer and more complex geopolitical relationships released by the end of the cold war. Turkey has been one state whose geopolitics have been especially profoundly affected by the breakup of the Soviet Union. New Muslim politics in the Balkans, the Caucasus, and Central Asia are now increasingly linked in one way or another to Turkish and European interests. The Muslim world is more interlinked than ever before—if only through conflict in some regions. We need to understand the new geopolitics of the post–cold war Middle East if we are to understand its impact on Southern Europe and U.S. interests.

Second, the final emergence of a likely comprehensive peace between Israel, the Palestinians, and the Arab states represents a major geopolitical watershed, nearly on a par with the fall of the Berlin Wall. Political relationships that have been frozen in the Middle East for half a century are now in the process of thawing. The longer-term impact on the region can only be dimly divined at this initial stage; the world will go on witnessing change in large and small ways all around the region as the longer-term impact of the peace settlement takes effect. The relationship of Europe and the United States to the region will also be directly affected.

One of the major impacts of Arab-Israeli peace on the Middle East will be to accelerate forces of change that have long been accumulating but have been suppressed. Most regimes in the region lack political legitimacy in the sense of representing their populations, and they are moving toward domestic crisis as they fail to meet growing economic and social demands; at the same time these regimes are increasingly less able to revert to outright repression as a means of solving longer-term problems. The Arab-Israeli confrontation in fact has been a boon to these despotic regimes, which have used it as a pretext for the imposition of powerful police state controls, calls for "eternal vigilance against the Zionist enemy," a race for arms, the elaboration of radical ideology, and the intimidation of neighbors in seeking to impose politically correct Pan-Arab ideals as defined by the radical states.

Now nearly all states in the region will be torn by political change that pushes in the direction of greater demand for increased political participation on the part of populations. If this trend was true before an Arab-Israeli settlement, it will be even truer now when the excuse for authoritarianism and "solidarity" is waning. These political changes will in turn provoke major social change as old elites lose their grip on power and are forced to give way to new groups, including ethnic and religious minorities. The end of the cold war had in fact already begun to weaken the position of many elites, since the external support they historically derived from either the United States or the Soviet Union—payment for their strategic allegiance— has now largely vanished. These changes, however disruptive, will inevitably come to the region, for the cold war and the Arab-Israeli conflict have been the two chief causes of oppressive government, extremism, and instability in the region.

It is thus good news that the way is being cleared for long overdue political evolution to take place in the region. Over the longer run such evolution will contribute to greater stability and rationality of government, diminished conflict, and diminished need for Western military intervention—which in every case leaves a baleful psychological legacy upon the region's peoples.

Economic change should also emerge from a new political framework. The region has been bound by ineffective state-run sectors that have made the economies of most states a shambles. These policies have also produced rising social discontent that is fodder for radical Islamist movements. But dictators in fact like the centralized economies that contribute to their overall control of the state and society and to the repression of independent sources of power within the state. Today there should be less excuse for highly authoritarian and centralized economies. One hopes that the creative forces of the region will be allowed to emerge and to improve the domestic economic situation in most states, especially those with large urban populations. It is therefore important for the West to work for and encourage this process of political and economic liberalization.

Yet however important the process of political liberalization is, over the short term it will not be smooth. On the contrary it will lead to short-term *instability* as societies face major political and social change. The political dominance of minorities in many states will inevitably give way to new social groups and classes that will assume a greater voice in the conduct of state policies. This change will in many cases be quite dramatic in character and may perhaps be resisted by many old elites. But the process is inevitable and cannot be put off. The good news is that these processes of change and instability no longer possess the global significance that they did during the East-West struggle. The West can now afford to permit and even encourage these long-range processes of change in the direction of political and economic liberalization, for over the longer run the Middle East will have no choice but to undergo these inevitable phases of economic, political, and social development. Their delay in many cases can only lead to even more explosive situations, for at the least democratic mechanisms provide ways of facilitating change, and these widespread changes are an integral part, for better or for worse, of what we all call "modernization."

Western Interests in the Middle East

What then are the interests of Southern Europe and the United States in looking at the Middle East? In brief, they may be summarized as involving oil, Israeli's security, the desire for stability, the spread of arms throughout the region, state-sponsored terrorism, economic development and trade, refugees and immigration, and Islamic fundamentalism.

Oil and Strategy

Historically, of course, the free flow of oil at "acceptable" prices has always ranked near the top of the list. Upon more careful examination, however, it appears that invocation of "oil" as a basic Western interest often conceals a much broader agenda of interests or goals. First one may query the degree to which the "flow of oil" to the West has ever been seriously threatened. It has been maintained over many decades through a variety of conflicts, including the Iran-Iraq war, during which for eight long years wellheads, oil refineries, oil terminals, and tankers were all targeted up and down the Persian Gulf—the ultimate horror scenario for Western oil planners and strategists. Yet that conflict did not fundamentally affect Western economies. To be sure, excess oil capacity existed in the market in that period. But the degree of redundancy of oil refineries, pipelines, and terminals and the fungibility of international oil sources make it ever harder for regional conflict to exert decisive impact upon the secure flow of oil to the West.

Western strategists have in fact often justified a broad range of political-military arrangements in the region on the basis of "protection of the flow of oil." Reality would suggest that more critical analysis needs to be devoted to this issue. The cold war called forth a complicated array of American involvements and commitments around the globe in the effort to check Soviet moves. The United States and the North Atlantic Treaty Organization (NATO) thus have had a variety of strategic reasons for maintaining allies, security treaties, bases, access rights, and prepositioning of military equipment, in the region. But today circumstances have changed with the end of the global cold war. If there are other broad strategic reasons for the maintenance of strategic relationships around the world, then they should be identified and justified in specific terms based on the new realities rather than imprecisely in the interest of "securing the free flow of oil."

Indeed over time the entire concept of "oil security" has been shifting. Fifty years or more ago physical possession of the oil fields and domination of all aspects of oil production were viewed as a strategic necessity. Later dominant control of the oil company was seen as the crucial element. Later still the maintenance of friendly rulers in those states was seen as the primary insurance. Yet over time the need for such stringent involvement has been systematically reduced, so that today all physical control and most operational aspects of foreign oil production are exclusively in the hands of foreign states and rulers, sometimes ones not even friendly to the West (such as in Iran, Libya, and Iraq). Indeed all the West seems concerned about today is that oil continue to be sold in a relatively open market.

What constitutes "oil security" in the next decade will therefore come under closer scrutiny as the geopolitics of the region moves toward change. The role of oil in Middle Eastern politics will require much new thinking.

Equitable and stable pricing structures will be a key demand of oil producers, and these should be of equal interest to Western consumers over the longer run. Redundancy of pipeline systems is another interest important to all. The emergence of oil from Muslim republics of the former Soviet Union involves new pipeline networks that relate to the present network as new lines emerge through Central Asia and the Caucasus to Iran and Turkey. The rapid expansion of the existing oil pipeline network eastward is just one facet of a Middle East undergoing broad redefinition. Changes in perception of oil supply problems will inevitably exert direct influence on the nature of Western policies in the region.

The Security of Israel

Historically the United States has always considered the security of Israel to be a major American goal in the Middle East. Close strategic ties with Israel have in fact assured that. Israel is more secure today in the region than ever before. Israel was also seen as an important strategic ally in the cold war context. With the end of the cold war, however, the strategic value of Israel to the United States in the Middle East diminished sharply. Given the volatile nature of the Arab-Israeli conflict, Israel under most circumstances would not normally have been the ally of choice for the United States when dealing with political crisis within the Arab world and seeking to maintain good ties with Arab oil-producing states. But the emerging Arab-Israeli peace settlement liberates the traditional U.S. relationship with Israel, making it more sustainable on the one hand and less strategically urgent on the other. Close ties with Israel no longer work directly at cross-purposes with U.S. relations with the Arab states. The zero-sum game quality of Arab versus Israeli ties is on the way to being alleviated. One can now imagine Israel gradually beginning to play a regional role in concert with other Arab states. This kind of involvement will have to come slowly and carefully in view of past sensitivities, but it will come. Some Arab states may then find that they have reason to establish working ties with Israel on a variety of issues, including first and foremost trade, but also technical assistance and cooperation, agricultural cooperation, perhaps export of technology, and eventually perhaps even security cooperation.

The Quest for "Stability"

Other American goals include the general desire for stability in a region of great economic importance that contains the greatest mass of arms of any region in the world. But even the concept of stability will require careful reconsideration. Suppression of political and social change is not synonymous with stability, as we have seen with the demise of the Soviet Union— long one of the most "stable" regimes in the world. Often only continuing and gradual change brings continuing true stability; political suppression brings explosion. We will need to reconsider the true meaning of long-range stability as the pressing need for political and economic reform emerges more strongly in a post–Arab-Israeli conflict environment. Stability today now requires measurement in terms of *liberalization,* with all its acknowledged short-term destabilizing effects.

Weapons Proliferation

Weapons proliferation in the region, especially the spread of unconventional weapons, will remain a major concern for both the United States and Europe. Southern Europe is especially exposed in that it will, within the next decade, if not earlier, be within range of Middle Eastern missiles that can carry weapons of mass destruction. Arms control in the region is thus a high priority. Weapons of mass destruction arguably pose a greater threat to the immediate neighbors of new nuclear powers than they do even to the West. The strategic environment for arms control will begin to change markedly if a new Arab-Israeli settlement proves enduring.

Terrorism

State-sponsored terrorism has been a broad concern of both the West and many states in the region for several decades. Successful identification of and response to these state sponsors, however, has served to reduce the incidence of terrorism in the region, at least against non–Middle Eastern citizens. Terrorism is increasingly confined to nonstate groups operating within existing states and against their own regimes, as in Egypt and Algeria. Although terrorism will remain a concern, in fact it is striking that the extent of terrorism has been as limited as it has, given the violence of political events in the region. Iranian terrorism during the Iran-Iraq war and Iraqi terrorism by Saddam Hussein during the Gulf War, for example, were far more limited than had been anticipated.

The West will necessarily remain concerned about the export of terrorism outside the Middle East. To the extent that it is state-sponsored, punitive response can be meted out to offending regimes. Nonstate groups, however, will always pose a threat and there will be little that Western states can do to limit it beyond the capabilities of regional governments themselves. As violent Middle Eastern politics extends itself outside the region, however, the chances are that terrorist actions among Middle Eastern groups themselves will be played out upon the European stage as well as in the region.

Economic Development and Trade

European trade with the Middle East—oil and guns excepted—has been relatively limited. With an emerging Arab-Israeli settlement, however, trade with Europe should increase sharply as Israel and Palestine become gateways for trade into the Arab world, unhindered by boycott and closed borders. The Maghreb in particular sees close economic ties with Western Europe as essential to its own development. In the past, economic ties with Europe have been vastly more important than trade among the Maghreb countries themselves.

Refugees and Immigration

Europe is deeply concerned with questions of economic development in the Middle East, especially in North Africa. Concern regarding demographic movement from the Middle East to Europe is especially great in Southern Europe, which is already the port of entry for most Arab migrants. European sensitivities to immigration problems and the cultural absorption of large numbers of Muslims also loom high on Europe's political and social agenda. The stability of the Middle East will have a direct affect on the immigration issue: desperate economic situations, or internal instability and civil conflict, will have a major "push" effect on potential immigrants to Europe.

Islamic Fundamentalism

Last, the United States and Europe share a concern for the spread of radical ideologies in the Middle East that can develop policies hostile to the West, destabilize the region, and spark regional war. Islamism[1] or "Muslim fundamentalism" ranks first as a radical ideology of concern because of its potential anti-Western orientation. How to live with political Islam is a particularly complex problem for the West. The most important characteristic of political Islam, however, is that it flourishes under circumstances of political, economic, and social hardship, as do most radical ideologies. Thus without some alleviation of these sources of discontent Islamists will make significant inroads in many countries.

Several other facets of political Islam require discussion. There is no monolithic movement within Islam. Islamist groups and movements vary considerably among themselves in their degree of radicalism and in their approach to democracy, political reform, liberalization, and relations with the West. Divisions among them tend to be most readily overcome and a united Islamic front produced when their activists suffer heavy repression from the state. At present in many countries, such as Egypt, Algeria, and Syria, the Islamists constitute virtually the only form of opposition to the state. When the state is incompetent, corrupt, and repressive and lacks political legitimacy in the eyes of the public, then Islamists attract a major degree of political support.

In the end political Islam is destined to emerge into Middle Eastern politics to one extent or another in almost every state. When it is repressed its appeal grows. Where it often lacks any comprehensive program of its own other than opposition to the obvious shortcomings of the state, it can fall back on simplistic slogans such as "Islam is the answer"; such mottos are easiest to invoke when these groups are declared illegal and banned. Only when Islamic groups and parties are allowed gradual, controlled entry into the political system—along with other repressed parties and groups—will they begin to fall into proper perspective on the overall political spectrum. In states where Islamist parties regularly contest elections, such as Turkey and Pakistan, they rarely fare better than 12 to 15 percent of the vote. Once they contend on the political scene and assume modest roles within the political system, it becomes evident that they possess few clear-cut programs, offer no magic answers, and possess the same failings as many other political groups. Many initially radical Islamic groups have also evolved politically and matured when participating in the political process, as they did in Egypt earlier, or have today in Jordan, Yemen, Turkey, Algeria, and Kuwait.

In short the only way in which political Islam will be "tamed" and able to take a normal place on the political spectrum is through its *gradual and controlled* entry into the political system. In states where it bursts forth onto the political system legally after years of repression and authoritarian government—as in Algeria—it almost invariably becomes the primary beneficiary of the backlash and can sweep the election and thus enter the political system under the most adverse circumstances, which play to its most radical and perhaps authoritarian forces.

The great art then for Western policy is to encourage gradual political reform that includes the Islamists. Under these circumstances radical Islam is not likely to become the dominant political voice in the Middle East.

Given the extreme deficiencies of the current regimes in Egypt and Algeria, and perhaps Tunisia and Syria, however, there is in fact a likelihood that political Islam might emerge supreme in one or another of these states in the next decade. There is little the West can do about this possibility except establish ties with all but the most radical groups. Western policies toward Islam and the Muslim world, after all, have a direct impact on how these movements perceive the West: they are highly sensitive to past Western colonial domination and to the powerful inroads of often negative aspects of Western culture into more traditional Islamic societies. Finally strong Western support for undemocratic and repressive regimes in the region leaves deep suspicions that the West has no genuine interest in the democratic process, only interests to be preserved via dictators if necessary.

In sum the phenomenon of political Islam is very complex and deserves a subtle and textured approach from the West. Otherwise talk of "a clash of civilizations" or of "Islam versus the West" can become a self-fulfilling prophesy. Europe will be affected by this phenomenon more directly than the United States as the new European order and its relations with the neighboring Muslim world are defined.

New Regional Political Configurations

As Europe is changing with the end of the cold war, so too the traditional view of what constitutes the Middle East has been changing, especially with the emergence of six new Muslim states on the territory of the former Soviet Union. The effects of these changing geopolitical configurations, among other things, extend the boundaries of "Middle Eastern politics" far to the East into western China, in a new Turco-Muslim cultural continuum. The geopolitics of Turkey, Iran, and the Gulf have been most directly touched. Let us examine the new shape of these new configurations.

Turkey

At the top of the list is the extraordinary transformation of Turkey, a state that has evolved from a geopolitical location at the "tail end" of Europe and NATO to become the center of a new Turkic-oriented world that stretches from the Balkans across the Caucasus and on into Central Asia and Chinese Turkestan. Europe's close relationships with Turkey therefore now inevitably draw Central Asian and Caucasian politics in important ways into the

European sphere. The republics of the former Soviet Union have in fact gained membership in the North Atlantic Cooperation Council—an astonishing fact that brings Tajikistan more formally into the councils of NATO thinking than Morocco, a stone's throw across the straits of Gibraltar from Spain. The Conference on Security and Cooperation in Europe is now deeply involved in attempting to adjudicate the Mountainous Karabagh conflict between Armenia and Azerbaijan. This conflict has the potential of embroiling Turkey, Iran, and Russia in ways that would have great negative impact upon the whole region.

Similarly, on Europe's doorstep, conflict in the Balkans is taking on a Muslim-Christian edge in Bosnia that can potentially drag diverse regional states, such as Turkey, Greece, Albania, and Bulgaria, into a third replay of the Balkan wars at the turn of the century. Turkey is one of the key factors in these conflicts, and its restraint has been important to the containment of the conflict. Bosnia, nonetheless, has had a major impact upon the entire Muslim world, being seen as a paradigm of Western indifference, if not hostility, to one of the last Muslim communities in Europe. This is the first time that the concept of Islam as part of geographic Europe has emerged since the beginning of the century, representing a new geopolitical extension of the Muslim world northward. If Bosnia is not dealt with justly, it threatens to become a "second Palestine" in terms of its emotive impact on Muslim-Western relations.

Turkey's influence finally extends to the creation of a Black Sea Consortium of all riparian states plus Armenia, Azerbaijan, Albania, and Greece. This organization promises to create new trade ties across the Black Sea that had been "frozen" by the cold war. The consortium could be an important factor in regional politics and could lead to cooperation on security issues as well.

Iran

The involvement of Iran in the politics of the Mediterranean has also grown considerably in the last decade. Tehran is represented in the Mediterranean with its strong and effective ties to Shi'ite groups in Lebanon. As Lebanon tries to rebuild itself and its mixed Christian-Muslim culture in the next decade with the end of the Arab-Israeli conflict, Iran's support for the long-oppressed Shi'ite community—the largest single group in Lebanon—will play a potentially significant role. Tehran's twenty year-old power in Lebanon has now been augmented by Iran's significant ties to the radical fundamentalist Palestinian organization Hamas. Hamas has declared its implacable opposition to the Palestine Liberation Organization accord with Israel. Although Iranian support has been significant in strengthening it, Hamas is more than simply the puppet organization of Iran.

Far less effective, but still symbolically important, are Iran's new ties to Sudan and fundamentalist groups operating along the Mediterranean in Egypt, Tunisia, and Algeria. In reality, the Islamist challenge to those states would be no less if Iran were to disappear tomorrow, but Iran helps encourage the concept of a broad international Islamist movement. Even worse Iran provides an excuse to these beleaguered regimes to blame all their domestic problems on external interference and to justify refusal to liberalize. Iran's policies thus have an indirect impact on issues of direct concern to a Southern Europe that is working for stability and development in North Africa.

Rethinking the Nature of the Persian Gulf

The Persian Gulf has, of course, always been an integral part of the interests of the West. But the very geopolitical meaning of the Gulf has also been affected by recent political changes in the area.

First, Iraq's adventurism has laid bare the deep ethnic and sectarian frictions that have been so exacerbated by the ruthless and destructive policies of Saddam Hussein. The country is at serious risk of partition; the Kurds have now attained quasi-autonomous status. Unless Iraq is able to rid itself of the most brutal regime in the history of the modern Middle East and adopt principles of democratic rule and federalism, the state is doomed to breakup. Such an eventuality has massive implications for the rest of the Middle East, for the Kurdish problem is really a paradigm for broader problems of ethnicity, sectarianism, separatism, human rights, democratic rule, and federalism that will challenge virtually all states of the region in the next decade. The resolution of the Kurdish problem will thus determine in which of two directions the situation will move: either the solution will be continued repression and denial of ethnic and sectarian differences—a course doomed to eventual collapse and civil war as in the former communist states—or democratic federalism will emerge, which meets the Kurds' own requirements for coexistence within the Iraqi state.

Whatever course is chosen in Baghdad, either way the issue has immense implications for the future of the territorial integrity of Turkey and Iran, both of which possess large Kurdish populations. Turkey is developing decent de facto working relations with the Kurdish entity in northern Iraq. But the process is delicate owing to the problems of Kurdish dissatisfaction within Turkey itself. Europe itself has already been affected by the problem because of the presence of nearly 2 million Turks in Germany, of whom one-third may be Kurds. The Kurdish problem has already negatively affected Turkish-German relations, and the battleground between Turks and Kurds has now extended to German cities. Turkey's application for membership in the European Union will also be profoundly affected by its handling of its own Kurdish problem. Europe is thus inescapably linked to this problem.

The extension of active Kurdish politics on the international level up from Iraq into Turkey and Iran has an impact on Iran beyond its own Kurdish population. The Kurdish area of Iran is contiguous and intermeshed with Iranian Azerbaijan. The emergence of an independent Azerbaijan in the former Soviet Union now also potentially challenges Iran's own integrity since Iran contains nearly twice as many Azerbaijanis as does Azerbaijan itself, raising questions about potential Azeri separatism in Iran over the longer run.

The Azerbaijan problem for Iran has broader implications since it threatens Tehran with the specter of "Turkish encirclement." Azerbaijan's strong Turkish orientation could place Turkey potentially on the side of Azerbaijani separatism if strongly nationalist-chauvinist elements were to come to power in Turkey. This rising tension may well eventually lead to serious Turkish-Iranian conflict in the future. Iran is also engaged in competition with Turkey in (largely Turkic) Central Asia. Iran will thus be highly preoccupied in the future with its northern borders, likely distracting some of its focus from the Gulf. More significantly, "Persian Gulf politics" has now clearly extended on up through Iraq into Kurdistan, Turkey, Iran, and the Caucasus. Europe will not be able to deal with these problems in isolation for they are all geopolitically linked.

Central Asia's five new Muslim nations have attracted much international attention, most of all, of course, in Turkey. Immediately after these states attained independence in 1991, Turkey sought to extend political, economic, and cultural ties to the area. It has done more than any other state to bring these states into the orbit of the outside world and is engaged in extensive projects in all the states. Washington expressed great interest in Turkey's role in the region, somewhat simplistically urging that Turkey be the model for the region in order to shut Iranian influence out. But the situation is considerably more complicated than mere rivalry between Turkish and Iranian models.

First, Turkey's ambitions in Central Asia cannot be fully sustained by the limited resources it possesses as a state. It is not in a position to channel significant sums into Central Asia. Joint ventures and educational, technical, and cultural assistance are Turkey's main attractions for Central Asia, as well as its role as a state with special sympathies and cultural ties in ways that can be helpful to Central Asia. The West is interested in extending some aid to the region via Turkey, which could also be helpful. But the Central Asian states themselves are not interested in committing to any particular bloc or political-cultural orientation that will in any way prejudice access to the goodwill or resources of any other state, including Iran. China, Japan, East Asia, India, the Arab world, the United States, and Europe are all potential sources of aid and trade. Central Asia can properly be expected to play the field to its own advantage.

Second, Iran cannot be ignored, however unattractive or negative its policies are perceived to be in the West. A glance at the map reveals that Iran represents the sole avenue for land access for Central Asia to the West apart from transit through Russia. Roads, rail lines, and pipelines via Iran are the logical way to get to the Persian Gulf, to Turkey, and onward to the West. No central Asian state will wish to damage its ties with Iran unless Iran should pursue policies hostile to the interests of Central Asia. So far that has not been the case; Iran has been cautious to pursue largely pragmatic policies in the area, despite accusations—highly exaggerated and inflammatory—by Uzbekistan about Iranian meddling in the Tajikistan civil war. In any case Iran will be more and more involved in the passage of oil and gas out of Central Asia and Azerbaijan into the Mediterranean outlets of Turkey's pipelines. Here again any Western interest and investment in the energy sectors of the Caucasus and Central Asia automatically require involvement in the problems of the Turkey-Iran axis.

Russia and the Middle East

Finally, all of these issues in the Balkans, the Caucasus, and Central Asia and on China's borders have a direct impact upon the emerging policies of Russia. Russia is still in a quandary about what its national interests may be in a post-communist world and with its new borders. Major debates are underway between those partisans of an Atlanticist foreign policy on the one hand and the "Eurasianists" on the other. The Atlanticists see Russia's future tied inextricably to the West in shared common political and economic values. This trend obviously represents the antithesis of the past and a rejection of all the values of the communist era.

The Eurasianists represent a diverse group that lacks any single coherent vision, but several key themes dominate. First, the fact that Russia is not a European but a Eurasian nation makes it inappropriate for Russia to pursue foreign policies that are in lockstep with European and American interests and policies. Although it is self-evident that Russia is an Asian continental power and would naturally have important interests and ties to the south and to China, Japan, and the Pacific to the east, this Eurasianist policy orientation says nothing about the political *values* that should guide and inform Russian foreign policy. Does Eurasianism suggest any distance from democratic values?

Second, Eurasianists stress the fact that Russia is still a great power and therefore that its interests by definition cannot mirror Western policies: Russia must have its own "independent" foreign policy. This approach at times almost seems to reflect difference for difference's sake—a desire to place distance between itself and the West, even where concrete differences of interest are not spelled out. This school also includes a number of thinkers who are strongly nationalist in outlook and stress deep ties with Slavic nations and the Orthodox Church—reminiscent of the nineteenth-century Slavophile school. Yet also implicit in this "Eurasian" tendency is the belief that Russia is somehow mystically linked with the East—going back to Orthodox Byzantium—and with the Islamic world—going back to the country's deep (and hostile) ties with the Tatars for so long. This line of thinking would place special emphasis on Russia's policies toward the Middle East, where Russia has had involvement dating from the early nineteenth century. The main question, however, is whether Russia would see its former radical clients—Libya, Iraq, Syria—as the natural focus of renewed Russian interest in the area, or whether it could work with all Muslim states in shared conjunction with the West.

If Russia suffers from uncertainty about its new place in the world, its own borders have been even more drastically affected. Russia's old international borders have almost completely vanished as the former Soviet republics, now independent, have become the new borders. Indeed when Russia speaks of its relations with the former republics it refers to them as the "near abroad" (*blizhnee zarubezhie*), as opposed to traditional foreign policy with the "far abroad." This distinction may be risky since it implies different treatment for the former Soviet republics within the shifting and uncertain parameters of the Commonwealth of Independent States.

These questions are not merely abstruse philosophical issues, for they not only have a direct bearing on Russia's overall orientation toward the West but also affect Russia's relations directly to its south and with the former Muslim republics. One point would seem clear at the outset: Russia's relations with the "far abroad" will inevitably be affected by its relations with the "near abroad," for the external world will be attentive to signs of resurgent Russian imperialism. Russia's relations with the Middle East cannot escape influence from the relations Moscow maintains with its former Muslim republics. Europe's interests with Russia are therefore directly linked to Russia's ties with the emerging world of the new Islamic politics.

How then will Russia view the upsurge of external states in the Caucasus, Central Asia, and the Black Sea? What of the Turkish challenge to Russian traditional influence in these areas? Turkish Prime Minister Suleyman Demirel (now president) several years ago urged the Turkic republics to consider forming a Union of Turkic States that potentially would end up reducing overall Russian economic and political influence in Central Asia. Although Russia need not think in former cold war terms of a Turkish-NATO "threat" to Russia in Central Asia, it still seeks dominant influence in the region in all areas including security (sometimes referred to in the West as the "Monroesky doctrine"). If Russia feels challenged by Turkish activism in the region, might it support Iran as a counterweight to Turkish influence there? How are we to interpret the July 1993 coup in Azerbaijan, in which the elected nationalist president, who had worked closely with Turkey and western oil companies was replaced (probably with Russian assistance) by a former senior communist who declared the need to reorient Azerbaijan's policies more closely with those of Russia? Turkey views this event as a direct setback to its own interests in Azerbaijan.

The chances are that as long as committed democrats are in power in Moscow, there should be no serious conflict between Russia and other outside powers in Central Asia. Yet the potential ethnic instability (including millions of Russians) in the region will also influence Russia's relations there and broadly affect Russia's relations with Turkey, Iran, Pakistan, India, and the Middle East. The greatest concern is that major instability in Central Asia could lead to Russian interventionism that would in turn lead to resistance in the region, creating a kind of "Islam versus Russia" scenario that would then feed intensified Russian chauvinism and imperialist expansionism. Such trends would have a major impact on Russia's relations with the West as well. Here again Muslim world politics in Central Asia now figures on the European security agenda.

Conclusion

Major new factors are thus emerging in the entire region from Europe to western China, creating new geopolitical realities that have a direct impact on European, southern European, and U.S. interests. These factors include the following:

—Europe's new process of self-definition, including the question of what its relationships with neighboring Muslim states will be.

—The new prospects for the Middle East that emerge from a budding Arab-Israeli peace settlement.

—The impact of new Muslim states in the former Soviet Union and their ties to the West, including those with Turkey and Iran.

—The uncertainties of the ethnic separatism now beginning to affect the Middle East directly, with Iraq as its first major victim.

—The role of an Iran that has still not fully emerged from the radical ideological focus of the revolution, despite many moderating trends.

—Turkey's new geopolitical centrality.

—The growing force of political Islam as it seeks to define new relationships with the West in a postcolonial period, some of the states being perhaps even hostile to the West.

—The demands for reform and political and economic liberalization in the Middle East, which will have an initially destabilizing influence on the area, thus affecting Western interests.

—The uncertainty of Russia's search for a new foreign policy.

Europe—especially Southern Europe—and the United States will thus find themselves involved increasingly in a geopolitically broadening Muslim world—in which even the distant borders of western China's Muslim population begin impinging upon the rest of the Muslim world all the way across to the Mediterranean states and their interests.

In the end the ultimate challenge for the West will be twofold:

—How to define its future relationship with the neighboring Muslim world—whether to favor a policy of inclusion or one of exclusion. There are major implications for either choice.

—How to assist in the evolution of these societies toward more stable, democratic orders on Europe's borders.

Achieving the latter goal will be tricky and rife with instability. The West will need to avoid the danger of embracing an artificial stability in the region, that is, keeping the lid on via acquiescence to repressive regimes. Such a policy only delays the inevitable and necessary processes of political and social change long pent up. If these forces are not allowed to evolve, already difficult problems will become even more explosive and produce more radical regimes. Over the next decade the only political force likely to emerge from repressive political orders is radical Islam. In sum although the broad course of events in the region is encouraging following its liberation from the cold war, the post–cold war challenge well exceeds in complexity that of the cold war itself.

Note

1. In this chapter *Islamism* refers to political Islam, or radical Islamic movements that seek direct political power. The term is not meant to refer to the body of traditional beliefs of most Muslims, to their belief in Islamic values, or even their desire to see them reflected in state policies; the term refers rather to those Islamic groups who advocate violence and who interpret Islamic politics in xenophobic or explicitly anti-Western, nonpluralistic, nondemocratic terms.

SIX

Efforts at Mediterranean Cooperation

Antonio Badini

THE MEDITERRANEAN has historically been an area of conflict, a hotbed of crisis, and a theater of war. Contrary to expectations, the end of the East-West confrontation and the establishment of the European Single Market have not yet produced any significant improvement in the relations between the two shores of the Mediterranean. No redistribution of wealth has taken place. The Southern Rim countries apparently have been left alone to confront difficult economic and social problems and an almost intractable political problem, internal dissidence.

Strong fundamentalist movements have sprung up in many Arab countries. They demand political power in order to change society radically. Most of the Islamic movements are rallying popular support against the forces of secularism or modernism. Repression cannot be the only way of confronting this religious upsurge, which clearly involves political ambitions as well.

Misperceptions make the task of promoting confidence-building measures on both sides of the Mediterranean difficult. In many countries on the southern shore, Islamic movements hold Western powers accountable for propping up local governments that they accuse of corruption, mismanagement, and conducting unfair and ill-advised policies. On the other hand, the West's perception of the South has been characterized by images of inefficiency-ridden countries, of fanaticism, of hostility toward Western values and interests, and of its being the hotbed of international terrorism. A disquieting factor is the emergence in many European countries of new forms of racism, fed by social crisis and expressed in hostility toward immigrants, especially those coming from the south of the Mediterranean.

If the trend is not reversed, racial and religious tensions will worsen, jeopardizing cultural and political pluralism and even peaceful coexistence within the region. As long as dangerous threats hang over the Mediterranean basin, many countries on both shores will remain vulnerable in an insecure and unstable political environment.

The most intractable challenge in the region—the mother of any future major crisis—is the alarming geographic mismatch between demographic pressures and technological and natural resources. Although the populations of European countries will remain unchanged, the working-age population in Southern Rim countries will double over the next ten to fifteen years. This could become an explosive factor of concern to the entire area.

Throughout the Southern Rim governments enjoy insufficient popular support. Although the population in much of the area may seem quiescent, militant forces are at work, seeking to capitalize on dissent, trying to turn discontent into destabilizing protest. The Moslem Brotherhood is winning greater support in Egypt. The Islamic Salvation Front, now banned in Algeria, continues to challenge the regime with killings and terrorist attacks. In response to Israel's efforts to repress opposition to its military occupation in the occupied territories and a part of Lebanon, Hamas, a radical group allegedly supported by Iran, has taken away much of the support formerly enjoyed by the more moderate Fatah, the major component of the Palestine Liberation Organization (PLO).

Although the magnitude of the problems confronting the area makes any rapid remedy—a quick fix capable of alleviating both malaise and misperceptions—illusory, some signs of positive change are in fact emerging.

The most striking is the agreement signed between Israel and the PLO establishing immediate Palestinian self-rule in the Gaza Strip and the West Bank city of Jericho, a historic deal that may lead to a wider peace settlement in the region. In addition Algeria is supposed to hold a constitutional referendum that might turn out to be a key element in getting the country back on the road to pluralism and democracy. Recent elections in Morocco have allowed opposition parties to gain a greater role in that country's parliament. The Jordanian and Tunisian governments have been working to improve national dialogue and reconciliation. Egypt is striving to devote more public resources to the neediest social strata in order to allay discontent.

But only greater and more effective involvement by the West can turn these signals into concrete results. The security of the region, which is important to the West, will depend upon the economic and social progress of its population. For that, Western capital and technology are fundamental. Furthermore, Western assistance, particularly if given within an institutionalized framework, could prove politically valuable by providing the assurance that is needed by the West's southern partners.

What is needed, in sum, is a strategy for dealing with the Southern Mediterranean countries that aims at establishing pluralist political systems governed by the rules of law and democracy, and market economies, and has the means to achieve these aims. Such a strategy does not exist today.

The Quest for a New Model of Mediterranean Partnership

What are the realities that a Mediterranean partnership must take into account? What of the efforts toward a partnership that have already been made? And what is the best prescription for action at this time?

The Worldwide Trend toward Regional Economic Integration

Regionalism has been developing worldwide over the last decade, with a distinct surge after the end of the cold war. It may constitute a new dimension of North-South relations.

The Asia-Pacific region provides the most telling demonstration of the force behind the new phenomenon. The striking aspect of the trend toward regional interdependence in the Asia-Pacific area is that it has been propelled by market forces operating within the multilateral free trade system.

The creation of the Asia-Pacific Economic Cooperation group (APEC), which includes highly industrialized countries, some of the most rapidly industrializing economies, and some less-developed nations, shows that regionalism is alive and well. The North American Free Trade Area (NAFTA) is further evidence pointing in the same direction.

Does this trend conflict with the concept of a global economy whose trading relations are conducted within the framework of the General Agreement on Tariffs and Trade (GATT)? The point can be argued from an economic standpoint; but from a political perspective regionalism has a positive attribute: it may well play a stabilizing role. The integration of China and Vietnam into the Asia-Pacific economy may have that effect; so, more arguably, may the reestablishment of close economic ties between Russia and the other states that have emerged from the former Soviet Union.

That being said, we must of course remain mindful of the possible harmful consequences of regionalism, constantly assessing the impact of regional integration on third countries, so that the new trend does not weaken GATT and infringe on the multilateral trading rules.

In the absence of a strong and strengthening GATT, regionalism could get out of hand; protectionist pressures could develop within the regional groupings, aimed at maintaining the discrimination inherent in preferential trade areas. The successful conclusion of the Uruguay Round will certainly serve as an important tool in keeping regionalism interwoven with, not destructive of, globalism.

The Desirable Shape of Regional Cooperation in the Mediterranean Basin

Unlike the East Asian economies, which have achieved spectacular growth over the last two decades, the economies of the Southern Mediterranean Rim countries are for the most part caught in a downward trend as far as their rate of growth is concerned.

The characteristics of the countries of the region seemingly are not conducive to regional integration. Natural resources are not uniformly distributed, and trade patterns are not moving toward greater interdependence. Trade barriers and the lack of economic complementarity and of transport infrastructure mean that better prospects for intraregional trade cannot be foreseen— unless, of course, something is done about these impeding conditions.

The diversity between the two sides of the Mediterranean, on the other hand, should be encouraging for flows of cross-border investments and production-sharing arrangements, as the Asian and North American examples suggest. However, the wide differences between North and South in the Mediterranean area in levels of industrialization, and especially sociopolitical systems and cultural traditions, seem to have negated the positive forces. As a result none of the efforts to promote the development of regional or subregional economic zones in the area have succeeded.

Indeed de facto economic integration in the Mediterranean area, simply as a result of the autonomous decisions of market operators, may never occur. Economic, political, social, and cultural changes need to take place if a framework is to exist within which the market can and will work. These changes require decisions and implementation by the governments concerned: first and foremost the governments of the Southern Rim, but also other governments that take an interest in the stability of the Mediterranean.

An approach based on agreements between governments, and involving measures such as the reduction of trade barriers, concessional aid, transfer of technology, and economic reforms, would more likely be fruitful if an economic entity of a certain size were created on the Southern Rim through some form of regional integration. This approach would, inter alia, help attract investments and management from abroad.

The Arab Maghreb Union (AMU) was established in 1989 by Algeria, Libya, Morocco, Mauritania, and Tunisia with the aim of gradually creating a common market modeled after the European Economic Community. This seemed to be the potential cornerstone of a large edifice, a catalyst for the long-awaited regional integration process. The AMU had the ambition to lay down the basis for an environment in which goods, capital, labor, and information would move freely across borders, and in which corporations would be encouraged to expand their horizons and promote global operations.

The Maghreb countries displayed imagination in perceiving, relatively early, the benefits of regionalism. Since then, however, their actual behavior has not shown an equivalent breadth of vision, nor has it been adequately consistent and effective. These failures in implementation, however, should not obliterate the value of the basic idea.

In the Mediterranean basin, regional integration would help bridge the gap between the reality of economic activity, which is increasingly internationalized, and the border consciousness of national political systems. Indeed progress toward increased economic interdependence is likely, in turn, to make countries in the area more willing to embark on a regional political dialogue designed to harmonize the rules of behavior of countries that have different social systems and political alignments.

Regional or subregional integration would have the more direct effect of promoting economic development, as well as the process of social and political harmonization. A first, important step in this direction is for the Southern countries to establish free trade with one another. Currently trade among the Southern Mediterranean countries accounts for no more than 5 percent of their total trade, whereas from 40 to 70 percent of these countries' trade is with countries of the European Union (EU).

Regionalism in the Mediterranean could increase national welfare by promoting greater intraregional trade and economic development. It could also act as a stepping-stone to freer trade in the future: it would provide member countries with a framework within which they could pursue wider liberalization.

Regional integration in the area might help overcome problems both within the region and between the region and the rest of the world. It could be the means for

—Alleviating political tensions and promoting closer political cooperation, as it would increase the involvement of each member in the others' trade and economic affairs.

—Building a consensus on issues of mutual concern in areas other than trade in goods and services, such as industrial development and regional security.

Furthermore, regional integration would increase the bargaining power of these countries: acting as a collectivity would shift the terms of trade in favor of the region in multilateral trade negotiations; strengthen it in seeking market access in the developed countries; and create a counterforce against the protectionism of others.

Integration, and even the prospects of integration, may encourage national governments to liberalize their economic policies and harmonize them with those of their neighbors, in order to enhance their competitiveness in increasingly global markets. Trade arrangements among the Southern Mediterranean countries could also help them reach new agreements and achieve concrete action on existing and imaginative, but so far ineffective, initiatives like the EU's Renewed Mediterranean Policy.

The Rationale for Joint Action

The unlikeliness of spontaneous growth in the Mediterranean area, given the circumstances that prevail there, and the desirability of using regionally oriented actions to stimulate growth, bring us to the question of the sort of cooperative regional framework needed to promote the economic and social development of the region and reduce the wealth and technology gap between the South and the North.

The challenge presented is of moment to countries lying outside the Mediterranean basin, and particularly to the EU and the United States. But although their support is needed, the interests of the countries of Southern Europe are so clearly and directly engaged that they should try to stimulate action. The countries concerned should reach a common understanding of the destabilizing threats in the area and reflect together on the role that a cooperative regional structure might play in preventing crises and preserving the peace. When they understand the issues and the scope for action, they should consult closely with the Southern Rim countries. Out of this process, it is to be hoped, will emerge policy guidelines for directing regional cooperation and for raising it to a level commensurate with the problems to be addressed.

It may well be asked why the United States should join in this effort; for years there has been a tendency to see relations with the countries on the southern shore of the Mediterranean as primarily a European concern. There are basically two reasons:

—The United States will, as a global power, be expected to intervene in case a serious military crisis or a threat to the peace should arise in the area. This suggests a continued and direct U.S. interest in the security of the region for the foreseeable future. Surely it would be better from the American point of view to avoid the necessity to intervene militarily. It is generally agreed that the growing discontent on the Southern Rim of the Mediterranean has two sources. One is the perception that the West ignores the aspirations of the Arab nation. The Israeli-PLO deal on Palestinian self-rule holds out a promise of meeting these Arab expectations, at least to some extent. But the other root problem threatening regional security, continuous economic and social degradation, still is awaiting a response; it is in America's *security* interest to participate in such a response.

—The United States is not just a global military power; it also has global trading interests. It has a big stake in maintaining and increasing access to overseas markets. If a regional trading scheme were to develop in the Mediterranean area, the United States would want to participate in order to protect access there for American goods and services. It could also hope that this market would, under the impetus of economic integration and development, become more significant and provide a return on greater participation in it. A special attraction is the rich and still inadequately exploited natural resource potential of some countries in the area.

The prediction that the trading world will be divided into spheres of influence dominated by the United States, Europe, and Japan is not persuasive. It is contradicted by the stronger and increasing force of globalism.

The concern in the specific case of the United States, that it will refocus its trade priorities on its North American neighbors, is myopic. Trade with these countries amounts to only 26 percent of the United States total; and trade with all of the Western Hemisphere accounts for only one-third of the United States' total exports and imports.

The United States cannot ignore its important trade and investment links elsewhere, especially with countries in the Pacific region and in Europe and its neighboring countries. NAFTA should not be read as a shift in U.S. policy from its central focus on multilateralism. President Bill Clinton's convening of an informal APEC summit in Seattle in November 1993 provided unequivocal evidence that America continues to look outward.

Other factors create a need for U.S. involvement. One is the inadequacy to date of European efforts. Both the Mediterranean policy of the European Community and the bilateral actions of European countries have fallen short of what is needed to stimulate the sort of economic dynamism that can be observed in other parts of the world.

Europe's inability to develop and carry out a solid, workable strategy for the region may in part be due to its preoccupation with other—too ambitious—schemes in recent years. The fall of the Berlin Wall gave rise within the EC to a sense of global responsibility and produced a flurry of premature initiatives and federalist designs.

In this respect the currency crises and lesser difficulties recently experienced within the European Monetary System may have a salutary effect. They have been a blow to EC dreams of power—a somewhat rude but perhaps stimulating awakening, bringing the Brussels Commission back to earth.

For the fact is that the EC, even if renamed the European Union, remains a regional power. As such, it must tailor its ambitions to fit within the perimeter of its concrete interests and of its ability to act. For its own security the EU should focus on its neighbors, to the east, but also to the southeast and south. In these areas the EU countries must be more assertive and show a readiness to assume risks and responsibilities as well as exert leadership.

The responsibility for security in the Mediterranean must ultimately be borne by all of Europe. If the EU wishes to maintain its cohesion and be a credible international actor, both politically and economically, all of its members must be as active and supportive as regards European involvement in the Mediterranean basin as the Southern European member states have been with regard to involvement in central and Eastern Europe and the former Soviet Union.

So far this has not been the case. It is true that the EC defined a new policy for the area—the Renewed Mediterranean Policy—but its actual implementation has to a large extent been sacrificed on the altar of strengthening central and Eastern European stability. The snarl within the Community, produced in particular by recurrent exchange market instability and growing unemployment, has worked very much to the detriment of cooperation with the Mediterranean countries.

It is important to stress that the need for a more consistent response of the EC as a whole to the problems of the countries on the southern shore of the Mediterranean in no way diminishes the need for Southern European countries to review their policy options. Up to now the Southern European countries have been unable to assume a leading role in reorienting the EC's priorities. They have failed to work out a cooperative approach. Instead they have regarded each other as rivals, not partners, and their competition has eliminated possibilities for joint or parallel action. A further barrier to the development of a cooperative approach has been France's determination to maintain hegemonic influence in Morocco, Algeria, and Tunisia.

Finally the Southern European countries have focused such efforts as they have made within Europe on obtaining a more favorable sharing of the financial benefits and burdens, with particular attention to the challenges and opportunities posed by the association with and possible entry into the EC of the states of the European Free Trade Association. This approach has not contributed to the development of cooperation among the Southern European countries focused on the regional problems of the Mediterranean area.

The Proposal for a Conference on Security and Cooperation in the Mediterranean

A discussion of the need for multilateral cooperation in the Mediterranean must take account of the most sweeping proposal for action of this kind yet advanced. The Italian-Spanish proposal for a Conference on Security and Cooperation in the Mediterranean (CSCM) can be interpreted as an answer to the need to ensure regional peace through a set of rules based on international legality and UN principles. The vehicle proposed to achieve these goals, the CSCM, was to mirror the open-ended, three-basket pattern of the Helsinki (Conference on Security and Cooperation in Europe [CSCE]) process, while adjusting it to the peculiarities of the Mediterranean region.

The proposal has many merits. It also responded to a number of quite understandable motivations. Basically the CSCM proposal called on Europe to assume primary responsibility in an area that is vital to Europe's security. Europe has experience, which it gained from the long and successful record of the CSCE, that could be applied in this case. It also has a unique heritage of historical ties with the countries on the other side of the Mediterranean that could be put at the service of this project.

Although the CSCM's scope is broad, participation in it, and its actual content, might develop incrementally. Thus the CSCM would not be a rigidly defined institution but a *process* for addressing the region's problems in a progressively more comprehensive way. It could also be a framework, or an umbrella, for specific mechanisms aimed at the solution of localized conflicts and crises.

More specifically, the CSCM's goals are

—To safeguard the security of all the countries in the region, within a general framework of arms control, with the aim of banning all weapons of mass destruction from the area, thus contributing to a greater degree of overall stability.

—To promote balanced economic and social development in the area, thereby gradually reducing disparities. This basket is essential if the CSCM is to achieve its fundamental goal of meeting the broad expectations of peoples of the area in material terms, by fostering codevelopment as a requirement for dealing with the economic, social, and demographic imbalances of the region.

—To create a framework within which diverse civilizations can coexist peacefully. The aim of this basket is to bring the peoples of the region closer together while respecting their cultural and religious identities. Through dialogue tolerance and understanding between societies would be promoted, to allow interchanges among the area's nations without compromising essential standards. This approach would narrow the intellectual distance and the gap of incomprehension currently separating the Western and Islamic cultures.

—To establish a more stable order in the area. This should be based on solidarity; cooperation should be fostered as an alternative to confrontation. This approach would lay the foundations for a new order, in which good-neighborliness, coresponsibility, and interdependence would prevail among all the nations of the region. It would ensure an active role for the Mediterranean and Middle East region within any new international order that may be fashioned. (It is worth noting that the current efforts to remove historical obstacles to resolving the Arab-Israeli conflict are producing breakthroughs that, it is to be hoped, will clear the way for a final settlement of that conflict.)

Toward an Intermediate Approach

The reaction to the CSCM proposal was on balance tepid, and some countries did not conceal their skepticism.

Italy, after gaining Spain's cosponsorship of the initiative, got active backing from Egypt and managed to obtain a "nonnegative" attitude on the part of France.

The United States, which regrettably had not been properly consulted before the idea was launched, feared that the Middle East peace process could get out of its hands and that it would lose control of the timetable for introducing stability into the whole region. (It also feared that the CSCM might turn into a mechanism for demanding the expulsion of outside naval forces from the Mediterranean—including the Sixth Fleet.)

Other governments, even among the Arab countries, thought that the initiative might draw attention away from the Arab-Israeli conflict while not seeming to offer a concrete option for settling the security issues of the area.

In retrospect the underlying concept of the initiative—that is, linking military security to an overall strategy of cooperation and partnership—still seems valid and may prove to be necessary in the future if a lasting and comprehensive peace settlement is to be found.

Subregional economic and technological cooperation, as part of a broad concept of security, constitutes an integral part of the current approach to a definitive settlement of the Middle East crisis. But the search for regional stability cannot be limited to portions of the region, however important they are. The proposed new relationship between the EU and the Maghreb countries on which the Twelve have been focusing for some time—an initiative now frozen because of UN sanctions against Libya—is a case in point. The desire that limited subregional initiatives not be exclusive and closed to broader developments underlay, for example, Egypt's recurrent attempts (to which there has now been a positive response by France and other Southern European countries) to revive its proposal for a Mediterranean Forum.

The Israeli-PLO rapprochement, by breaking the logjam in progress toward an overall solution to the Middle East crisis, could allow the forces for peace in the region to operate and put the CSCM exercise on more solid footing. However, uncertainties and fears should not be underestimated. Nor should the repercussions of the rise of Islamic radicalism be overlooked. Even though the horizon is less clouded, the hopes created by the historic Israeli-Palestinian deal are still fragile, and the final settlement of the Middle East conflict still seems to be a long way off.

The complexity of the CSCM could still be a drag on reaching solutions to critical issues. At the same time it is imperative that the vicious circle of political instability, social turmoil, wasted resources, and an arms race be broken.

The countries that have a more direct interest in the region's stability— starting with the United States, the EU, and the individual countries of

Southern Europe—must send a convincing message of understanding and support, as part of a joint strategy with the Southern Rim countries to make the latter less vulnerable to outbursts of frustration and despair.

If we want the Southern Rim countries urgently to assume more responsibility for the region's overall security, a step that implies action on the environment and on human rights as well as controls over arms proliferation, we should act to promote an increase in overall wealth—on both sides of the Mediterranean. This pressing requirement, which cannot be postponed until the time when the CSCM becomes possible and appropriate, should be met by an intermediate approach.

The Creation of an Alliance for Progress

The Mediterranean runs the risk of remaining excluded from the phenomenon of regionalism, which appears to many developing countries to be the best route to integration into the world economy—the best way of plugging into the world's wealth circuit. So far no regionwide attempt has been made to liberalize trade, to reduce tariff barriers, and to narrow differences between national legislation on issues critical for a common market. Only politically motivated subgroupings have occasionally been created, such as the Arab Consultative Council. However, these have been short-lived and ineffective, except for the Arab Maghreb Union (AMU). Even though poor in results, it so far constitutes the leading example of lasting cooperation.

Although the AMU represents the only serious attempt to establish a subregional integrated area in the Southern Rim, it has made little real progress toward the reduction of intraregional tariff and nontariff barriers to trade and toward the implementation of guidelines on infrastructure, production sharing, and transportation policy. The Union is a long way away from achieving a full-fledged free trade area or customs union, and the idea that it would create a common market seems, as of today, absolutely unrealistic.

As already noted, market forces (unlike the case in other regions of the world) have not been able to produce a real process of integration in the Mediterranean. No formal integration can be contemplated in the area unless and until greater similarity is achieved in such areas as trade and economic regimes, political institutions, and culture. The big, almost intractable, problem posed in the Mediterranean is how to weld together so disparate a group of countries through a structure of cooperation.

For a number of reasons I believe that, under the present circumstances, it would be best to think in terms of a loose institutional framework. The past provides evidence that political impulses have failed to propel market forces in the desired direction and that the benefits from integration were inadequate to mobilize the political will of the countries concerned. What is needed is a mechanism that permits differential treatment while encouraging gradual harmonization and that is capable of fostering a stronger interaction between policies, incentives, and market response.

In order to contain social and economic decline in the Mediterranean region, to restore some confidence and dynamism to the integration process, and, possibly, to prepare the ground for future, more ambitious formal agreements like a revised and refined Conference on Security and Cooperation, a new Alliance for Progress should be launched. The interests they share should lead the countries on the two shores of the Mediterranean, plus the EU as a whole and the United States, to join together to turn the risk of an era of confrontation into a prospect for peace and prosperity.

What I am proposing is more akin to a group of like-minded nations than to a new multilateral institution; indeed it would seek primarily to catalyze and mobilize the existing institutions that should be concerned with the problems of the Mediterranean, but that have so far given them inadequate and uncoordinated attention. But to the extent that what I propose seems to be an institution, I am not ashamed; relations between the South and the North of the Mediterranean are in need of some sort of bridge, of a demonstration that the North is not indifferent to the concerns of the South, and what I propose aims to meet this need.

The Alliance might opt for an evolutionary approach aimed at creating the conditions for economic integration. It should be based on a concept of partnership. Its main purposes could be

—To promote numerous cultural exchanges (involving, for example, research institutes and universities, writers, and artists) in order to improve mutual understanding and trust.

—To encourage dialogue between the two shores (with a stress on enhancing cooperation in the context of a shared responsibility).

—To accelerate investments in and transfers of technology to the Southern countries in order to broaden and diversify their productive base.

—To allow greater market access in the North for goods and services produced in the Southern countries.

Only with a well-conceived and credible strategy can the Northern countries hope to convince the Southern countries' governments to agree to rules and principles consistent with durable and sustained development.

The first objective in this respect is to prove that the bad state of the Southern Mediterranean economies is due to delay in undertaking effective reform. These economies should become more definitely market oriented.

At the same time economic growth has to be planned in such a way as to reduce disparities and to foster human development (for example, housing, health care, education). This is the counterpart, and balance, to the demands made by the Northern countries that the Southern countries improve their human rights performance.

Social stability in these countries depends very largely upon the success of efforts to provide a dignified way of life for the underprivileged. To achieve such success the Northern members of the Alliance should be ready to propose policies and mobilize financial and technological flows.

But international assistance can hardly be expected to produce a breakthrough as long as corrupt and obstructive regimes persist, fanaticism and radicalism block improvements in the status of women, and faulty economic policies smother growth. If it is true that democracy without social and economic progress may prove illusory, the reverse is also true: is *durable* economic development possible except in a democratic and open society?

Scope and Characteristics of the Alliance

Although membership must in principle be open to all the countries of the two shores of the Mediterranean, a limited number of specified countries of the hinterland of the Mediterranean, and the United States, accession would in fact be conditional upon countries' agreeing to a formal declaration stating their commitment to the universal principles of freedom, the rule of law, human rights, and respect for international law. In addition acceding states would have to have adhered to the Treaty on the Non-Proliferation of Nuclear Weapons and would have to declare their readiness to combat the proliferation of weapons of mass destruction and missiles. They would also state their readiness to play a constructive role in the international community and behave in a way that was consistent with the maintenance of peace and stability. No country against which UN Security Council sanctions are in effect could accede; and the membership of countries that at any time did not fully respect UN Security Council resolutions could be suspended or revoked.

These are but the essential conditions for acceding to the Alliance. Enjoyment of full membership would depend on the extent to which countries provided good government and pursued the reforms necessary to achieve market economies.

For their part the Northern nations would have to agree on a common program to support reforms in the South, a program consisting of both concessional aid and loans, as well as assistance for training; improvement of technical, managerial, and banking expertise; transfer of technology and skills; investment facilitation; and granting of trade preferences. The aim would be to promote a growing role for the private sector and the reduction of state control and participation in the economy.

The design of the Alliance should be flexible enough to reflect the realities of the region and the wide variety of situations existing there, without losing sight of the ultimate goal of a more integrated community. Since there is no single model that fits all of the Southern Rim nations, it would be advisable for the Alliance to adopt a "variable geometry" approach. Care should be taken, however, in selecting specific options. Above all actions should not be taken that might be perceived as divisive, or that could deepen rather than narrow the disparities among the Southern countries. A "hub-and-spoke" kind of agreement, to which the EU Commission seems to be resorting in implementing the Renewed Mediterranean Policy, should be avoided.

It is inevitable that the EU, because of its economic and technological weight, its geographic proximity, and its traditional interests in the area, will function as a magnet. But it, individual Southern European countries, and the United States should refrain from applying overly different provisions to each "spoke" country. To do so would in the long run generate rivalry among Southern nations and frustration among the less-favored nations, which would feel themselves discriminated against. Graduation of incentives appears necessary at the beginning to take into account differences within the region, but this should be designed so as to promote eventual harmonization and agreement, even among those countries that cannot initially meet the conditions for full membership.

The opposite extreme—the "convoy" approach—has equally to be avoided. It means reducing the speed of the integration process to the rate of progress of the most slowly evolving participant. In effect it can punish other countries for the problems raised by one country. Thus the "Five plus Five" process has been stalled by Libyan behavior.

Two alternatives remain that provide the desired flexibility. The first— the concentric circles approach—puts a hard core of fully participating countries at the center, with more loosely linked countries gravitating around them. The second approach envisages a string of "inner core" countries spread across the different areas within the region.

The basic difference between the two approaches is that in the first countries are ranked—and divided—according to their similarity to the "model" countries, or their capacity for reform, whereas in the second subgroupings are based on geographic proximity or cultural and historical ties. Examples of the latter could be the AMU or the subregional cooperative arrangement devised as part of the Middle East peace process.

In the second approach the group, not individual countries, becomes the object and subject of the cooperative process. For such subregional groups to be vital and fruitful, their members must be economically complementary to one another, so that trade relations develop among them. The subgroup must also have some collective raison d'être or distinctiveness in trading with other groups or external partners. It would be up to the Alliance's Steering Committee to make sure that the subgroups met these tests or to take corrective measures to do so.

In my view the second approach seems to be less contentious and easier to put into effect. It has the merit of contributing to what in any case should be encouraged, the formation of aggregations within the framework of the Alliance. It may encourage the participation of the maximum number of countries. Finally it has the advantage that smaller economies would have a means, through the subregional groupings, to make their voices heard and get better protection.

The makeup of the groupings merits careful study. However, purely for illustration, one might think of three subregional groupings:

—The first, western, grouping might be made up of Portugal, Spain, France, and Italy to the north, and the so-called "Petit Maghreb" countries—Morocco, Algeria, and Tunisia—to the South.

—The second, central, grouping might be open to the membership of the countries of the former Yugoslavia, Greece, Libya, Egypt, and Mauritania (included among the African, Caribbean, and Pacific group of developing countries by the EU).

—Last, in the east, there could be the subregional grouping associated with the Middle East negotiations.

Malta could be offered a choice of joining either the western or the central grouping.

Cross-participation would be possible if it were in the interest either of a subregional grouping or of the overall collective effort. Countries whose participation in more than one grouping would meet one or both of these tests include the United States, the EU (as a whole), Egypt, France, Spain, Portugal, and Italy.

In the aftermath of the Israeli-PLO peace deal, the third, Middle Eastern, subgroup is bound to attract the greatest flows of financial and technical assistance. However, it would be a mistake to direct all the efforts to that area to the exclusion of the others. An evenhanded approach aimed at promoting greater openness and pluralism in the whole region would ensure a more solid consensus and support for the Middle East peace prospects because it would contain the hotbeds of radicalism and religious fanaticism.

The Alliance's Priorities and Operations

The Alliance's basic strategy should aim at improving the standard of living of the Southern Rim countries by policies ensuring a better balance between population growth and resources. Connected to this is the concept of sustainable development, and the need to assess the environmental impact of development initiatives, and indeed of any economic reforms. Attention to social, cultural, and scientific aspects and effects must be an integral part of the Alliance's coordinated policies.

Although specific actions may well differ from country to country, the following "core" program should be the key part of the Alliance's strategy:

—Advancing market reforms and the privatization of the economy.

—Increasing regional agricultural production to meet to a greater extent the food demand of the local population.

—Phasing in environmental protection guidelines as part of the process of industrial and economic restructuring.

—Creating new job opportunities, especially for young people.

Achieving sustainable development in the region will be an enormously expensive undertaking. In this light the Alliance should be considered as a kind of catalyst, and the initial contributions of its Northern members as seed money making possible the mobilization of human and financial resources from other sources, both multilateral and bilateral. To this end the Alliance should promote an Interagency Unit and a Mediterranean Banking Institution.

The Interagency Unit

The aim of the Interagency Unit would be to increase and coordinate the programs for the region of multilateral organizations. It should be a high-level, policy-oriented, interdisciplinary group, jointly responsible with the Alliance's Steering Committee for planning, coordinating, and monitoring. It should be composed of a representative from each of the institutions operating in the region, including the International Bank for Reconstruction and Development (IBRD), the International Monetary Fund (IMF), the Food and Agriculture Organization, the European Investment Bank (EIB), the International Fund for Agricultural Development (IFAD), and the United Nations Environment Programme.

The Bretton Woods institutions (the IBRD and the IMF) have been accounting for nearly two-thirds of the multilateral funds devoted to the countries on the southern shore of the Mediterranean. Their policies and practices therefore heavily color multilateral development lending to the countries under review. The region's other main sources of multilateral financing are, in descending order, the EIB, the African Development Bank and Fund, the IFAD, the Islamic Development Bank, the Special Fund of the Organization of Petroleum Exporting Countries, and the Arab Fund for Economic and Social Development. These institutions help shape projects. They play a useful but not critical role in the region's overall external financing.

There is a rather clear-cut distinction of roles and functions between the IMF and the World Bank on the one hand and development financing from other multilateral sources on the other. The Bretton Woods institutions give priority to financial stabilization and structural adjustment and bring a strong policy emphasis to both overall strategies and individual lending operations, whereas the other multilateral agencies are essentially geared to the support of individual projects, mostly on the basis their financial, technical, and microeconomic merit.

The different vocations and policy objectives of the various institutions encourage the search for close coordination from the outset of actions they take simultaneously. The World Bank and the EIB have recently jointly financed the Environmental Program for the Mediterranean, which may provide a good example for future joint ventures. (The areas of interest of the two institutions have differed somewhat: the World Bank focused more on water, land, and rural management issues through a broad range of agricultural and forestry projects, whereas the EIB has lent funds primarily for water management and pollution control.)

The IFAD, the African Development Bank and Fund, and the Arab Fund for Economic and Social Development have achieved some success. Overall lending has, however, been so small that it has not had any noticeable impact on the key development issues in and prospects for the region. The organizations' impact could be increased if their lending were carried out in parallel or jointly with the Bretton Woods institutions. Financial stabilization and project financing are, in fact, two complementary activities that should be undertaken in close, finely tuned connection with one another, both for the sake of efficiency and to have a significant positive impact on the recipient country.

The distinctive roles and vocations of the multilateral financial institutions operating in the area can be of great advantage as long as the resulting mix of policy and project financing addresses the priority issues adequately and in a coordinated way.

The task of the Alliance's Steering Committee would be to review, together with the Interagency Unit, how specific policies have responded to the area's most pressing problems, and how better to meet future challenges through concerted effort. A new emphasis should be placed on regional integration through cross-sectoral and transnational initiatives with the aim of ensuring consistent application of policy directives and guidelines in the regional subgroupings, and also of helping the transfer of experience gained in one subgroup to the others.

Let me draw on my experience as a "Sherpa"—one of the seven persons who, on behalf of the heads of government of the seven most advanced industrial economies, prepare the annual economic summits. At a certain point an impasse was reached between Russia and the IMF: Russia could not make the reforms required by the IMF without financial assistance; the IMF would not provide financial assistance unless the Russians made the reforms. The G-7 Sherpas, conscious of the importance of Russian stability, stepped in and persuaded the IMF to introduce a new "systemic transformation facility," a way to allow the Russians to adjust some macroeconomic policies so as to pave the way for a standby agreement. What I envisage is the Alliance's Steering Committee acting as we Sherpas did, providing political input and innovative schemes to the financial institutions represented on the Interagency Committee.

The Mediterranean Banking Institution

The Mediterranean Banking Institution would parallel other regional banks such as the African Development Bank and the Asian Development Bank. The argument for establishing this new bank has been further strengthened by the creation of the European Bank for Reconstruction and

Development. It is important not to aid the East by diverting funds from the South, to the detriment of the European security position in the Mediterranean.[1]

Debt and development in the Mediterranean areas of Africa and Asia are problems of common concern to North and South. A regional development bank able to operate on the pattern of the Inter-American Development Bank and of Japan's Overseas Cooperation Fund seems indispensable for channeling new financial resources to these countries for infrastructure investments, and for supporting productive investments by insurance guarantees and cofinancing.

In the long run the economic development of the Southern Rim countries will depend on their ability to become competitive exporters. However, for many years to come, despite the favorable outcome of the Uruguay Round, it will be difficult to expand exports from the Southern Rim to the North. This prognosis leaves a vital gap to be filled by strengthened and extended financial assistance.

Even assuming continuance of financial flows from existing multilateral institutions at present levels, the countries of the Southern Rim will continue to be plagued by severe population pressure (with the prospect of rapid demographic growth into the future) and by high levels of unemployment. The migratory flows resulting from these demographic and employment problems are putting heavy pressure on the labor markets of the countries on the Northern Rim of the Mediterranean, especially France, Italy, and Spain.

Furthermore, the pressure on natural resources is causing severe environmental degradation, with implications for the entire Mediterranean region, especially as regards water management. In 1990 the European Investment Bank and the World Bank launched an initiative to curb and reverse the trends of environmental degradation in the Mediterranean. The joint initiative of the EIB and the IBRD has produced the important Mediterranean Environmental Technical Assistance Program.

The Alliance for Progress should address the environmental issue by ensuring, as soon as possible, the signing by the Mediterranean countries of a new charter applying the major conventions adopted at the Rio Summit to the region and providing a compliance and enforcement timetable.

The Alliance must, more particularly, make sure that the Global Environmental Facility, after its pilot phase, earmarks a special fund for the Mediterranean to address such issues. It could function as a mechanism to secure effective and efficient implementation of assistance, as well as provide financial resources. Likewise a special section for the Mediterranean should be set up within the UN Commission on Sustainable Development.

The employment and environmental problems of the countries of the Southern Rim are the real challenge for the area's development and for development finance. A regional bank might fill the gap between that challenge and the resources otherwise available to meet it.

Concluding Remarks

Dealing with the problems of the Mediterranean area is an integral part of a strategy that aims to put world stability on a solid basis. The region remains a key element in European security, and its stability is a necessary condition for a durable, peaceful settlement in the Middle East and the Gulf area.

Countries in the Southern Rim are now facing enormous challenges on many fronts, beginning with the economic.

Security and stability are more and more linked to social and human development. The southern shore of the Mediterranean continues to lag behind the pace of progress and increasing wealth achieved by the northern shore. The governments of the Southern countries have to intensify their processes of reform in order to usher in political pluralism and orient their economies to the market. However, there is no chance that this effort will succeed without sizable and continuous support from the international community.

There is a need, furthermore, to reverse the trend toward a corrosive climate of mistrust and to lay down the basis for a new partnership.

For all these reasons a strong and credible initiative should be launched as soon as possible, so as to seize the unique opportunity created by the Israel-PLO peace deal. The Alliance for Progress, complex though it may seem, would be a credible and viable intermediate step toward the integration of the countries of the southern shore into European development and security mechanisms.

The subregional cooperation that is beginning to develop as a result of the breakthrough in the Middle East peace process fits perfectly into the framework of the proposed Alliance. The Alliance, if properly implemented, will benefit the countries of the region by the strengthening of their market positions and by the synergies that will be realized. Economic progress, in turn, will be the basis for pluralist, more open societies fully respectful of individual and collective rights, the necessary precondition for creating a "community of destiny" in the region.

I do not contend that the Alliance is the only possible way to achieve such a community. But I am convinced that individual nations and existing multilateral institutions have not so far faced up to the need for action. The Alliance seeks to meet that challenge.

Note

1. The EC's financial focus on Eastern and central Europe was already clear in 1990, when it spent $100 a person on that part of Europe but only $10 for each African. See Yves Boyer, "Europe's Future Strategic Orientation," *Washington Quarterly,* vol. 16, no. 4 (Autumn 1993), p. 151.

Part Two

SOUTHERN EUROPE
AS PART OF EUROPE

SEVEN

Southern European Countries in the European Community

Dimitri Constas

IF A DISTINCT identity of the Southern European Community members (SECM) exists at all, it is more the result of images held by outsiders regarding the region and the common features and interests of its component parts than the outcome of historical, cultural, and geographic realities. In the period after bipolarity a number of such external perceptions exerted constructive influences on the SECM regarding their common needs and concerns and joint efforts to fulfill them. The collapse of the Eastern Bloc and the Soviet Union set the stage for the full restoration of centuries-old channels of communication between Eastern and Western Europe, where, unlike the North-South divide shaped by such features as the Alps, there are no great geographic barriers obstructing interaction.

Apprehensions that diversion of European Community (EC) attention to the East will deprive the SECM of valuable resources underlined the need for coordination of a number of current and future Community policies.[1] The acceleration of the process of European integration decided at Maastricht in Decemember 1991 led to a timetable for attaining some quite ambitious economic targets prior to each of the main stages in the evolution of the European Union (EU; the title now adopted by the EC). This development, in turn, implied that unless the less-developed member states, like the SECM and Ireland, prevented the diversion of Community funds supporting economic and social cohesion to other targets, their place in the future Union could be insecure.

The author wishes to acknowledge the assistance he received from Ada Marcoyianni, a research assistant at the Institute of International Relations, Panteion University, in the documentation of this chapter.

Furthermore, with perceptions of a military threat from the East fading away, indirect security challenges, such as religious fanaticism, nationalist claims, illegal immigration, and terrorism, along with potential direct security threats from third mediterranean countries (TMC) and the Middle East were rapidly upgraded on the agenda of European security considerations.[2] Such issues were quite familiar, throughout the cold war years, to nations in the South, where, with the possible exception of Italy, perceptions of an immediate threat to national security from the Warsaw Pact never dominated domestic political debate. Developments in the East presented the SECM with novel opportunities to bring their views on security closer to those of the Northern members.[3] The dynamics of this convergence became evident prior to and during the Maastricht Treaty deliberations and contributed to the delicate balance of views on Common Foreign and Security Policy (CFSP) reached at Maastricht. One should point out in that respect that unless this process continues to produce concrete results the long tradition in the South of bilateral security arrangements with the United States, the superpower dominating the Mediterranean, could seriously undermine the course of European integration.

The identity of the SECM can also be deduced from certain objective criteria, especially geographic location and stage of economic development, and most appropriately from a combination of the two. The application of the geographic criterion to current EC members suggests five prospective candidates for the SECM category: Portugal, Spain, France, Italy, and Greece. However, France, although it is undoubtedly a Southern and a Mediterranean nation, is equally an Atlantic and a Northern one, as well as the state that since the foundation of the EC has strived to preserve as its cornerstone the Common Agricultural Policy, traditionally attuned more to the interests of the North than to those of the South.[4] Table 7-1 shows a classification of the five prospective SECM based on their share of payments from the European Agriculture Guidance and Guarantee Fund (EAGGF) and the European Regional Fund. The first fund supports the export or the destruction of surplus EC agricultural produce as well as its private storage; the second finances projects that could contribute to economic growth in the less-developed regions of the EC. There are great variations concerning the share received by each of the five from the EAGGF: France is first, followed at a distance by the second, Italy, and the fourth, Spain. Greece is only seventh and Portugal is a distant eleventh. On the contrary there is much more evident homogeneity among a group of four members concerning their common interest in securing EC financial

Table 7-1. *Payments to Five SECM from EC Agricultural and Regional Funds, 1991*

Member state	European Agriculture Guidance and Guarantee Fund (Guarantees)			European Regional Fund		
	Amount (million ECU)	Percent of EC total	Rank among EC	Amount (million ECU)	Percent of EC total	Rank among EC
Portugal	316.4	1.00	11	971.2	18.74	2
Spain	3,300.3	10.46	4	1,488.8	28.74	1
France	6,332.7	20.08	1	323.2	6.23	7
Italy	5,347.0	16.96	2	710.8	13.72	3
Greece	2,211.8	7.01	7	537.2	10.37	4
EC total	31,527.6			5,179.9		

Source: "Annual Report of the Board of Auditors for the Financial Year 1991," *Official Journal of the European Communities* 330 (December 15, 1992), p. 15 (Greek Edition).

support for their underdeveloped regions: Spain is first, Portugal is second, Italy is third, and Greece is fourth, whereas France is only seventh in that respect.

Using the mixed criteria of geographic location and regional underdevelopment I would therefore limit the inquiry into the policies of the SECM within the EC to Portugal, Spain, Italy, and Greece, and with considerable hesitation I would exclude France. Although not an SECM in a strict sense, France is the one nation among the EC's "big three" (along with Germany and United Kingdom) that, on a great number of issues, follows policies supportive of Southern interests. This is particularly the case with regard to "widening," that is, enlargement of the EC, an issue on which France has taken a cautious position giving priority to strengthening internal cohesion.[5] It is also the case concerning the development of an EC Mediterrranean policy as well as inter-Mediterranean trade, in which France is the most important partner for the Maghreb countries.[6] On the other hand, although France was originally a strong supporter of extending the boundaries of the Community southward, it mounted the strongest opposition to the accession of Spain, at least until the socialist victory of François Mitterrand in the French presidential elections of 1981.[7]

Furthermore, France, where immigration from the Maghreb has been perceived as an internal and external challenge, has been instrumental in introducing the concept of a "threat from the South" into contemporary European security considerations and in encouraging a "redefinition of security in which economic and social issues are being given greater importance," thus leading the way to the convergence between Northern and Southern perceptions on security.[8]

It may be pertinent to suggest at this point that Germany, a non–Southern European great power, also has shared interests with the SECM that could lead to tactical alliances in important issue areas. For instance, following unification, Germany's eastern provinces (the former German Democratic Republic) qualify for assistance from EU structural funds, a fact that may add Germany to the supporters of an active "cohesion policy" for the Union. At the same time Germany favors immediate enlargement of the Union to include the wealthy European Free Trade Association (EFTA) countries, which could share with Germany part of the cost for implementing such a policy. As will be discussed later in this chapter, the SECM, although unwilling to endorse Germany's preference for a quick expansion of the EC toward the East (Hungary, Poland, and Czechoslovakia), have no objection in principle to accepting more wealthy Northerners into the Union, if the latter are prepared to make substantial contributions to the structural funds.

Finally Italy—whose stronger credentials on both grounds (location and regional underdevelopment) make it part of the SECM group—has, in the period since the entry of Spain into the EC, gradually relinquished to the latter leadership on "Southern issues," like cohesion within the Community, and tends to follow less distinct and more balanced positions. This is a development that stems both from the accentuation of its internal "north-south" economic and political divisions and from broader foreign policy considerations of the post-bipolar era.[9]

This chapter attempts, using available data, to investigate SECM attitudes primarily in three areas of profound common interest: Mediterranean policy, enlargement, and evolution of the European Union. It also reviews briefly SECM positions related to a CFSP for the European Union and makes an effort to test the compatibility of prevailing trends in that area with long-term SECM economic and political interests.

A final issue could be raised at this point. Is the SECM a mere subdivision of the "small EC members" category? In other words, do the SECM act in typical "small country" fashion by pursuing external balance for their economic and security needs through the formation of an alliance to safeguard their interests from the "imperialism" of much more powerful groups like the "big three"? The answer to this rather simplistic question is negative. The well-known difficulties of classifying states as "small" versus "big" are even more pronounced within the EU because of the great variety of issue-areas that fall within the competence of the Union, a factor that renders meaningless the task of measuring state power in each one of them and that contributes to the ever-changing patterns in alliance formation. This is quite clear in the case of the SECM group. Even on those very few issues that could be crudely reduced to "small versus big" questions, like the expansion of weighted voting in decisionmaking within the Union or the right of the "small" states to hold the presidency in an enlarged Union, it would be inappropriate to classify all members of the group in the "small" category. Although Greece and Portugal will find themselves more at ease within an alliance that includes Denmark, Ireland, Belgium, or even Luxembourg, this will hardly be the case with Italy and Spain. In fact the identity of the SECM is a function of objective common features like relative economic underdevelopment, geographic location, and geostrategic interests, as well as of external perceptions of group identity along with shared objectives on a limited range of EC issue-areas. It is not the result of their being part of the "small" category of a clear-cut "small state versus big state" division within the Union.

Southern Attitudes and Policies

Let us now examine SECM attitudes and performance with regard to Mediterranean policy, the enlargement of the EU, and the EU's development.

The Development of a Mediterranean Policy

The 1980s witnessed a rapid deterioration of economic conditions in the TMC. Some of the causes of this deterioration—such as overpopulation, inadequate political systems and public administration mechanisms, shrinking fresh water resources, growing external public debt (see table 7-2), and domestic consumption of agricultural products that reduced income from exports—are independent of EC-related developments. The accession to the Community of Greece (1981) and, much more important, Spain and Portugal (1986) has had adverse effects on TMC exports of agricultural products to the Community.[10]

At the same time the enlargements gave birth to a much more homogeneous and determined SECM group whose members—their historic links with the TMC and their concern for preserving stability in the region notwithstanding—have had both the ability and the resolve to discourage excessive Community concessions that would be potentialy detrimental to

Table 7-2. *Total External Debt Ratios of Selected Third Mediterranean Countries*

	Total external debt as percent of:				Total debt service as percent of exports of goods and services		Interest payments as percent of exports of good and services	
	Exports of goods and services		Gross national product					
Country	1980	1989	1980	1989	1980	1989	1980	1989
Algeria	130.0	248.8	47.1	56.8	27.1	68.9	10.4	19.1
Morocco	223.8	328.4	53.1	98.4	32.7	32.2	17.0	18.4
Jordan	79.2	246.0	. . .	181.2	8.4	19.6	4.3	11.7
Tunisia	96.0	136.7	41.6	71.9	14.8	22.6	6.9	8.5
Egypt	208.4	333.6	95.0	159.0	20.8	20.5	9.0	10.3
Syria	82.3	. . .	21.0	47.1	11.4	. . .	4.7	. . .
Turkey	332.9	190.0	34.3	53.8	28.0	32.1	14.9	14.1

Source: World Bank, *World Development Report 1991: The Challenge of Development* (Oxford University Press, 1991), pp. 250–51.

their vital economic interests. Two of the new members also brought with them their disputes with the TMC: the Greek-Turkish conflict over Cyprus and the Aegean and the Spanish-Moroccan territorial dispute over Ceuta and Melilla.

The Community, by far the most important trade partner of the TMC, had failed to provide through its Mediterranean Policy sufficient financial support to stimulate economic growth. In the period 1979–87 the EC, collectively or through individual contributions of member states, provided aid amounting to 17 percent of the total development aid given to the TMC, compared to 31 percent given by the United States and 28 percent by the Arab members of the Organization of Petroleum Exporting Countries. During the same period underdeveloped countries in Latin America and Asia received 21.5 percent of total EC development aid; African, Caribbean, and Pacific countries close to 67 percent and the TMC only 11.5 percent.[11]

Emigration to the "affluent" Mediterranean North and the rest of the EC became an irresistible remedy to economic stagnation and demographic explosion in the TMC, and it is expected to assume alarming proportions in the years to come. The situation in the eastern Mediterranean is as grave as that in the western Mediterranean. There are considerable similarities concerning economic conditions and population growth, as well as nutrition, health, and education, between the two parts of the Mediterranean. Although the population of the SECM (including France) will increase from 1989 to 2025 by an average of only 5 percent, in the same period the population of the nine TMC will increase by an average of close to 90 percent. Turkey, an eastern TMC, will see its population grow from 55 to 93 million, the largest share of any single country in the total population growth of the Mediterranean (see table 4-1).

As for immigration, in 1990 "foreign residents in EC countries" totaled 13 million persons, or 4 percent of the population, of which 8 million came from outside the EC. About half of these immigrants originate from the TMC, namely North Africa, areas of the former Yugoslavia, and Turkey. It is well known that the country that absorbs most of this immigration flow is not a member of the SECM group but the former West Germany, where the foreign resident population has risen from 4.5 million in 1980 to 5.2 million (or 8.4 percent of the total population) in 1990. Turks in (West) Germany amount to 1.7 million or 32.6 percent of the foreign population in Germany and 21.2 percent of that in the entire EC.[12]

Economic stagnation, overpopulation, and concerns about imminent massive population movements from South to North, along with the rise of Islamic fundamentalism, political instability, and a rapid deterioration of the environment in the TMC, provided powerful incentives for a reconsideration of the EC's Mediterranean Policy, which, by and large, consisted of a "set of association and cooperation agreements drawn up in the second half of the 1970s."[13] The initiative for a new policy came not only from the SECM but also from the prosperous North, which is more attractive to immigrants, and especially Germany, whose society and economy already reflect the pressures placed on them by the new entrants.[14]

The "new" Mediterranean Policy would promote three main objectives:

—Preferential treatment of industrial and agricultural products of the TMC so as to secure access to EC markets.

—A significant increase (close to 40 percent) in financial aid to the TMC, which should increase agricultural and industrial productivity and improve technical and professional training.

—Encouragement of regional economic cooperation among the TMC, development of human resources, incentives to support private business and investment, and protection of the environment through a "horizontal" program of financial assistance benefiting all of the TMC.

The European Investment Bank would play an important role in the action plan through loans that would reach 1.8 billion ECU in the period 1992–96.

During the negotiations for the Renewed Mediterranean Policy (1990), the SECM kept their distance from EC Commission proposals that made overly generous trade concessions to the TMC on products that would compete with their own. The Italian presidency, however, followed a more balanced policy in line with broader Italian objectives, especially with regard to the western Mediterranean (like the "Five plus Five" initiative) as well as the Mediterranean as a whole. To ensure that the Policy would be adopted within its term, Italy did not align with the rest of the SECM group and pressed hard for a compromise formula. On the other hand, northern EC members like United Kingdom, the Netherlands, Belgium, Denmark, and Germany were quite keen to endorse trade liberalization but unwilling to consent to large increases in financial aid to the TMC, regarding which there were no objections by the SECM.[15] (An additional complicating factor was Greece's position, in line with its traditional policy of linking Turkey's access to Community funds and policies with positive steps toward the solution of the Cyprus problem, that both provisions on financial protocols and those on the "horizontal policy" be drafted in a way that would not benefit Turkey.) With neither side ready to pay the cost of postponing or canceling an important package deal with the South, the Renewed Mediterranean Policy, with minor changes, was finally approved in December 1990.

The difficulty of disassociating political aspects of cooperation with the TMC from economic aspects became apparent within the next few months when the European Parliament rejected the financial protocols with Syria and Morocco owing to the failure of these countries to guarantee satisfactory protection of human rights. It should be noted that Morocco was one of the countries that had participated from the beginning in an initiative undertaken by the countries of the western Mediterranean, at a meeting in Rome in March 1990 that included France and three countries of the SECM group (Italy, Spain, and Portugal) as well as the members of the Arab Maghreb Union (Mauritania, Morocco, Algeria, Tunisia, and Libya), to institutionalize a political dialogue on economic, environmental, cultural, and social questions that could evolve into a Conference on Security and Cooperation in the western Mediterranean.

The Gulf War early the following year and the enduring crisis in the former Yugoslavia showed that the division of the Mediterranean into western and eastern areas might, in the short run, safeguard cooperation experiments in the former but in the long run would prove shortsighted and counterproductive. It took only a few days for radical messages to reach from Bahgdad to Algeria and Morocco and even to the streets of Paris, and only a few weeks for refugees from Yugoslavia to spread into Western Europe.

With hopeful prospects for peace in Bosnia and the Arab-Israeli dialogue closer to a settlement than ever before, there appears to be a historic opportunity for a comprehensive Mediterranean policy that would address the "threat from the South" by economic as well as political means. The convergence of interests between northerners and the SECM in meeting effectively this challenge might even smooth the way for the application of the CFSP provisions of the Maastricht Treaty.[16]

Deepening versus Widening of the European Union

The acceleration of the process of European integration, institutionalized at Maastricht, and the claim of the poorer members for more resources to strengthen socioeconomic cohesion conflicted with the aspirations of central and Eastern European and Mediterranean countries, which turned to the EC for economic and political support and eventually full membership and saw their hopes withering away. Discrepancies between applicants from those regions and those from the rich EFTA nations were embarassingly visible—for example, $33,000 and $23,000 per capita gross national products (GNP) in Switzerland and Scandinavia, respectively, versus $1,600 in Poland and Turkey—thus posing for EC decisionmakers some very real moral, political, and economic dilemmas.[17]

The experience with German reunification—a unique kind of "widening" that was accomplished within a few weeks without the usual protracted accession procedures—with its negative effect on European Monetary Union and other aspects of cohesion, complicated the debate on enlargement, inevitably linking it with the broader budgetary questions of the EC.

The views of EU members concerning enlargement divide them into two groups. The first comprises states that for a variety of reasons are in principle in favor of enlargement, although, by and large, they tend to have in mind specific states or group of states. Perhaps the state most committed to enlargement in general is the United Kingdom: "The British government's interest in increasing this intergovernmental cooperation within the Union framework is widely believed to be a primary reason for its attachment to enlargement." Germany also supports enlargement, particularly, however, in the direction of neighboring Austria and Switzerland as well as the Baltic republics. Denmark is particularly keen to end the "artificial division of the North" by admitting the rest of the Nordic countries to the EU, a prospect also attractive to the Netherlands, but not at the risk of threatening existing EU structures or the future evolution of the Union.[18]

The other two Benelux countries take an even more cautious line and with the much more outspoken SECM (including France) and Ireland form a strong opposition group. The group's negative stance, however, becomes more flexible in the case of EFTA members, whereas the SECM would also endorse parallel negotiations for the admission of at least one Mediterranean country: Malta.[19] Greece will almost certainly argue that Cyprus, more prosperous than Malta with a 1989 per capita GNP of $7,040 versus Malta's GNP of $5,830, should not be penalized for a division imposed on it by force following the 1974 Turkish invasion. Nevertheless, the SECM and Ireland would oppose any new membership that would place considerable burdens on EC finances:

> The poorer nations in the Community, relapsing into economic stagnation, demand more money for regional aid and structural assistance from the richer north and from the new applicants in EFTA. That is their price to negotiate an enlargement of the EC. . . . [With] a GNP per capita less than half that of the northern members of the Community they are in no hurry to admit the poorer countries of Eastern Europe and the Mediterranean, or to sacrifice their slice of the perennially contested EC budget.[20]

At the Lisbon Summit in June 1992 the Commission submitted to the Council a report on enlargement that the latter accepted in principle.[21] The report made it explicit that "widening must not be at the expense of deepening" and that negotiation should await not only the ratification of the Maastricht Treaty but also the completion of the negotiation on the second package of financial and structural measures. In its evaluation of applicant countries the report is in the mainstream of member state opinion in concluding that EFTA members will pose fewer problems and that an unspecified period of preparation would be necessary for the rest. As for the procedure for enlargement, the Commission hints that some kind of evaluation of applications in groups would be convenient and appropriate. This echoes Gianni de Michelis's notion of "groupings of states" visualized as three concentric circles. The center circle would consist of the EC and EFTA, the next of the countries of central and Eastern Europe, and finally the outer circle of the remaining members of the Conference on Security and Cooperation in Europe.[22]

A similar concept, which in fact postpones to an unspecified date the accession of all but the wealthiest of applicants, has also been voiced by EC Commission President Jacques Delors and has received a warm response by the SECM.[23]

In short the seven EFTA members, who already accepted more than 60 percent of the *acquis communautaire* through the European Economic Area (EEA) Treaty of May 1992, and whose accession will increase the EC population by only 10 percent, appear to be the most likely new EC members. To strengthen even further their candidacy and help appease SECM concerns that their membership will pave the way for a two-speed Community, the EFTA members agreed during the EEA negotiations to contribute to the financial solidarity of the Community by setting up "an EEA cohesion fund for the benefit of southern EC members and Ireland."[24] Accession negotiations with Austria, Sweden, Finland, and Norway were in fact concluded in March 1994 in time for entry into the EU on January 1, 1995, subject to referenda in the applicant countries.

As for the other groups, central and Eastern Europeans will have to content themselves for several more years with EC assistance through the European Bank for Reconstruction and Development, as well as trade and cooperation agreements that in some cases could take the form of the more ambitious and deep-seated association agreements known as "Europe Agreements."[25] All three current Mediterranean applicants have association agreements with the Community that envisage development into customs union and possible accession.

There is a broad consensus today that of all the prospective applicants, Turkey is the country least likely eventually to become a member of the Community: "EC governments would, by and large, prefer the Turkish application to go away."[26] Besides the traditional references to the Cyprus problem and the Greek objections, in recent years additional reasons are more openly and frequently cited to support the view that the prospects for Turkish membership are worse today than before the Gulf War, including the following: "it has by far the largest population of all potential applicants" and the fastest rate of population growth; "it is very poor" and "not wholly European"; "it has failed to establish a full democratic regime"; "it will be increasingly difficult for EC members to accept the additional . . . exposure in the Middle East that Turkish membership would imply"; and "the status of the Kurds within its borders represents a newly-stated barrier."[27]

The end of bipolarity and of Turkey's vital role in the Alliance as a front-line state with the longest borders with the Soviet Union may explain the unusual frankness and vigor with which arguments against Turkish membership are put forward and defended. Perhaps the most accurate picture of the actual dilemmas that Turkey, a regional military superpower, encounters in the post-bipolar era is the one conveyed in the analysis of a distinguished Turkish scholar, Duygu Sezer:

> Differences of a political nature, namely, Turkey's exclusion from the EC and the Greek-Turkish Conflict, also help to draw a wedge between Turkey and the rest of the countries in the region. Turkey's particular social and economic problems, more specifically, its relative underdevelopment, the revival of Islam and its adverse record in human rights, are features that are more commonly found in the south than in the north. In other words, in many ways Turkey is south, whereas the rest of Southern Europe is north; *this means that it presents them with the types of challenges that they fear might come, for example from North Africa.* [my emphasis][28]

Turkey's post-bipolar dilemmas are also dilemmas for the Community. Regardless of the eventual fate of the Turkish membership bid, there can be no comprehensive and effective EC Mediterranean policy addressing the political, economic, and security dimensions of the "threat from the south" that would exclude Turkey. Greece can and should not stand in the way of such a policy provided that its legitimate security concerns are taken into account in the new EC system of CFSP. This is particularly pertinent in view of Part III of the Petersburg Declaration, adopted by the Western European Union (WEU) Council of Ministers in June 1992. The Declaration deprives members of the WEU (and, of course, Greece, after its accession to that organization) of the right to invoke the WEU Treaty's security guarantees in disputes with a member of NATO, such as Turkey. As Edward Mortimer points out, "this is not very satisfying for Greece, which regards possible Turkish aggression as the most serious threat to its security, and looks to both NATO and the WEU for insurance against it; and, indeed, the Greeks can argue that the *Petersburg formula is tantamount to declaring that NATO allies are free to attack each other*" (my emphasis).[29]

The Evolution of the European Union

The Intergovernmental Conference (IGC) on the Political Union and the deliberations and consultations that preceded it provided important incentives to member states to formulate positions on the different aspects of the European Union.

Table 7-3 presents those positions in a simplified fashion. Nevertheless it clearly shows that, despite similar backgrounds and needs, the SECM managed to form a homogeneous front on only two out of the six major items debated and decided upon at the IGC. One of these two, the "principle

Table 7-3. *Southern European Countries' Positions on Certain European Union Issues*[a]

Issue	Spain	Portugal	Italy	Greece
Codecision for the European Parliament	In favor	Opposed	In favor	In favor
Federalism	In favor	Opposed	In favor	In favor
Principle of subsidiarity	In favor	In favor	In favor	In favor
Majority vote in CFSP	Ambivalent[b]	Opposed	Ambivalent	Ambivalent
Inclusion of defense in CFSP	In favor	Opposed	Ambivalent	In favor
More cohesion money	In favor	In favor	In favor	In favor

a. All ratings are based on post-1989 documented positions of members. Valuable information for this table was drawn from F. Laursen and S. Vanhoonacker, eds., *The Intergovernmental Conference on Political Union* (Maastricht, The Netherlands: European Institute of Public Administration/Martinus Nijhoff, 1992).

b. "Ambivalent" means either that there is not sufficient evidence to establish a state's position on the issue or that available evidence does not place it unequivocally in either the "in favor" or the "opposed" category.

of subsidiarity," was an important but by no means feverishly contested issue. The principle, inserted in article 3b of the Treaty on European Union, states that "in the areas which do not fall within its exclusive competence, the Community shall take action, in accordance with the principle of subsidiarity, only if and insofar as the objectives of the proposed action cannot be sufficiently achieved by the Member States and can there-fore . . . be better achieved by the Community." The proposal repre-sented a shrewd move by Commission President Delors[30] to counter growing hostility against initiatives taken by Brussels bureaucrats; the only remarkable thing about it is that it won easy approval by the most antifederalist of members despite its wide recognition as one of the central principles of federalism.[31]

The area of social and economic cohesion constitutes by far the most characteristic common policy of the SECM and one that has been pursued with considerable success. Although funds and policies to support the less wealthy countries and regions of the EC predated Spanish and Portuguese accession, it was the prospect of their eventual membership that gave new momentum and vigor to such Community actions. The prospective entry of these two countries into the EC led in July 1985 to the adoption by the Council of Ministers of the Integrated Mediterranean Programs (IMP) with the aim of improving the socioeconomic structures of certain regions in France, Greece, and Italy and overcoming the adverse impact of the second enlargement on their economy. Table 7-4 shows the considerable financial benefits that each of those countries has gained as a result of the IMP.

Table 7-4. *Distribution of Integrated Mediterranean Program Payments*
Millions of ECU

	Payments			
Member state	By December 31, 1989	In 1990 and 1991	In 1992	Total
Greece	1,987.6	5.2	7.2	2,000.0
France	782.6	16.8	44.1	843.5
Italy	1,009.6	246.9	. . .	1,256.5
Total	3,779.8	268.9	51.3	4,100.0

Source: "Annual Report of the Board of Auditors for the Financial Year 1991," *Official Journal of the European Communities* 330 (December 15, 1992), p. 171 (Greek Edition).

As regards Greece in particular, the successful pursuit of the IMP marks an important turn in the policy of the socialist government, from making unilateral claims to offset the potentially negative effects of accession on the Greek economy to acting collectively in support of broader EC policies ("Southern interests") that could eventually be beneficial to Greece.[32]

The Single European Act, approved almost a year after the second enlargement (July 1987), enacted regional policy as primary Community law and emphasized its role in promoting economic and social cohesion; at the same time it required the restructuring and coordination of all EC funds that affected regional development (European Agricultural Guidance and Guaranties Fund, Social Fund, European Regional Development Fund).[33] A few months later, in February 1988, the European Council agreed with the Commission's proposal to approve the first Delors Plan to finance the reform of the Common Agricultural Policy and the structural funds. The new regional policy took effect in January 1989, with its main beneficiaries (as shown in table 7-5) being the SECM and the United Kingdom. The advantages of this development were considerable but insufficient to remove the obstacles to full participation in the European Union that the SECM and the other less wealthy members encountered.

The Spanish threat to veto the entire Maastricht Treaty unless important steps were taken to address economic and social cohesion is symbolic of the importance attached to this issue by the SECM and Ireland, which became known as "the cohesion countries."[34] It is also symbolic of the leadership role that Spain undertook with considerable success in the IGC negotiation regarding "Southern issues."[35] A few weeks before the Maastricht Summit (November 10, 1991) a special meeting took place between Commission officials and representatives of Spain, Portugal, Greece, and Ireland at which Spanish delegates exerted strong pressures for the endorsement by

Table 7.5. *Payments to Member States from the EC Regional Fund, 1987–91*
Millions of ECU

Fiscal year	Belgium	Denmark	Germany	Greece	Spain	France	Ireland	Italy	Luxembourg	Netherlands	Portugal	United Kingdom	Nonavailable grants	Total
1987	23.0	16.6	73.4	293.9	345.3	311.2	134.7	563.5	3.8	19.6	222.7	526.7	0.6	2,535.0
1988	29.6	10.1	96.9	312.6	543.5	436.3	136.9	597.4	7.4	13.3	330.7	577.8	0.3	3,092.8
1989	40.6	14.8	163.8	418.4	980.0	284.2	191.3	787.3	1.2	28.9	396.9	612.4	0.3	3,920.0
1990	43.6	18.9	88.6	543.2	1,406.9	331.3	250.2	910.2	0.4	32.7	451.9	464.6	11.6	4,554.1
1991	46.4	11.3	94.8	537.2	1,488.8	323.2	411.9	710.8	18.3	34.6	971.2	530.1	1.3	5,179.9
Total	183.2	71.7	517.5	2105.4	4,764.6	1,686.2	1,125.0	3,569.2	31.0	129.1	2,373.4	2,711.5	14.0	19,281.8
Percent of total payments	1.0	0.4	2.7	10.9	24.7	8.7	5.8	18.5	0.2	0.7	12.3	14.1	0.1	100.0

Source: "Annual Report of the Board of Auditors for the Financial Year 1991," *Official Journal of the European Communities* 330 (December 15, 1992), p. 132 (Greek Edition).

President Delors of a "maximalist" Spanish proposal asking, inter alia, for the setting of a fifth economic resource proportional to the economic capacity of each member state, for a special fund to help implement social cohesion, for a revision of the system of EC's "own resources," and that "structural funds . . . be doubled and be implemented with flexibility."[36]

The Spanish proposal met with strong resistance from Northern members and was not accepted as such. Nevertheless, the results of the solidarity among SECM during the IGC were by no means negligible. They included the following:

—A decision was made to set up, before December 31, 1993, a new Cohesion Fund to provide "a financial contribution to projects in the fields of environment and trans-European networks in the area of transport infrastructure.

—The objective of social and economic cohesion became the subject of a special protocol as well as of specific provisions in the Treaty (articles 130a–e).

—In the protocol a commitment was made both to review the operational effectivenes and size of the structural funds and to satisfy the Spanish demand for correcting "regressive elements existing in the present own resources system."

—Finally a Delors II Plan was announced that will lead to further financial transfers to the poorer regions of the Community.

As already mentioned the field of economic and social cohesion represents the only area in which a solid SECM bloc has operated within the EC. Regarding "co-decision" by the European Parliament—a new provision (article 189b of the Maastricht Treaty) under which in certain cases of disagreement between the Council and the European Parliament the latter will have a veto—the Portuguese had a number of reservations consistent with their preference for the maintenance of the present institutional balance in the Community.[37] In addition satisfaction with the intergovernmental aspects of the Community system and special relations with the United Kingdom led Portugal to take a low-key but negative attitude regarding explicit reference, in the Maastricht Treaty, to a federal goal for Europe.

Ratings concerning SECM cohesion and solidarity in foreign policy, security, and defense-related issues are much more discouraging. Portugal was against majority voting in the CFSP field, but it would consider it for the future provided that the "one country, one vote" rule would apply.[38] Greece's position on this issue, rated "ambivalent" in table 7-4, might have hardened even further against relinquishing the national veto in view of the incoherence of EC policy on the former Yugoslavia and its own vital interests in the region.[39] Spain was also in favor of preserving unanimity in decisionmaking on CFSP but agreed that abstentions should not hinder a decision.[40]

The extension of CFSP to include defense found the SECM even more divided. Spain is the country among the four SECM that has taken the most unequivocal stance in support of a defense dimension for the Community,[41] with Greece—after the conservative victory in the polls in 1990—following at a very close distance.[42]

Portugal, on the other hand, has adopted a view that is very close to the United Kingdom's position that "it is too soon to integrate the WEU into the EC and that NATO should remain as the main defense organization in Europe."[43] Finally Italy, as shown by the Anglo-Italian Declaration on European Security and Defense[44] (October 5, 1991) and its general attitude during the IGC, has great difficulty choosing between the option of "an independent European security pillar and the Atlanticist option."[45]

The Divergence of Security Perceptions

The disparity of the SECM's views on the evolution of a security and defense dimension for the European Union, amply demonstrated during the IGC, is a natural reflection of their diverse historical experiences and contemporary needs and priorities. Since this subject is dealt with at length in other chapters of this volume it suffices here to summarize briefly some of the factors that accentuate this divergence of perceptions and attitudes as well as their implications.

The SECM represent a heterogeneous group of states from the point of view of size, location, security needs, and military capabilities. Their membership in collective defense mechanisms (NATO and, with the exception of Greece, the WEU) founded in order to deter distant "threats from the East" had meager results in stimulating perceptions of a common security and defense identity. As long as the "central front" mentality dominated allied strategic doctrine and military planning, SECM apprehensions over indirect, or even direct, security threats emanating from their adjacent regions—the Mediterranean and the Middle East—would have to be downplayed as marginal or even parochial preoccupations. The absence of institutionalized structures of collective defense capable of addressing such issues further enhanced the already dominant American position exemplified in the bilateral defense and cooperation agreements linking the SECM with the Western superpower.

Those bilateral arrangements, besides their concrete economic and military benefits, were conceived by the smaller SECM as supplementary safety valves elevating their national posture vis-à-vis powerful neighbors like Spain and Turkey, which also retained their own bilateral institutional ties with the United States in the security and defense fields. Certainly Portugal has apprehensions of potential Spanish economic and political domination over the whole Iberian penninsula.[46] However, these are not comparable to Greece's fears, rooted in the 1974 precedent in Cyprus, that her adversary, Turkey, could once more resort to military force as a means of settling bilateral disputes. The weight of the "Turkish threat" for Greece as well as the inadequacy of NATO guarantees to provide an effective deterrent led that country to forewarn its partners in IGC negotiations that it would veto all Maastricht agreements unless it was allowed to join the WEU.[47] The demand was officially justified by reference to the rapidly deteriorating situation in Yugoslavia, but there was little doubt in anybody's mind that Turkey was the true reason for the Greek intransigence.[48] Spain's dispute with Morocco, also a country with special ties to the United States, over the Ceuta and Melilla enclaves (North African territories falling outside both NATO and WEU areas of responsibility) provides additional evidence regarding the insufficiency of existing multilateral security arrangements as well as the importance of America's role as an external balancing actor in SECM conflicts with the TMC.[49]

The short period of time separating the collapse of the bipolar world order and the IGC was not enough to allow the SECM to absorb the new realities and reexamine their policies and commitments. The SECM would be delighted to draw the attention of the rest of the EC to their traditional concerns over economic, demographic, political, religious, and even military developments in the Mediterranean, but they would find it especially hard to agree among themselves on the specific geographic origins of related "threats" and even harder to agree on priorities. It was nevertheless natural for Spain to take the lead in supporting an independent defense option for the European Union. Spain, unlike Italy, was not preoccupied with dilemmas of the "Atlanticist" versus "European" variety, and although large, self-confident, and ambitious, it was apprehensive of its vulnerability to indirect and even direct security challenges from the South and eager to draw Northern EC members behind a collective security defense scheme that would reduce unilateral dependence on the United States. Still, in the aftermath of the Gulf War, challenges from the South have yet to assume proportions that would motivate a joint SECM and possibly EC-wide reaction.

At the same time rapid developments in the Balkans further underlined the peculiarity of the position and security needs of Greece, the eastern Mediterranean member of the SECM group, which saw its immediate environment dramatically reshaped as a result of regime changes in Albania and Bulgaria and the war in the former Yugoslavia. Greek failure to draw the rest of the EC behind a policy that would resist the rapid disintegration of Yugoslavia or to win the endorsement of its position regarding the use of the name "Macedonia" by the Former Yugoslav Republic of Macedonia made Greek policymakers increasingly skeptical over the prospect of transferring sovereign foreign policy prerogatives to a European Union unable or unwilling to understand Balkan realities.[50]

In short the SECM do not have the shared perceptions regarding the inadequacy of current multilateral arrangements to cope with immediate security threats common to the group that would be the basis for an SECM foreign policy and defense identity, which would subsequently merge with broader EC security considerations. Even in cases like those of Greece and to a much lesser extent Spain, in which an SECM does have specific and urgent reasons to explore alternative security arrangements, it will face, as a rule, negative or reserved reactions from EC partners unwilling to entangle themselves in geographically distant disputes that could escalate into armed conflicts.[51]

Concluding Remarks

The preceding analysis sustains the view that indeed the SECM operate as a pressure group in certain areas within the European Union. Their combined efforts have already influenced policies related to economic and social cohesion and the TMC and could prove in the future a decisive factor on decisions concerning enlargement. Nevertheless the two factors that have brought the members of the group closer in the post-bipolar era—the accelerated pace of integration set at Maastricht and the prospect of diverting resources and offering EC partnerships to the new democracies in Eastern Europe—were not strong enough to change traditional SECM attitudes and policies so as to create a united front on the vital issues of the evolution of the Union.

In that respect the SECM appeared trapped in a vicious circle. For the European Union to continue benefiting SECM economies it would have to survive in international competition. But in order to survive it would need to strengthen its internal political and economic cohesion and acquire competences that would allow it to deal collectively and effectively with major foreign policy and security issues. The SECM would certainly like to see an EU properly endowed to redistribute wealth and bridge economic differences between its north and south, and they appreciate the additional security that their membership in a strong European Union implies in connection with challenges from the TMC. Nevertheless they maintain the hope that they might have some or all of those benefits without substantially sacrificing their sovereign prerogatives or changing their traditional policy patterns in multilateral or bilateral commitments regarding security and defense. Even an SECM like Greece, eager to utilize the advantages of taking part in a Union endowed with a CFSP, would hesitate, for example, to loosen its bilateral ties to the United States before such a CFSP had taken shape and proven its effectiveness—an unlikely development should the majority of EC partners, including the major ones, share this attitude. One should add at this point that the forthcoming enlargement of the EU in the direction of the traditionally neutral EFTA members like Austria and Switzerland could add to the problems that the CFSP has encountered owing to lack of substantial SECM support, and, of course, the negative position of the United Kingdon and the other Atlanticists.

Failure of the European Union to make progress in both its economic and political dimensions, including an efficient CFSP, would pose insurmountable obstacles in promoting development and stability both in east-central Europe and south of the Mediterranean. Thus in Edward Mortimer's words Europe could revert "to its prewar status of mutually hostile nation-states"—a prospect that should worry all EU members regardless of wealth or particular national objectives.[52] The SECM have much at stake in a strong and effective European Union. Recent spectacular developments leading to a settlement of the Arab-Israeli conflict pave the way for a more energetic and comprehensive EU policy for the whole Mediterranean. They also present the SECM with an unprecedented opportunity to take the lead in that direction, to revive their own special identity, and, in cooperation with likeminded powers such as France, breathe new life into and open new horizons for the CFSP arrangements of the Maastricht Treaty.

Notes

1. A. de Vasconcelos, "Portugal: A Case for an Open Europe," outline of a paper presented at the conference "The Community, the Member-States and Foreign-Policy: Coming Together or Drifting Apart?" sponsored by the European Policy Units of the European University Institute, Theatre-Badia Fiesolana, July 1–3, 1993.

2. Ian O. Lesser, *Mediterranean Security: New Perspectives and Implications for U.S. Policy* (Santa Monica, Calif.: RAND, 1992), p. 21.

3. A. de Vasconcelos, "The Shaping of a Subregrional Identity" in R. Aliboni, ed., *Southern European Security in the 1990s* (London: Pinter, 1992), pp. 17–18.

4. See M. V. Agostini, "Italy and Its Community Policy," *International Spectator,* vol. 25 (October-December 1990), p. 349.

5. See N. Nugent, "The Deepening and Widening of the European Community: Recent Evolution, Maastricht and Beyond," *Journal of Common Market Studies,* vol. 30 (September 1992), p. 311, and related analysis later in this chapter.

6. L. Guazzone, "The Mediterranean Basin," *International Spectator,* vol. 25 (October-December 1990), p. 305.

7. A. G. Ibanez, "Spain and European Political Union," in F. Laursen and S. Vanhoonacker, eds., *The Intergovernmental Conference on Political Union* (Maastricht, The Netherlands: European Institute of Public Administration/ Martinus Nijhoff, 1992), p. 101.

8. See Lesser, *Mediterranean Security,* p. 50.

9. See R. Aliboni and others, "Three Scenarios for the Future of Europe," *International Spectator,* vol. 26 (January-March 1991), pp. 4–24, especially pp. 21–24.

10. Alan Swinbank and Christopher Ritson, "The Common Agricultural Policy, Customs Unions and the Mediterranean Basin," *Journal of Common Market Studies,* vol. 27 (December 1988), pp. 97–112. See also M. Plummer, "Efficiency Effects of the Accession of Spain and Portugal to the EC," *Journal of Common Market Studies,* vol. 29 (March 1991), pp. 322–23.

11. C. Tsardanides, *The "New" Mediterranean Policy of the European Community and Greece* (Athens: Hellenic Center for European Studies/Papazisis, 1992), p. 25 (in Greek).

12. United Nations Population Fund, *The State of World Population—1993* (New York, 1993), p. 16.

13. Guazzone, "The Mediterranean Basin," p. 305.

14. A. Menon, A. Forster, and W. Wallace, "A Common European Defense?" *Survival* vol. 34, no. 3 (Autumm 1992) pp. 103–04.

15. See in detail Tsardanides, *The "New" Mediterranean Policy,* pp. 42–46, 50, and 62–63.

16. See on this point R. Aliboni, "Southern European Security: Perceptions and Problems," in R. Aliboni, ed., *Southern European Security in the 1990s* (London: Pinter, 1992), pp. 12–13.

17. W. Goldstein, "Europe After Maastricht," *Foreign Affairs,* vol. 71, no. 5 (Winter 1992–93), p. 129.

18. A. Michalski and H. Wallace, *The European Community: The Challenge of Enlargement* (London: Royal Institute of International Affairs, 1992), pp. 7 and 56–57. The quotation is from p. 57.

19. Nugent, "The Deepening and Widening of the European Community," p. 323.

20. Goldstein, "Europe After Maastricht," p. 127.

21. See text in Michalski and Wallace, *The European Community,* appendix 3, pp. 157–67.

22. G. de Michelis, "Reaching out to the East," *Foreign Policy* 79 (Summer 1990), p. 45.

23. Vasconcelos, "The Shaping of a Subregional Identity," pp. 26–27.

24. Michalski and Wallace, *The European Community,* p. 43.

25. Michalski and Wallace, *The European Community,* pp. 113–14, and Nugent, "The Deepening and Widening of the European Community," p. 319.

26. Michalski and Wallace, *The European Community,* p. 56.

27. I. Lesser, "Turkey and the West After the Gulf War," *International Spectator,* vol. 27 (January–March 1992), p. 35. The first and second listed reasons are from Nugent, "The Deepening and Widening of the European Community," p. 323. The remaining ones are from, in order, Vasconelos, "The Shaping of a Subregional Identity," p. 17; Lesser, *Mediterranean Security,* p. 88; and Michalski and Wallace, *The European Community,* p. 10.

28. D. Sezer, "Prospects for Southern European Security: a Turkish perspective," in R. Aliboni, ed., *Southern European Security in the 1990s* (London: Pinter, 1992), pp. 133.

29. E. Mortimer, *European Security After the Cold War,* Adelphi Paper 271 (London: International Institute for Strategic Studies, 1992), p. 61. For the opposite view see Menon and others, "A Common European Defense?" pp. 113, 116.

30. Goldstein, "Europe After Maastricht," p. 128.

31. F. Laursen, "The Maastricht Treaty: A Critical Evaluation," in F. Laursen and S. Vanhoonacker, eds., *The Intergovernmental Conference on Political Union* (Maastricht, The Netherlands: European Institute of Public Administration/ Martinus Nijhoff, 1992), p. 259.

32. D. Constas, "Greek-Foreign Policy Objectives: 1974–1986," in S. Vryonis, ed., *Greece on the Road to Democracy: From the Junta to PASOK 1974–1986* (New York: Caratzas, 1991), p. 50.

33. N. Mousis, *European Community: Institutions and Policies* (Athens: Papazissis, 1991), p. 175.

34. Laursen, "The Maastricht Treaty," p. 257.

35. E. Barbe, "Spain and European Political Cooperation," summary of a paper presented at the conference "The Community, the Member States and Foreign Policy: Coming Together or Drifting Apart?" held at the European University Institute, July 1–3, 1993. Ireland also benefited from Spanish tactics: see C. Wijnbergen, "Ireland and European Political Union," in F. Laursen and S. Vanhoonacker, eds., *The Intergovernmental Conference on Political Union* (Maastricht, The Netherlands: European Institute of Public Administration/ Martinus Nijhoff, 1992), p. 136.

36. Ibanez, "Spain and European Political Union," pp. 108–09.

37. F. X. G. M de Meirelles, "Portugal and European Political Union," in F. Laursen and S. Vanhoonacker, eds., *The Intergovernmental Conference on Political Union* (Maastricht, The Netherlands: European Institute of Public Administration/Martinus Nijhoff, 1992), pp. 183–84. On the position of the other SECM see F. Laursen, S. Vanhoonacker, and R. Wester, "Overview of the Negotiations," in F. Laursen and S. Vanhoonacker, eds., *The Intergovernmental Conference on Polit-*

ical Union (Maastricht, The Netherlands: European Institute of Public Administration/ Martinus Nijhoff, 1992), p. 16.

38. Meirelles, "Portugal and the European Political Union," p. 185.

39. D. Tsakaloyannis, "Small States and Collective Security: The Case of Greece," summary of a paper presented at the conference "The Community, the Member States and Foreign Policy: Coming Together or Drifting Apart? held at the European University Institute, July 1–3, 1993, p. 5.

40. Ibanez, "Spain and European Political Union," p. 105.

41. Ibanez, "Spain and European Political Union," p. 105.

42. A. Hartog, "Greece and European Political Union," in F. Laursen and S. Vanhoonacker, eds. *The Intergovernmental Conference on Political Union* (Maastricht, The Netherlands: European Institute of Public Administration/ Martinus Nijhoff, 1992), p. 94.

43. Meirelles, "Portugal and the European Political Union," pp. 185–86; see also A. de Vasconcelos, "Portugal and European Political Cooperation," *International Spectator,* vol. 26 (April-June 1991), pp. 127–40.

44. France saw the joint declaration as calling into question the French aim of an autonomous European security identity, submitted together with Germany, and reacted very strongly; see E. Martial, "France and European Political Union," in F. Laursen and S. Vanhoonacker, eds., *The Intergovernmental Conference on Political Union* (Maastricht, The Netherlands: European Institute of Public Administration/Martinus Nijhoff, 1992), p. 123.

45. E. Martial, "Italy and European Political Union," in F. Lauersen and S. Vanhoonacker, eds., *The Intergovernmental Conference on Political Union* (Maastricht, The Netherlands: European Institute of Public Administration/ Martinus Nijhoff, 1992), p. 150. For an analysis of the Italian attitude see Lesser, *Mediterranean Security,* pp. 68–69, and Agostini, "Italy and Its Community Policy."

46. See S. Vanhoonacker, "A Critical Issue: From European Political Cooperation to a Common Foreign and Security Policy," in F. Laursen and S. Vanhoonacker, eds., *The Intergovernmental Conference on Political Union* (Maastricht, The Netherlands: European Institute of Public Administration/Martinus Nijhoff, 1992), p. 28. Also see Meirelles, "Portugal and the European Political Union," p. 179; and Lesser, *Mediterranean Security,* p. 31: "Portugal's traditional wariness of Spain continues to make itself felt in the political, economic and cultural realms, despite recent initiatives aimed at improving bilateral ties. It also exerts identifiable, if waning, influence on strategic thought. In particular, the continental dimension of Portuguese defence planning has long incorporated what some observers have termed the 'theory of the Spanish danger,' reflected in the Portuguese military structure adopted in the 1980s."

47. See Hartog, "Greece and European Political Union," p. 94, and Laursen and others, "Overview of the Negotiations," p. 20.

48. See note 29 and related text.

49. Lesser, *Mediterranean Security,* pp. 41–42.

50. See also note 39 and related text.

51. See note 29 for the Greek experience, and E. Regelsberger, "Spain and the European Political Cooperation—No Enfant Terrible," *International Spectator,* vol. 24 (April-June 1989), p. 123.

52. Mortimer, "European Security After the Cold War," p. 68.

EIGHT

Southern European Countries and European Defense

Fernando Rodrigo

MY PURPOSE is to explore whether there is something separate and differentiated enough within the North Atlantic Treaty Organization (NATO) or within the European Community (EC) to justify speaking about a Southern European dimension in European security policy. Or are we are dealing with an artificial topic that many of us have contributed to creating and expanding during the last few years?[1]

A passage from Philippe Schmitter's introduction to *Transitions from Authoritarian Rule: Southern Europe* could be useful as the beginning of our reflection:

> The countries on the northern rim of the Mediterranean have long been the "stepchildren" of the study of Western European politics and society. With the notable exception of Italy (and then only since its democratization after World War II), they have been routinely placed outside the mainstream of inquiry and generalization about political developments in that part of the world. Scholars shied away from studying them. Textbooks simply ignored their existence. Classification systems assigned them the status of "exceptions," or simply placed them in the ignominious category of "other." . . . The conviction grew that they somehow did not belong in Western Europe. Spain and Portugal were placed on the other side of the Pyrenees, "in Africa." Greece, when it fell to the despotism of the colonels, became Balkan. Turkey, despite all its efforts at Western secularization and modernization, was exiled to the Middle East.[2]

What those countries had in common was their shared marginality in relation to the mainstream of Western politics, as a result of their slow pace of economic development, the singularities of their political systems, and their dubious position at the end of World War II.

But are these negative characteristics, which could have identified them as a group in the early 1980s, still alive and important today? All those countries, after all, have established democratic political systems, have joined the EC, and have gone through a period of impressive economic growth. Or, as a result of the "normalization" of their internal and external policies, have these countries chosen different paths, in accordance with their different interests and values?

From the Southern Region of NATO to Southern Europe

How has Southern Europe evolved from being simply a military region peripheral to Europe?

When NATO Is Not Enough

If there was a Southern Region during the 1960s and 1970s, it existed only in strategic terms and it included with Italy all the backward countries on the northern shore of the Mediterranean (Portugal, Spain, Greece, and Turkey) that were integrated into the West because of their links with the "strategic federator," the United States.[3]

Strategically speaking, however, there was not an autonomous Southern Region. It existed only because of its importance for the defense of the central front, which was the raison d'être of NATO. In fact, the Southern Region consisted of four separate military theaters: Italy, Greece and western Turkey, eastern Turkey, and the Mediterranean Sea.[4]

If these countries belonging to the Southern Region had something in common, it was the perception that their security concerns were not fully met by NATO and in some cases were even in conflict with the interests of the most important country in NATO, the United States. But this perception was normally the consequence of a long process with different origins in each country.

In Greece, the origin of the conflict with NATO was the support given by the United States to the military dictatorship at the end of the 1960s and the lack of support given by the United States and other NATO members to Greece in its conflict with Turkey over Cyprus in 1974. The Greeks discovered that more than twenty years of alignment with the Western powers and dependence on the United States had not given them the capacity of defending their territory against external threats.[5]

That discovery led to the withdrawal of Greece from the integrated military structure of NATO and the termination of the 1973 home-porting agreement with the United States. At the same time Greece began to develop an autonomous security policy and made defense from the perceived threat from the east, Turkey, the focal point of its military organization. This crisis kept Greece alienated from NATO and the United States during the second half of the 1970s. The victory of the Panhellenic Socialist Movement party in the 1980 general elections prevented the normalization of these issues during the 1980s as well.[6]

In Portugal the relationship with NATO had also been mainly a bilateral, Luso-American affair. As Thomas C. Bruneau has pointed out, "Despite joining NATO as a charter member in 1949, the main contribution of Portugal in the Alliance was the provision of facilities on the mainland and access to bases and other facilities in the Azores by the United States in accordance with the terms of a bilateral agreement first signed in 1951."[7]

This very limited involvement in NATO virtually disappeared with the outbreak of colonial conflicts in 1961, and Portugal remained only a nominal NATO member until these colonial wars came to an end as a consequence of the 1974 revolution.

The conflicts that had existed between Premier Antonio de Oliveira Salazar and the United States government because of the colonial wars, and the role that the United States played during the 1974 revolution and afterward, produced a period of exceptionally good relations between the two countries but failed to bring about a change in the bilateral nature of the relationship.

During the 1980s the "special" relationship with the United States deteriorated as democratic Portugal sought a broader relationship with the United States, while the United States remained very comfortable with the status quo. That situation led Portuguese governments to adopt a more pluralistic approach in their foreign and defense policies, relying more on multilateral frameworks such as NATO, the EC, and the Western European Union (WEU) and emphasizing the importance of independent policies in some areas of the world of special relevance for Portugal, like Brazil, Angola and Mozambique, and the Middle East. Nevertheless Atlanticism has remained one of Portugal's defining characteristics.[8]

Spain was linked to Western security only through the defense agreements signed in 1953 with the United States, and its main contribution, as in the case of Portugal, was to provide facilities for the U.S. armed forces. This connection between the regime of Francisco Franco and the United

States was a liability for the United States when Franco died in 1975. Nevertheless all the political forces, even the Communist Party, understood that in order to have a peaceful change of regime, Spain had to maintain the status quo in this respect. Therefore, the government of Juan Carlos I signed a treaty of friendship and defense with the United States in September 1976 that was mostly an extension of the previous one.

But when this treaty had to be renegotiated in 1981, the Spanish government of the Unión de Centro Democrático thought that the time had come to alter the bilateral relationship and to establish one that was more balanced. This reequilibration would only be possible, in the government's view, if the relationship with the United States were placed within a multilateral framework. Spain applied for NATO membership in 1981 and became a member in May 1982, at the same time that a new and more balanced defense agreement was signed with the United States.

This process of normalization of Spanish security policy was interrupted because of the reaction of the socialists and communists, who perceived that step as a serious alteration of the status quo and as a threat to the security of Spain, which had no interests in the East-West conflict. These positions, after a momentous campaign, obtained the favor of public opinion and were an important element in the overwhelming victory of the Partido Socialista Obrera Español (PSOE) in October 1982.

When the PSOE arrived in government, Felipe González began to understand the importance of maintaining Spain within the same security framework as the other Western countries and designed a strategy to ensure Spanish membership in NATO in exchange for nonmilitary integration into the Alliance and the withdrawal of important U.S. military forces from Spain.[9]

This strategy allowed González to win a referendum on NATO membership in 1986 and led to a period of crisis in the relationship with the United States. Finally in January 1988 the United States government agreed to withdraw the 401st Tactical Fighter Wing from Torrejon near Madrid, and at the end of 1988 a new defense agreement with the United States was signed.[10]

The case of Italy is different from those of Greece and Spain and closer to that of Portugal, because in Italy too the relationship with the United States and membership in NATO are key elements of foreign and security policy that command wide support among political elites and the public at large. NATO membership was an important element of Italy's international legitimacy during the 1940s and 1950s, and support for U.S. military requirements within and outside the Alliance was taken for granted.

In the 1950's, the Mediterranean was considered an "American lake." The "threat from the south" had not yet entered NATO terminology. . . . No military requirements other than those deriving from the Alliance's operational planning were envisaged . . . and no scenarios of bilateral crisis outside the Atlantic context were imaginable. . . .

It is even arguable that up until about 1979, Italy did not really have its own military policy but merely copied that of NATO.[11]

External developments like the Camp David agreements and Israel's invasion of Lebanon led Italy in the 1980s to develop a more active and independent policy in the Middle East and to elaborate an autonomous approach toward those areas of the Mediterranean that potentially presented risks for Italian security and were not covered by NATO planning.[12]

This autonomous course produced some important crises between Italy and the United States, as was shown during the U.S. management of the hijacking of the *Achille Lauro* in 1985 and the air raid on Libya in April 1986. These incidents led to serious conflict with the United States government and raised questions about its use of the NATO bases on Italian territory for "out-of-area" purposes without obtaining the prior authorization of the Italian government.

The Europeanization of the South

Nevertheless this common feeling of dissatisfaction with the security arrangements established during the cold war was not enough to produce a sense of shared identity among the countries of Southern Europe. Only the integration of these countries into the European Community during the 1980s meant a step in that direction. EC membership meant for them, more than an opportunity for building up a Southern European caucus, the possibility of formulating a more autonomous and pluralistic foreign and defense policy, particularly through their participation in European Political Cooperation (EPC), which was strengthened in 1987 thanks to the Single European Act.

Entry into the EC became the main objective of the foreign policy of these countries after their successful return to a democratic system of government during the 1970s. Greece appllied for membership in 1975 and became an EC member in 1981. Portugal and Spain applied in 1977 and became members in 1986. Entry into the EC provided them with a unique framework for developing a more autonomous approach to foreign policy without creating many problems with the United States, because the EC was not competent in the security and defense areas. They became less dependent on the United States in economic and political terms and obtained new sources of information as well as new foreign policy capabilities thanks to their participation in the EPC, without affecting their security compromises with NATO and the United States.

Turkey suffered during the 1970s from problems similar to those experienced by other countries in the south of Europe. The breakdown of its democratic regime in 1980 as well as its conflict with Greece interrupted its rapprochement with the EC, always problematic for cultural and economic reasons.[13] Therefore Turkey could not develop a new international identity during the 1980s and it remained in the "Southern Region," while the other countries transformed themselves into "Southern Europe." As Duygu Sezer has put it, "in many ways Turkey is south, whereas the rest of Southern Europe is north."[14]

Back to the Periphery?

The almost simultaneous arrival in the EC of Greece, Spain, and Portugal tilted the balance of the Community toward the Mediterranean but was not enough to create a Southern European caucus within the EC, at least vis-à-vis foreign and defense policies. The creation of this group was a reaction to the events in central and Eastern Europe in 1989 and particularly the fall of the Berlin Wall in November of that year.

The negotiations that led to the signing in Moscow in September 1990 of the treaty that gave the green light to the unification of Germany produced an earthquake that shook all the countries in the EC. The effect of this earthquake in the Southern European countries of the EC, particularly those situated in the western corner, was especially intense, arousing fears that an EC that turned toward its eastern borders could forget about its southern dimension.

Thus all the Southern European countries supported the idea of deepening the Community before any enlargement could take place, although the idea of convening an Intergovernmental Conference on Political Union divided the Southern caucus, with Portugal remaining in the reluctant camp with Great Britain and Ireland.[15]

These policies were intended to prevent the isolation of the Southern European countries from the changes occurring inside and outside the EC. But they did not address the question of the future of EC relations with the non-EC Mediterranean countries, which was one of the main concerns of Portugal, Spain, Italy, and Greece.

This concern lead to a new activism on the part of these countries vis-à-vis the countries of the southern shore of the Mediterranean that contributed decisively to creating a sense of shared identity and produced the perception in the other EC countries that a Southern European caucus existed, at least with reference to Mediterranean affairs.[16]

Southern Europe and the Debate over European Security

Nevertheless the debate over a Common Foreign and Security Policy (CFSP) that was a consequence of the Intergovernmental Conference on Political Union very soon jeopardized the illusion of the existence of Southern Europe as a group that pursued similar policies within the EC.

The Southern countries were members of an EC that only painfully coordinated the foreign policies of its members but lacked the competences to formulate and implement a common foreign policy and to deal with the military aspects of security. The only European institution with competence for dealing with defense matters, the WEU, had no formal connection with the EC and possessed no operational capacity of its own. Therefore the interest of Portugal, Spain, and Greece in membership in WEU was more for the sake of attaining another symbol of their new European identity than because they were looking for an alternative to the existing defense arrangements.[17]

But all this changed with the prospect of establishing a European Union (EU) with a more vigorous international dimension. The debate soon turned around the idea of transforming the intergovernmental mechanisms of the EPC into an element of the EC process and the abolition of restrictions on the examination of security problems.

One of the first contributions to this debate came from Greece and presented an important change in the way Greece approached the Community. It was a consequence of the existence of a new government in Greece after the April 1990 general elections that resulted in Constantine Mitsotakis's replacing Andreas Papandreou, who had remained in office for ten years, as prime minister. Only one month after taking office, the Mitsotakis government released an important memorandum on "Progress Towards Political Union," in which it stressed that "application of the principle of subsidiarity leads to the conclusion that external policy is one of the areas where joint action is more effective than action by each individual Member State."[18]

This view, although it did not imply the incorporation of the EPC into the EC framework, was very far from the traditional mistrust of the Papandreou governments toward the EPC on the ground that it implied a threat to Greek sovereignty in foreign affairs.[19]

The Gulf War

The invasion of Kuwait on August 2, 1990, had a direct impact on the debate over a CFSP. In the first months of the conflict the performance of the EC and the WEU was certainly impressive. The foreign affairs ministers of the Twelve, after several meetings of the EPC, decided to convene on August 21 a ministerial meeting of the WEU, to which the EC countries that were not members of the WEU (Ireland, Denmark, and Greece), plus Turkey, were invited.

This WEU ministerial meeting, because of the EPC's lack of competence in military matters, decided to coordinate the naval forces sent by member countries in order to apply the embargo ordered by the Security Council. Therefore on August 27, for the first time in the recent history of the organization, the chiefs of staff of the WEU countries met to draft a document on coordination, and on August 31 a permanent unit was established in Paris with coordination activities to take plce on the spot. Thanks to this umbrella provided for the WEU, Portugal, Spain, and Greece participated in the Gulf coalition.

As a consequence of this practical example of a CFSP, many declarations were made in favor of the development of an independent European security and defense structure within the future European Union. Yet the situation changed when the crisis with Iraq became an open military conflict and the problems that the Twelve had in developing an independent diplomatic course became evident. The important role played by the United States and the divisions between Britain and France cooled the enthusiasm of many countries for an independent defense policy for the future EU.[20]

The Role of the WEU

In the aftermath of the Gulf War the debate centered around the role that the WEU should play in the security dimension of the Union. Italy, which then held the presidency of the EC, expressed, as early as September 18, 1990, its will "to transfer to the Union all the competences presently being exercised by [the] WEU."[21]

Britain led the countries that were against the WEU's being swallowed up by the future EU and that stressed the importance of the WEU as a bridge between the Union and NATO.

The Community was once more divided between Europeanists and Atlanticists, and Southern European countries were equally divided, over a spectrum that ran from the more Europeanist views of Spain and Greece to those of Portugal, which were more supportive of the Atlantic perspective:

> Although the Portuguese government appreciates that the need for an agreed European security policy was apparent during the Gulf crisis and regards it as a necessity, the main lesson it tends to take from these events is that its view of the fundamental role of the United States in European and out-of-area security was fully vindicated, and that one must stress the eminently national character of defence issues.[22]

Italy finally became a middleman between both options with the Anglo-Italian Declaration on European Security of October 1991. This foreshadowed the compromise reached in Maastricht, which was to develop a CFSP as an intergovernmental process with decisions made by consensus and to maintain the WEU as a bridge between NATO and the EU.

Only with the election of Bill Clinton as president of the United States were American reservations regarding a European foreign and security policy dropped. The quarrel among European members of NATO, and particularly among the Southern European members, has come to an end. In this respect the Declaration of the Heads of State and Government participating in the NATO summit of January 1994 finally settled the dispute by stating the following:

> We give our full support to the development of a European Security and Defence Identity which, as called for in the Maastricht Treaty, in the longer term perspective of a common defence policy within the European Union, might in time lead to a common defence compatible with that of the Atlantic Alliance. . . .
>
> We support strengthening the European pillar of the Alliance through the Western European Union, which is being developed as the defence component of the European Union. . . .
>
> We therefore stand ready to make collective assets of the Alliance available, on the basis of consultations in the North Atlantic Council, for WEU operations undertaken by the European Allies in pursuit of their Common Foreign and Security Policy.[23]

The End of the Cold War

Defense policies of the Southern European countries changed fundamentally during the 1990s as a consequence of the end of the cold war, not
because of the debate about the future of European security. For these
countries the end of the cold war meant the end of politico-ideological
limits to their foreign policies and therefore allowed them to develop a more
active and independent foreign policy.

As noted earlier in this chapter, if these countries of the Southern Region
had something in common, it was the perception that their security concerns
along the North-South divide of the Mediterranean were not met either by
NATO or by the EC. Thus in the late 1980s and early 1990s they have used
their new freedom of action to develop a foreign and security policy more
oriented toward meeting the risks from the south, not only in military terms
but also in political and economic terms.

Nevertheless the new leverage in foreign policy has had very different
consequences for the Southern European countries, because some of them
(like Greece and Turkey) have had to face a hostile international environment, first with the Gulf War and after that with the war in Yugoslavia, as
well as with the new situations in the Caucasus and in the Middle East. Not
only are they divided from the other European countries over the Balkans,
but Turkey is confronting a whole new world:

> Within a few years of Gorbachev's coming to power, Turkey's geopolitical environ-
> ment began to change in three out of four directions of the compass. To the north-
> west, truly independent Balkan states have emerged. . . . Directly to the north, Turkey
> has an opportunity for direct relations by sea with a newly independent Ukraine and
> a distinct new Russian entity. To the northeast, three independent states have ap-
> peared on the scene in the Caucasus with whom Turkey has already established
> direct relations. Further to the east, five independent Muslim states have emerged in
> former Soviet Central Asia. . . .
>
> Even to Turkey's south, while no new states have yet emerged, a far more
> difficult situation has arisen in the Persian Gulf with the Gulf War. . . . And an
> Arab-Israeli peace process also may open possibilities of new relations between
> Turkey and the Arab world.
>
> Turkey is thus surrounded by new opportunities and potential new problems.[24]

It is possible to see the different effects of the end of the cold war in the
Southern European countries by examining table 8-1, which is based on
figures from the International Institute for Strategic Studies publication *The
Military Balance*. Although all of them are seeking to reduce the weight of

Table 8-1. *Evolution of Southern European Defense Expenditures as Percent of Gross Domestic Product*

Country	1985	1991	1992
Spain	2.4	1.7	1.7
Italy	2.3	2.1	2.0
Portugal	3.1	3.2	2.9
Turkey	4.5	5.1	4.7
Greece	7.0	5.4	5.6

Source: International Institute for Strategic Studies, *The Military Balance 1993–1994* (London, 1993).

defense expenditure in relation to their gross domestic production, Greece and Turkey continued to devote a large percentage of their national income to defense.

However, for Portugal, Spain, and Italy the overall importance of military force declined in the new international environment. These countries were more ready to use military force in a limited way in a multilateral framework like the United Nations or the Western European Union than they had been before for collective defense within NATO, as the participation of Spain and Portugal in the embargo against Iraq clearly shows.[25]

In any case NATO has also developed a new strategic concept (approved at the meeting of the Atlantic Council held in Rome in November 1991) that puts more emphasis on the economic, social, and environmental elements of defense, and a new structure of forces that stresses the importance of rapid deployment rather than of availability of large numbers of troops.

All these factors have had a great influence on the missions, size, arms procurement, and training of armed forces, and indirectly on conscription. Public debates over how to combine the famous peace dividend with the reorganization of the armed forces have taken place in all these Southern European countries.

Portugal

As Alvaro Vasconcelos has pointed out, "The end of the cold war, the disappearance of a common threat and its substitution by a myriad of threats and challenges, the uncertainties about the US presence in continental Europe, and the efforts undertaken to bring about the existence of a European Defense Identity, have undermined the basic pillars and the widespread consensus on which Portugal's Defense and Security policy was founded."[26]

Thus in recent years a profound revision of Portuguese security and military policies has begun to take place, as the approval of a new Strategic Concept of National Defense by Parliament in 1993 reveals. In the new strategic concept the Portuguese government takes account of the new strategic challenges and for the first time acknowledges the effects of Portugal's membership in the European Community and the Western European Union on its security policy. It considers as objectives of national defense not only the preservation of the Atlantic links and Portugal's contribution to the new definition of NATO but also the participation in the process of European integration, including the security and defense aspects.

The strategic concept stresses the importance of the armed forces as a tool of Portuguese foreign policy and attaches great importance to the participation of Portugal in multilateral operations far from its borders in the context of NATO, the WEU, or the UN. Special importance is also given to the Mediterranean dimension of Portuguese foreign and security policy and particularly to the relationship with Morocco and other Maghreb countries.

The revision of the Portuguese security policy has not been only conceptual; it also affects the whole of the armed forces. In 1993 Parliament approved a law that provides funds for military acquisitions until 1997. The law is an important step in the process of modernization of the armed forces; the number of military personnel will be cut almost by half, being reduced in the next three years from 65,000 to 35,000, and the period of military service has already been reduced to only four months of conscription. This law is a turning point in the evolution of Portuguese military policy because the funds approved will be provided by the state budget and not from the economic compensation provided by the United States under its base agreement with Portugal.

Spain

The changes in the international environment resulted in the approval in 1992 of a new "Directiva de Defensa Nacional" (DDN) by the Spanish prime minister and of a new "Directiva de Defensa Militar" (DDM) by the minister of defense. These are the main documents establishing the guidelines for developing defense and military policies.

The new DDN is especially illustrative of the changes that have taken place in Spain's defense policy since the referendum on NATO membership held in 1986, the year in which the previous DDN was approved. At that time the almost exclusive concern of the Spanish armed forces was the defense of Spain's "area of strategic interest," which meant the Spanish side of the Iberian Peninsula and the Balearic and Canary islands. This was also understood to be the main contribution of Spain to the common defense under NATO.

The new DDN explains that the security of Spain is not only related to the defense of territory; it speaks also of the importance for Spain of the European strategic landscape and of other world crises that could affect its security.[27] This statement reflects the experience of the Gulf War, when Spain participated in the enforcement of the embargo on Iraq ordered by the Security Council, and also of the numerous peacekeeping operations in which Spain has taken part in Central America, Angola, Mozambique, Namibia, and Yugoslavia under UN mandates. As a consequence of this international experience the Spanish government decided in January 1992 to create a Rapid Reaction Force under the Army's chief of staff, to be used for national emergencies but also to be deployed as part of multinational contingents in the context of NATO, WEU, or UN operations.

The DDM has approved a number of extraordinary measures with the aim of adapting the structure and deployment of the armed forces to the new international environment, particularly the decision to reduce the size of the armed forces to 180,000 from the 227,096 approved in 1991.[28] The debate over changes in conscription policy reached Parliament, where all the political parties agreed to develop a new model of the armed forces, to be composed half of professional soldiers and half of conscripts.

Italy

In Italy the London NATO Declaration of July 1990 was the beginning of an effort to develop a new defense model, which was presented by the defense minister, Virginio Rognoni, to Parliament in November 1991, after some delay resulting from disagreement among the chiefs of staff of the different services. The new model pointed out the disappearance of the threat from the North and East with the dissolution of the Warsaw Pact, the Soviet Union, and Yugoslavia and the growing importance of the risks from the South. The army has accordingly already eliminated a quarter of its units and changed its structure to gain flexibility as well as capacity for rapid deployment for national as well international emergencies.[29]

The defense budget has been frozen at the level of 1990 (although the new model required an increase of 27 percent in real terms), and the size of the armed forces is to be reduced from 360,000 to 287,000. The period of military service has been reduced to ten months from twelve; at the same time a target of 45,000 professional soldiers has been set.[30] Italy has not participated directly in peacekeeping operations in the former Yugoslavia because of its proximity, but since the early 1980s it has frequently participated in this kind of multinational operation, and in recent years it has been present in Lebanon, Iran and Iraq, Mozambique, Kurdistan, and elsewhere.

Conclusions

The reactions to the Gulf War as well as the debate over a Common Foreign and Security Policy have shown us that it is not easy to speak of a common perception among Portugal, Spain, Italy, and Greece regarding European security. In fact there are many elements of conflict among the Southern European countries on this question.

However, the Southern European countries have in recent years been very active in promoting forums for emphasizing their common concerns with respect to the Mediterranean aspects of European security. At the moment this approach is stalled because of unfavorable developments in the Maghreb, the Balkans, and the Middle East, and it is very unlikely that the four Southern European countries will succeed in the near future in building a framework capable of addressing so many different concerns.

Nevertheless they will remain concerned about events in the Southern Rim of the Mediterranean because important challenges could come from there in the years to come. However, a clear distinction should be drawn between the countries of the western Mediterranean, which do not now have any real conflict with any Maghreb country, and Greece and Turkey, which not only have historical conflicts with each other but also are suffering from the spillover effects of the wars in the Balkans and the Caucasus.

Notes

1. See Roberto Aliboni, ed., *Southern European Security in the 1990s* (London: Pinter, 1992); John Chipman, ed., *NATO's Southern Allies: Internal and External Challenges* (London: Routledge, 1988); Ian O. Lesser, *Mediterrranean Security: New Perspectives and Implications for U.S. Policy* (Santa Monica, Calif.: RAND, 1992).

2. Philippe C. Schmitter, "An Introduction to Southern European Transitions from Authoritarian Rule: Italy, Greece, Portugal, Spain, and Turkey," in Guillermo O'Donnell, Philippe C. Schmitter, and Laurence Whitehead, eds., *Transitions from Authoritarian Rule: Southern Europe*, (Johns Hopkins University Press, 1986), p. 3.

3. Alvaro Vasconcelos, "The Shaping of a Subregional Identity," in Aliboni, ed., *Southern European Security in the 1990s*, p. 19.

4. John Chipman, "NATO and the Security Problems of the Southern Region: From the Azores to Ardaban," in Chipman, ed., *NATO's Southern Allies*, p. 38.

5. See Ellen Laipson, "U.S. Policy Towards Greece and Turkey since 1974," and Athanasios Platias, "Greece's Strategic Doctrine: In Search of Autonomy and Deterrence," in Dimitri Constas, ed., *The Greek-Turkish Conflict in the 1990s: Domestic and External Influences* (London: Macmillan, 1991), pp. 164–82 and 91–108.

6. See Thanos Veremis, "Greece and NATO: Continuity and Change," in Chipman, ed., *NATO's Southern Allies*, pp. 236–86.

7. "Defense Modernization and the Armed Forces in Portugal," Naval Postgraduate School, 1992.

8. Alvaro Vasconcelos, "Reorganization of Portuguese/US Security Relations," in José Calvet de Magalhaes, Alvaro Vasconcelos, and Joaquim Ramos Silva, eds., *Portugal: An Atlantic Paradox* (Lisbon: Institute for Strategic and International Studies), 1990, p. 51–68.

9. See Angel Viñas, "Spain and NATO; Internal Debate and External Challenges," in Chipman, ed., *NATO's Southern Allies*, 1988, pp. 140–94..

10. Fernando Rodrigo, "End of the reluctant partner: Spain and Western Security in the 1990s," in Aliboni, ed., *Southern European Security in the 1990s*, pp. 99–116.

11. Maurizio Cremasco, "Italy: A New Role in the Mediterranean?" in Chipman, ed., *NATO's Southern Allies*, pp. 199–200.

12. Ettore Greco and Laura Guazzone, "Continuity and Change in Italy's Security Policy," in Aliboni, ed., *Southern European Security in the 1990s*, p. 69–85.

13. See Ali Karaosmanoglu, "Turkey and the Southern Flank: Domestic and External Contexts," in Chipman, ed., *NATO's Southern Allies*, p. 287–353; Constantine Stephanou and Charalambos Tsardanides, "The EC Factor in the Greece-Turkey-Cyprus Triangle," in Constas, ed., *The Greek Turkish Conflict in the 1990s*, pp. 207–30; Ilkay Sunar and Sabri Sayari, "Democracy in Turkey: Problems and Prospects," in O'Donnell, Schmitter, and Whitehead, eds., *Transitions from Authoritarian Rule: Southern Europe*, pp. 165–86.

14. Duygu Bazoglu Sezer, "Prospects for Southern European Security: a Turkish perspective," in Aliboni, ed., *Southern Europe: Security in the 1990s*, p. 133.

15. See Finn Laursen, Sophie Vanhoonacker, and Robert Wester, "Overview of the Negotiations," in Finn Laursen and Sophie Vanhoonacker, eds., *The Intergovernmental Conference on Political Union* (Maastricht, The Netherlands: European Institute of Public Administration/Martinus Nijhoff, 1992), p. 16.

16. Esther Barbé, "España y el Mediterraneo en el Nuevo Equilibrio Europeo," in *Annuario Internacional CIDOB 1990* (Barcelona: Fundació CIDOB, 1991), pp. 75–82.

17. Portugal and Spain became full members of the WEU in March 1990; they had taken part in WEU activities since November 1988.

18. See the Greek memorandum, "Contribution to the Discussions on Progress Towards Political Union," in Finn Lauersen and Sophie Vanhoonacher, eds., *The Intergovernmental Conference on Political Union* (Maastricht, The Netherlands: European Institute of Public Administration/Martinus Nijhoff, 1992), p. 281.

19. Arthur den Hartog, "Greece and European Political Union," in Finn Lauersen and Sophie Vanhoonacker, eds., *The Intergovernmental Conference on Political Union* (Maastricht, The Netherlands: European Institute of Public Administration/Martinus Nijhoff, 1992), pp. 90–93.

20. Laura Guazzone, "Italy in the Gulf Crisis," in Nicole Gnesotto and John Roper, eds., *Western Europe and the Gulf* (Paris: Institute for Security Studies of the Western European Union, 1991), pp. 71–87.

21. See the Italian proposal, "Common Foreign and Security Policy" in Finn Lauersen and Sophie Vanhoonacker, eds., *The Intergovernmental Conference on Political Union* (Maastricht, The Netherlands: European Institute of Public Administration/Martinus Nijhoff, 1992), p. 292.

22. Alvaro Vasconcelos, "Portugal, the Gulf Crisis, and the WEU," in Nicole Gnesotto and John Roper, eds., *Western Europe and the Gulf* (Paris: Institute for Security Studies of the Western European Union, 1991), p. 121.

23. Declaration of the heads of state and government participating in the meeting of the North Atlantic Council held at NATO Headquarters, Brussels, January 10–11, 1994, *Survival*, vol. 36, no. 1 (Spring 1994), p. 163

24. Graham E. Fuller, "Turkey's New Eastern Orientation," in *Turkey's New Geopolitics: From the Balkans to Western China*, ed. Graham E. Fuller and Ian O. Lesser (Boulder, Colo.: Westview Press, 1993), 37.

25. Rodrigo, "The End of the Reluctant Partner," in Aliboni, ed., *Southern European Security in the 1990s*, pp. 99–116.

26. Alvaro Vasconcelos, "Portugese Security Policy: The Euro-Atlantic Dilemma," Lisbon, 1994.

27. *Las Fuerzas Armadas Españolas Hoy* (Madrid: Ministerio de Defensa, 1993).

28. *Memoria de la IV Legislatura* (Madrid: Ministerio de Defensa, 1993).

29. Virgilio Ilari, "La politica militare italiana," in Istituto Affair Internazionali, *L'Italia nella politica internazionale, Anno dicianovesimo, 1990–1991* (Milan: Franco Angeli, 1993), pp. 253–75.

30. Roberto Ilari, "La politica militare italiana," in Istituto Affari Internazionali, *L'Italia nella politica internazionale, Anno ventesimo, edizione 1993* (Rome: SIPI, 1993), pp. 203–29.

Part Three

SOUTHERN EUROPEAN RELATIONS WITH THE UNITED STATES

NINE

Southern Europe
and the United States:
The Community Approach

Roberto Aliboni

IN EURO-ATLANTIC GEOPOLITICS, Southern Europe comprises the rim of countries lying on the southern flank of the Atlantic Alliance, from Portugal to Greece and Turkey. During the cold war—to which the concept of Southern Europe is very much linked—Southern European foreign and security policies were shaped by three factors: national interests, the Atlantic Alliance, and the European Community. The Community, although for different reasons and in varying conditions, has played a unique role in working out new democratic institutions and contributing to economic development in all the Southern European countries. Assuming that changes presently arising from the end of the cold war are bringing about new and different options for Southern Europe, what will be the weight and merit of continued membership in the Community (newly renamed the European Union)? The relevance of a Community approach to Southern Europe is the subject of this chapter.

Three arguments will be presented: a general interpretation of the international role of Southern Europe; an examination of challenges arising in the regional areas close to Southern European countries; and a discussion of Southern Europe's Community approach and its implications for transatlantic relations and the United States.

The Southern European Role: Centrality and Marginality

Southern Europe's participation in the Euro-Atlantic institutional network proved very beneficial to the countries belonging to the area. As a result of their Euro-Atlantic integration, the Southern European countries have been able to develop economically and to mature as viable democracies. Still their political and economic weaknesses continued to characterize their participation in the life of the Euro-Atlantic alliances.

Their marginality has been stressed by all analyses devoted to Southern Europe.[1] They suggest that despite remarkable growth and modernization, major structural weaknesses and imbalances have persisted in these countries, relegating them to a marginal role on the international stage. But this marginality is relative and differs depending on whether it is considered from the perspective of the North Atlantic Treaty Organization (NATO) or that of the Community.

Within the framework of NATO the role of the Southern European countries during the cold war can be considered both marginal and central. Their more or less peripheral location with respect to the main threat emanating from the communist bloc (away from the central front) entailed a certain distance from the political center of the Alliance as well. On the other hand, although they were militarily and politically marginal within the circle of the Alliance, the Southern European countries were geographically central with respect to the regions south of the Mediterranean. In other words Southern Europe was marginal with respect to the global dimension of the Alliance, but central from a geopolitical point of view.

This centrality had a dual dimension: within the Alliance, with respect to Southern Europe's role as NATO's southern flank, and outside the Alliance, with respect to relations with the regional countries not included in the Alliance's jurisdiction. This has always led to overlapping between "area" and "out-of-area" roles and ambiguities in the Southern European countries' relations with the United States, depending on whether the latter wore its NATO or its national hat.

Political marginality pertained more to the Atlantic circle than to the European one. Within the Community, there is no doubt that the Southern European countries have gained significant political weight and enjoyed a substantial role despite their relative economic weakness and the centrality of the Paris-Bonn axis. Their membership in the Community helped the Southern European countries to perform a much more significant international role than they would otherwise have had individually.

One consequence that is relevant here is that the solidarity extended by the Community has given the Southern European countries the possibility of compensating for their marginality within the Atlantic Alliance. In particular European solidarity eased the management of contradictions arising from the bilateral and multilateral dimensions (that is, centrality versus marginality) of the security relationship between the Southern European countries and the United States at the southern fringe of the Alliance. In a broad sense the existence of European solidarity made it easier for Southern Europe (and, broadly speaking, for all the European members of the Atlantic Alliance) to resist recurrent pressures from the United States for NATO to get involved in "out-of-area" operations. In particular controversies stemming from Mediterranean and Middle Eastern crises, in which the United States acted as a global power enforcing its national security goals from military bases located in Southern Europe, were also made more manageable by the existence of this Community solidarity.

It must be pointed out that during the successive U.S. interventions in the Mediterranean and the Middle East that punctuated the 1980s, Community solidarity was manifested, but subject to the limits of the so-called European Political Cooperation (EPC), an intergovernmental diplomatic cooperation empowered to do little more than make declarations. Unless the spirit of the 1991 Maastricht Treaty is fully enforced, the Community is not endowed with substantive instruments of foreign and security policy. Thus, as important as Community solidarity may have been up to the end of the 1980s, it has proved limited. As a result the EPC was able to attenuate, but not to eliminate, the situation of marginality and centrality shared by the Southern European countries on the southern rim of the Alliance's territory.

As limited as its political backing might have been, in the cold war international context the Community approach did manage to alleviate Southern Europe's predicament in two ways. First, within the European Community itself the Community approach gave Southern Europe a political weight and an economic support that would otherwise have been very difficult to achieve. Second, the upgraded political status and external solidarity extended by the Community as a whole helped Southern Europe to play a significant international role at large and to manage the ambiguities of the individual Southern European countries' security relations with the United States in the Mediterranean, at the border with territories and challenges outside the NATO area.

The existence of a more extended and penetrating institutional framework has made it possible for Southern Europe to enjoy more substantial political parity in the Community than in the Atlantic circle. This is not to say, however, that the Southern European tendency toward marginality has been absent in the Community. Such marginality has always been apparent with respect to the more economically homogeneous areas of central and Northern Europe and to the special political relationship between France and Germany.

Therefore, to complete the picture, it should be noted that Southern Europe's strategy of using the Community to compensate for its marginality in NATO or centrality in the Mediterranean has also sometimes worked in reverse. That is, Southern Europe used relations with the United States to compensate for marginality in the Community. This was particularly the case for Italy, where an "American party"—as opposed to a "European" one—has always had remarkable influence and a strong role in shaping both domestic and foreign policies.

Though it would be fatuous to talk about a Southern European model, there are some regularities in the international predicament of the Southern European countries that are worth pointing out:

—There is a tendency to compensate for marginality either in NATO or in the Community by stressing relations with the Community and NATO, respectively.

—There is a tendency, somewhat reminiscent of third world political patterns, to combine global marginality with regional and geopolitical centrality.

—There is a tendency to compensate for weaknesses in bilateral relations with the United States by drawing support from the Community multilateral context.

Is this combination of marginality and centrality coming to an end in the post–cold war situation? The fluidity of such a situation does not allow for a clear-cut response. The apparent loosening of the Euro-Atlantic framework may increase marginality and weaken the Southern European countries both regionally and within the Euro-Atlantic circle. On the other hand Southern Europe's proximity to the regions south of the Mediterranean and to the Balkans may increase its centrality and attenuate its marginality, as these regions are becoming increasingly central from both an international and a Euro-Atlantic point of view.

What is new with the end of the cold war is the nature of Southern Europe's centrality. Whereas this centrality was essentially geopolitical and regional during the cold war, it seems that it has more of a global flavor in the present situation. With respect to the new kinds of risks, tensions, and threats pointed out by the NATO strategic concept worked out at the December 1991 Atlantic Council in Rome, Southern Europe emerges as a central area. The same is true with respect to the "new arc of crisis" singled out by the Western security community, although in both cases Southern Europe is only a segment of the whole Western area that is exposed to the new dangers.

This is not to exclude a Southern European tendency to remain marginal within the changing Euro-Atlantic context. However, this tendency toward marginality combines with a stronger centrality. It is evident that this stronger centrality might be used by Southern Europe to compensate for its marginality.

Before examining the new interaction of opportunities and liabilities that present international developments are offering Southern Europe, we must consider the regional situation around Western Europe, that is, the determinants of its new international situation.

Regional Developments around Western Europe

Even before the end of the cold war there were significant new developments in the regions south of the Mediterranean. Some of these developments are merely the continuation of trends that were already at work in the past; others are new. With respect to old trends, the essential change is that the end of the cold war dissipated military threats coming from the Soviet presence in the Mediterranean area and the risks of horizontal escalation. From a regional point of view, however, old regional sources of instability persist and the new ones are not kept in check by the cold war "order." Adding to this southern instability, as a consequence of the collapse of the former Yugoslavia, further sources of instability and concern have emerged in southeastern Europe. Southern Europe is at the juncture of these two arcs of crisis.

The factors contributing to instability and affecting security across the Mediterranean, especially in North Africa, the Middle East, and the Gulf up to Central Asia, have been explored by a number of works in the recent years.[2] These factors are summarized later in this chapter.

Broadly speaking, socioeconomic conditions in the regions south of the Mediterranean, particularly in key countries like Algeria, Egypt, and Iran, are not improving. Although it will decrease slightly in the mid- to long term, demographic pressure remains very high, leading to unemployment, particularly among young people. Migration, increasingly discouraged by both European and Arab states, can ease the situation only to a limited extent. These socioeconomic conditions favor political radicalism, in particular political Islam or Islamism.

The number of adherents of Islamism—from mainstream parties like the Muslim Brothers (now represented in several legislative bodies and even governments) to clandestine and terrorist groups—is increasing almost everywhere, including Saudi Arabia, and its spread is encouraged by the radical international postures assumed by Iran and Sudan. In the space of a few years, religious radicalism has also become a factor in the Maghreb countries, a development that is of particular concern for a number of Southern European countries.

Religious radicalism is the response of frustrated people to old and new crises in the region, like the Arab-Israeli dispute and Iraq's inconclusive crisis. It is also the response to the failure of nationalism to give Arabs and Muslims an economic and political status commensurate with the important cultural and historical heritage of the Arab and Islamic peoples. Islamism wants to achieve the goals nationalism proved unable to, and it considers the West as its enemy. Unlike nationalism, however, Islamism is not striving to gain political and economic parity with the West, but to assert its diversity. The feeling of Islamists toward the West ranges from "separateness" to hostility. Prospects for international cooperation are therefore bound to be limited. Antagonism and conflict are bound to be the rule.

This new political antagonism in combination with the hostility inherited from postcolonial nationalism promises to make Islamism particularly difficult to deal with as a factor in international conflict. Today, in addition to conflicts fueled by nationalism (as in the case of Saddam Hussein's Iraq), Islamism is trying to destabilize secular regimes (such as Egypt, Tunisia, and Algeria), often by using democratic institutions, and also nonsecular regimes (such as Saudi Arabia and Kuwait). It is constantly narrowing the freedom of non-Muslim communities in the Middle East by the gradual Islamization of society, as in Egypt.

This situation of turmoil in the region is bringing about terrorism and other forms of low-intensity violence. It may bring about conflicts that will involve the West or oblige it to intervene. From the Western point of view, however, the most worrisome trend arising from today's relatively impotent Islamist hostility is that it is leading to an increase in the quantity and quality of arms in the region. Islamism is not a military threat today, but it may become one tomorrow.

The end of the cold war has brought about an initial arrangement between Israel and the Palestinians, and the beginning of a normalization between Israel and the Arab countries. The peace now emerging within the context of the Arab-Israeli crisis is a crucial development for the stability of the region. It would be highly premature to speak about the stabilization of the region, however, because of the possible Arab-Israeli normalization. Apart from political instability in the Gulf, the trend that is bringing about instability in the whole of the Arab-Muslim area, cutting across its various regions, is now Islamism and its combination with nationalism. The predictable opposition to the Arab-Israeli normalization from Islamists and other rejectionist quarters may intensify the radical tendencies already at work in the region. This will keep the area in a state of instability (and require effective management from the West).

As for the crisis brought about by the collapse of the former Yugoslavia and by the Serbian combination of aggressive nationalism and communism, it is only partly linked to instability in the regions south of the Mediterranean by the presence of a Muslim component to the crisis—the Muslim people in such areas as Bosnia, Sandjak, and Kosovo—making Muslim and Arab countries feel that they are involved.

In principle this linkage is not enough to merge the two theaters of crisis, but such a merger is not to be excluded either. In fact the tendency toward a linkage between the crisis in southeastern Europe and crises in the regions south of the Mediterranean is reinforced by similarities in their ideological and socioeconomic matrixes. There is the same intolerance arising from an exasperated search for identity. This intolerance, like that in the Arab-Muslim area, gives rise to significant displacement of people, environmental damage, and economic instabilities. Most important, because of present conflicts in the Balkans and the Western inability to manage them, Balkan Islam may well turn into Islamism. This development would merge the crises in Balkans and the areas south of the Mediterranean.

The former Yugoslavia and other areas previously included in the Soviet Union, like Transcaucasia or Tajikistan, may be considered today as part of an enlarged notion of what is meant by "out-of-area." Some have referred to the "Mediterraneanization" of the areas that were peripheral to the former Soviet Union.[3] The notion of a new arc of crisis extending from Morocco to the former Soviet Union is now widely accepted.[4] Threats and tensions arising from different areas within the new arc of crisis are not necessarily likely to merge, but they pose the same kind of challenges and threats to the West and the international community. A new notion of "out-of-area" is emerging, in which areas that were once part of the Eastern bloc are now considered part of an expanded "out-of-area" region, with important differences but also important similarities among its countries. The multidimensional threat described by the new 1991 strategic concept of the Atlantic Alliance refers to the regions both east and south of Western Europe, that is, to the entirety of the new "out-of-area" region.

As we have already noted, Southern Europe's geographic exposure with respect to this new "out-of-area" region and the global significance of that region in the present international situation make it more central than it had been in the cold war. But is this centrality more regional or global in nature?

Despite the presence of important unifying factors among the various components of the new "arc of crisis" (particularly in southeastern Europe and along the rim of the Russian Federation), it is very clear that is divided into an eastern and a southern segment, both preserving important distinctive characters and problems. For Southern Europe, one element of centrality in this situation is its location at the juncture of these two segments.

From the point of view of the West as a whole, the eastern segment is more important than the southern one. This perception may marginalize Southern Europe within the global circle, according to the traditional pattern. But Western assessments of the eastern segment of the arc of crisis differ: the United States, like Germany and other continental European countries, has greater concern for the eastern segment than for the southern one. Although the United States has a global concern for the southern segment, Germany is relatively unconcerned with this area. This different strategic emphasis between Northern Europe and the United States may have important consequences for Southern Europe.

Finally it should also be noted that not all of the Southern European countries are equally positioned with respect to this new arc of crisis. Italy and Greece are more exposed than Portugal and Spain. The latter two countries are definitely more interested in the Maghreb than are the former. This situation entails different regional and global involvements and different alliances within the Euro-Atlantic circle of the two groups of Southern European countries we have just mentioned.

Southern Europe's Community Approach

Clearly Southern Europe is not equipped to cope either militarily or politically and economically with challenges presently emanating from the other side of the Mediterranean and the wider arc of crises lying east and south of the Euro-Atlantic ensemble. The individual Southern European countries may each perform a role in dealing bilaterally with a given country, for example, Italy with Albania or France with Algeria. They might even work effectively in some regional grouping, as in the case of the so-called "Five plus Five" in the western Mediterranean—a cooperative scheme that is now, however, at a standstill. But unless they go their own way by adopting some futile form of nationalism, the backbone of their policy toward the new "out-of-area" region will be provided by their Euro-Atlantic multilateral tradition.

Within this Euro-Atlantic tradition the case for reinforcing the European Community, implementing the Maastricht Treaty and emphasizing the Community approach seems strong. Broadly speaking, a Community approach would increase Southern Europe's ability to deal with challenges from the Mediterranean and the Balkans. A strong Community means a capacity to extend enhanced economic, financial, and social cooperation to the countries around the Mediterranean. By and large this cooperation is deemed very important in helping these countries to stabilize and, therefore, in reinforcing the security of both Southern Europe and the Community. The development of the so-called Common Foreign and Security Policy (CFSP) envisaged by the Maastricht Treaty should offer the European Union a possibility for both multiplying its cooperation efforts and using cooperation to improve its security. The Maastricht Treaty also gives the Community the chance to add a policy of military insurance to the cooperative dimension of its security policy, thanks to the development of a common European defense within the framework of the Western European Union (WEU), designated by the Treaty to act as the military arm of the European Union.

In principle the Community approach, particularly if the Community is truly upgraded into a European Union, would offer Southern Europe an optimal combination of marginality and centrality with respect to the global circle. The existence of a CFSP would reduce differences between eastern and southern priorities among member states; Mediterranean, Balkan, and Eastern policies would emerge as different dimensions (of course with different weights) of a coherent CFSP of the European Union. A reinforcement of Community solidarity would lessen Southern European risks of marginality with respect to a weaker Community dominated by an eastward priority. On the other hand risks associated with centrality in the Mediterranean would be compensated for by the possibility of sharing them with the Community's partners. Finally the development within the European Union of common foreign, security, and defense policies toward the arc of crisis—in this case especially its southern branch—would lessen Southern Europe's traditional bilateral exposure to either conflict or collusion with the United States.

The Community's prospects in the post-Maastricht era are not very bright. Assuming that a Community approach will be feasible, however, the question that must be discussed in this chapter is the impact of the Community approach on the transatlantic dimension.

Impact on Transatlantic Relations

The eventual strengthening of the CSFP and the WEU as a result of an emerging European security identity has always raised mistrust in Washington. It is feared that a duplication of integrated commands could weaken NATO and its American leadership and bring about political divisions among allies.

Developments in Europe before and after the signing of the Maastricht Treaty and the national security policy that the Clinton administration is gradually working out suggest that the sense of the transatlantic security debate is changing.

The compromise outlined by the Maastricht Treaty on the CFSP and European defense is heavily biased in favor of the creation of a NATO European security pillar rather than a security pillar of the European Union. The integrated command remains firmly with NATO, and the WEU is being developed as a framework for coordinating a varying combination of Western European military forces strictly coupled with NATO. The Franco-German Eurocorps, which was regarded at the outset as a European counterweight to the integrated Atlantic defense, has been linked to NATO and is now emerging as an element of a wider French rapprochement with the Alliance. The joint military operations in the Adriatic Sea and on the Danube River arranged by the WEU in connection with the Yugoslav crisis and the support provided by NATO to implement the flight exclusion zone over Bosnia, however effective they may be, are emerging as complementary factors in a useful division of labor rather than as competitive developments. The endorsement of Combined Joint Task Forces (CJTF) on the occasion of the January 10–11, 1994, Atlantic summit in Brussels shows that NATO is acquiring more military flexibility while remaining politically integrated, and that the idea of an operative Euro-American division of labor is gaining support. In the CJTF scheme American transport and logistic capacities will be made more easily available for supporting missions upon which NATO will decide jointly and that European forces will carry out under ad hoc integrated commands.

In summary, because of these developments the debate that took place in 1991–92 about the risks that a stronger European security and defense identity would pose for NATO now seems obsolete. If the common European security and defense policy continues to develop along present lines, the Community approach that Southern Europe may be willing to pursue is not bound to have any negative effects on transatlantic relations. It would be consistent with a largely convergent U.S.-European policy.

The line of reasoning that has been developed so far, however, assumes an American strategy of multilateralism, that is, a U.S. willingness to continue to play an important international role and share institutions and decisions with European and other Western countries to enlarge and consolidate the role of democracy and liberalism in the world.[5]

Although limited by a harsh redefinition of the extent of U.S. international engagements and of U.S. priorities, the U.S. international commitment is very clear. President Clinton's multilateralism shares the need for domestic renewal with isolationist streams of opinion, but his renewal is intended to implement strategic interdependence rather than independence. Consequently a U.S. strategy of multilateralism can be reasonably assumed. However, the international setbacks suffered by the new administration in its first year, particularly in Somalia, and its oscillations with regard to the role that the United Nations was thought to play in U.S. foreign policy, have been so severe that the boundary between devolution and disengagement is not very clear. For example, many have regarded the CJTF concept as an accelerated U.S. disengagement, although it has been construed as a reshuffling of U.S.-European relations within the Alliance.

Therefore the transatlantic context may be marked by a weak multilateralism. This may prove to be not substantially different from a strategy of selective unilateralism, that is, one emphasizing the preservation of U.S. global advantages and leadership, although within the limits permitted by economic and financial constraints. Both strategies may lead to forms of devolution to Europe coupled with policies either incapable of fostering a Community reinforcement (weak multilateralism) or aimed at preventing the strengthening of a European Union and keeping it divided and relatively weak (unilateralism).

In the Mediterranean a weak U.S. multilateralism, as well as some kind of U.S. unilateralism, would oppose Southern Europe's Community approach or would feel hurt by the possible success of such an approach.

The U.S. argument against Southern Europe's Community approach stems from the dual nature of the Mediterranean as a dimension of both allied and national security. A more cohesive European security identity, as consistent as it may be with NATO, may eventually interfere with U.S. national missions and the global presence of the United States in regions south of the Mediterranean, reduce U.S. freedom of action, or weaken NATO support for such an American presence. This scenario may arise in the future if the trend toward a strong reduction in the U.S. military presence on the European continent is coupled with American will to maintain a constant naval presence in the Mediterranean. In such a scenario a strong Community approach on the part of Southern Europe may prevent the United States from enjoying the combination of allied and bilateral relations that usually makes the management of the Mediterranean area easier.

A last case to be listed is that of a Community unilateralist strategy, to which Southern Europe would strongly adhere with its Community approach. Unless the United States adopted an isolationist policy, such a development would lead to U.S. attempts to hinder the Southern European Community approach against a backdrop of wider transatlantic tension. However, the case for an emerging European unilateralism is very weak.

The conclusion to be drawn from this brief discussion of the transatlantic implications of a Southern European Community approach is twofold. If U.S. multilateralism succeeds a Southern European Community approach may contribute to a better U.S.-European division of labor, and Southern Europe's relations with the United States would not be subjected to ambiguities and contradictions. If U.S. unilateralism prevails, or if the U.S. multilateralist strategy is weakly implemented, a Community approach would bring about conflicts and difficulties.

But the conclusion cannot be black and white. Even with a U.S. multilateralist policy and a reinforcement of the European Union defense and security role, it may be that the United States will always prefer more flexibility in its policy toward regions south of the Mediterranean and in its relations with the Southern European countries. Such a U.S. wish may be matched by the difficulty that the Southern European countries will always encounter in fully integrating the Mediterranean issue into the CFSP's priorities, that is—to put it very simply—in making the Mediterranean as important to their Northern partners as Eastern Europe is.

This conclusion may be reinforced by elaborating on Southern European attitudes. How univocal would Southern Europe's preference be for a Community approach? The thrust of a Southern European country's policy will not be an absolutely pro–United States or pro-Community stance; rather it will insistent on trying to reconcile Europeanism with Atlanticism. This has always been Italy's position, and it will probably continue to be so. This position is due to the factors already noted in the first section of this chapter. It is true that the marginality or centrality of Southern Europe within the global circle brings about difficulties that can be compensated for by the reinforcement of Community links; nonetheless, marginality within the Community can be compensated for by the existence of strong links with NATO and the United States. This means that, as strong as the case for a Community approach may be, Southern Europe will always reconcile it with a U.S. and NATO approach. There is no clear-cut solution to Southern Europe's dilemma: a Community approach strong enough to bring about a conflict with the United States is not expedient for Southern Europe, nor is a bilateral relationship with the United States strong enough to cut Southern Europe out of the Community.

Turkey in Southern Europe's Community Approach

One aspect of this discussion that deserves further attention is the role that Turkey may play in Southern Europe's Community approach and its implications vis-à-vis the United States. There is an asymmetry in Turkey's status in the European Union and NATO that makes an important difference.

Turkey, although not exactly a European country, is a pivotal NATO member associated with the Community, and it has always been included in the concept of Southern Europe during the cold war. At the end of the 1980s, however, pessimism about the possibility of its joining the Community in the foreseeable future, and changes brought about in Turkey's geopolitical position by the end of the cold war, shifted Turkey from the European circle to a more Turkish-centered role.[6]

This higher international profile for Turkey emerged during the 1990–91 Gulf War because of the important role it played in supporting the effort carried out by the United States-led coalition against Iraq, both politically and militarily. The importance of Turkey's role in the U.S. view was also being enhanced by the Turkish drive toward Central Asia: Turkey's presence in this area after the collapse of the Soviet Union was regarded as a stabilizing factor and a counterweight to Islamist and other radical influences in the region. Referring to this new Turkish role, Washington criticized the fact that Turkey was excluded from the security and defense institutions that the Community was envisaging at the intergovernmental conferences that were to lead to the Maastricht Treaty. The sense of the U.S. argument was that by excluding an important transatlantic ally like Turkey, the Community drive toward a European security and defense identity would prove to be fractious with respect to the Atlantic framework.

With the lessening of the controversy about the European defense pillar polemical exchanges about Turkey have also disappeared. Turkey has been included as an associated member in the WEU. On the other hand its role in Central Asia has proved more problematic than expected. Contrary to the American enthusiasm for new Turkish protagonism, it may be that a stronger European connection is a necessary condition for the effectiveness of a Turkish Central Asian role and for the prevention of Central Asian Islamism and nationalism from having a negative impact on the secular and democratic Turkish state.

The U.S. insistence that Turkey be included in the Community security and defense dimension as a Western or Atlanticist "guarantee" is part of a temporary polemical development that has already rapidly declined. However, the developments previously referred to show that Turkey may emerge as a special dimension in Southern Europe's Community approach and the possible related United States-Community tensions.

What role would Turkey play with respect to Southern Europe's Community approach? What would the implications be for the United States?

Let us first imagine Southern Europe's Community approach as a factor in an emerging unilateralist European Union. A unilateralist Union, committed to managing crises in neighboring regions within a framework of decoupling transatlantic relations, would probably be interested in strengthening its relations with Turkey because of the key role that country plays with regard to the Balkans, Transcaucasia, and the Middle East. Consequently it would include Turkey as a member, or it would reinforce Turkey's associated status.

Unless the United States opted for an isolationist strategy, it would also be interested in Turkey whether the U.S. approach were unilateralist or multilateralist. It is likely that the U.S. interest would even be magnified by the fact that Turkey would serve as a surrogate for the regional logistic support that a unilateralist European Union would downgrade. Thus Southern Europe's Community approach to a unilateralist European Union would make Turkey, among other tensions, a bone of contention between the

United States and the European Union. If the U.S. strategy were unilateralist, serious and determined efforts on the part of the United States could be envisaged, not only to prevent Turkey from being included in the European Union but also to prevent or hinder Southern Europe's Community approach.

It cannot be overlooked that the integration of Turkey into the more unilateralist and assertive European Union assumed here would call for a change in Community countries' attitude toward Turkey's membership that would be so radical as to be difficult to imagine. Greek hostility to Turkey and German fears about integrating the large Turkish community now merely viewed as "guests" in the country seem insurmountable obstacles to the inclusion of Turkey in the Southern Community approach, even if a unilateralist and assertive Community were to emerge.

All in all, both the case of a unilateralist Europe and the attempt to include Turkey in such a Europe hardly seem realistic. If they were the attempt to include Turkey might produce intra-Community rifts that would weaken rather than reinforce the European Union.

As already noted when outlining Southern Europe's Community approach in general terms, the scenario that seems to prevail under present conditions is a multilateralist one, on the side of both the United States and the emerging European Union. As was also noted, there are weaknesses in the implementation of current multilateralism because neither the United States or the European Union has determined the extent of its commitment. However, NATO's decision about the CJTF may represent the first step toward an operative devolution, which would allow for continued political cohesion. In summary, the multilateralist case can be safely assumed.

In this scenario Turkey's strong bilateral relationship with the United States, its membership in NATO, and its status of association with both branches of the European Union (the European Community and the WEU) combine to link the country firmly to the ensemble of Euro-American security institutions. In principle this link does not need further reinforcement, although present relations between Turkey and the Community must be improved to become viable: in particular, Greek opposition to the normal working of existing economic and financial understandings between the Community and Turkey ought to be overcome. A Southern European Community approach would probably be reinforced and would in turn contribute to strengthening transatlantic relations, if it were construed as fostering Turkey's linkages to Community institutions. This implies that Southern European governments should assume a more resolute attitude toward Greece.

Conclusions

In the new post–cold war context, Southern Europe's situation of geopolitical centrality with respect to "out-of-area" problems and marginality with respect to European and Western institutions is not fundamentally changed.

Geopolitical centrality is increasing, but the tensions between U.S. or European loyalties that such a development might bring about for Southern Europe are compensated for by a convergent evolution within NATO. A first devolution from the United States to the European Union is taking place without implying any significant discontinuity from the point of view of the Alliance's political cohesion.

This evolution makes any Southern European Community approach consistent with broad U.S. interests and security requirements. The Community's reinforcement coupled with a strong U.S.-European convergence within the Atlantic circle represents an optimal situation in which Southern Europe can improve its ability to deal with challenges emanating from the southern shores of the Mediterranean.

However, many factors, and in particular the strong European Union and NATO focus on the eastern branch of the arc of crisis, may result in an important qualification to this conclusion. As noted previously, even with a United States-European Union convergence within the Atlantic Alliance, one may easily expect that the United States will still prefer to have some more flexibility in its policy toward regions south of the Mediterranean and in its relations with the Southern European countries. This would cause traditional problems and well-known dilemmas for the Southern European countries.

Notes

1. Roberto Aliboni, ed., *Southern European Security in the 1990s* (London: Pinter, 1992); Douglas T. Stuart, ed., *Politics and Security in the Southern Region of the Atlantic Alliance* (Macmillan, 1988); John Chipman, ed., *NATO's Southern Allies: Internal and External Challenges* (London: Routledge, 1988).

2. Roberto Aliboni, "European security across the Mediterranean," Chaillot Paper (Paris: WEU Institute for Security Studies, 1991); Ian O. Lesser, *Mediterranean Security: New Perspectives and Implications for U.S. Policy* (Santa Monica, Calif.: RAND, 1992); Bertelsmann Foundation, Research Group on European Affairs, "Challenges in the Mediterranean—The European Response," paper presented to the Conference of Barcelona, October 7–8, 1991; Yves Boyer, "Europe's

Future Strategic Orientation," *Washington Quarterly,* vol. 16, no. 4 (Autumn 1993, pp. 141–53.

3. Reinhardt Rummel, "The Global Security Architecture and the Mediterranean," paper presented at the international conference on "The Mediterranean: Risks and Challenges," Istituto Affari Internazionali, Rome, November 27–29, 1992.

4. This notion was elaborated at the annual conference of the International Institute for Strategic Studies in Zurich, September 12–15, 1991; see G. Joffé's and C. Gasteyger's papers in "European Security and the New Arc of Crisis," papers 1 and 2, and also Z. Brzezinksi, "The Consequences of the End of the Cold War for International Security," in *New Dimensions in International Security,* Adelphi Paper 265 (London: International Institute for Strategic Studies, 1992), pp. 53–68, 69–81, and 3–17. Also see R. D. Asmus, R. L. Kugler, and F. S. Larrabee, "Building a New NATO," *Foreign Affairs,* vol. 72, no. 4 (September-October 1993), pp. 28–40. The latter article distinguishes between a southern and an eastern section of the arc.

5. Current American schools of thought on international policy and European relations are outlined in R. D. Asmus, "The Rise—or Fall?—of Multilateralism: America's New Foreign Policy and What It Means for Europe," paper presented at the IAI-SWP international conference on "Security in Europe after the Cold War: What Role for International Institutions?" Rome, December 10–11, 1993.

6. See Ian O. Lesser, *Bridge or Barrier? Turkey and the West After the Cold War* (Santa Monica, Calif.: RAND, 1992); Graham E. Fuller, *Turkey Faces East: New Orientations Toward the Middle East and the Old Soviet Union* (Santa Monica, Calif.: RAND, 1992); Paul B. Henze, *Turkey: Toward the Twenty-First Century* (Santa Monica, Calif.: RAND, 1992). The idea of a new self-centered Turkey, energetically projected from various directions, has been proposed especially in U.S. quarters, in the wake of the role played by Turkey in the 1990–91 Gulf War (and with a polemic intention toward the non-role played by the European Community). More recently the U.S. press has reported some skepticism about Turkey's ability to meet U.S. expectations; see Alan Cowell, "Turkey Loses Its Allure as a Patron in Central Asian Nations," *New York Times,* August 4, 1993, p. A3.

TEN

Southern Europe and the United States: The Bilateral Approach

Jaime Gama

IT IS VERY difficult to speak about matters such as relations between the United States and Southern Europe in terms of a final model, because the situation is not stable and the only certainty is that we can have no certainty. This generalization is certainly valid for the area of international relations.

Despite the growing importance of the actions of international organizations for Southern Europe and even the Mediterranean, there is a continuing role for the bilateral dimension. In fact the new international context created by the changes that have taken place in East-West and North-South relations is propitious for a new function for the bilateral dimension.

There are two parallel developments. On the one hand the call for multilateralism is growing, and on the other national governments are forced to make essential choices at the national level.

The relationship between Europe and the United States, specifically that between Southern Europe and the United States, is not an exception to the general rule. On the one hand the area of influence of international organizations is growing; on the other states preserve their ultimate freedom to make foreign policy decisions autonomously.

The End of the Cold War and Southern Europe

Southern Europe is a zone of great diversity. The pressure exerted by the Soviet Union on Southern Europe, especially Turkey, Greece, and Italy, and its diplomatic and naval presence in the Mediterranean, contributed to the homogeneity of the area. Even during the cold war, situations arose such as the dispute between Greece and Turkey, the departure of France from the military organization of the Atlantic Alliance, and the entry of Spain into the North Atlantic Treaty Organization (NATO) without incorporation into the integrated military structure. The disintegration of Soviet power accentuated the overall tendency of Southern Europe toward diversity, by removing a pressure that previously served as a stimulus to solidarity and promoted a relative convergence of interests. The conflict in the Balkans, and the divergent positions that are being taken in relation to it, are the clearest examples of the deterioration of the cohesive effect of the Soviet threat.

Southern Europe has been transformed into a stage for armed confrontation on a large scale that risks spilling over the borders of the former Yugoslavia. On the other side of the Mediterranean there is a slow erosion of the political systems and ideologies that carried out the decolonization of North Africa and, sporadically or continuously, maintained an active military relationship with the Soviet Union. The future of the Arab countries of North Africa—their demographic, economic, and social problems; their migratory currents; and the spread of fundamentalism—has planted itself at the heart of the worries of Southern Europe, if not as a direct military threat (which for the moment it is not) then at least as the risk of a difficult relationship.

To this scenario of uncertainty characterizing Southern Europe at the end of the cold war there is added the entire problematic situation of the Middle East, along with the tensions in the Gulf and the war in the Caucasus, not to lose sight of issues such as the future of formerly Soviet Central Asia and such transitory problems as the operation in Somalia.

The concentrated Soviet military threat, which lay to the north, has therefore been succeeded by a chain of instability that stretches horizontally across the Mediterranean, making it one of the most pronounced foci of risk on the international scene today. I do not see this situation becoming a threat of comparable seriousness to the previous one, but this chain of instability poses new problems and calls for new answers.

The Southern Flank of the Atlantic Alliance fulfilled functions complementary to those of the central front, as well as dealing with the naval threat in the Mediterranean itself. It is now being thrust into a new role. It is clearly moving into the position of a border facing a whole area of instability. This situation is totally different from the previous one and clearly justifies the need to construct a diplomacy, a security policy, and a defense.

For that reason the Southern European countries have in recent years been carrying out military modernization programs, although there is a limitation as far as defense expenditures are concerned. We can note that this sort of financial constraint is not inconsistent with the improvement of restructured programs that are clearly oriented to this new type of risks. An analysis of the military program laws in several of these countries reveals a new type of investment more related to air defense capabilities, to area naval protection, and to rapid deployment forces for close intervention in the neighboring areas. All the other categories in the military budgets, oriented toward large-scale conflict in central Europe, have been reduced and have been balanced by increases in programs oriented toward these new types of options.

The same trend is apparent when we analyze what is happening to the NATO structure in the southern area. There is a rebuilding of the Allied Forces Southern Europe (AFSOUTH). AFSOUTH was previously oriented toward two types of missions: reinforcement of the northern area and intervention in the Mediterranean. Now AFSOUTH is being oriented both to containment toward the South and to acting as a corridor within which forces can be moved in a crisis situation, for example from Portugal to Turkey. This is totally different from the previous organizational concept of AFSOUTH, which was much more oriented to deploying troops northward from the border of Italy.

I also see a profound restructuring of goals by the United States with respect to the region. The new objectives of the United States are not as contentious as were in their day the objectives of combating communism or Soviet expansion in the area. Rather they constitute arbitration of intra-European and intra-Arab disputes in the region, in order to preserve free access, project force in the region, and use the region as a base for action to contain crises in nearby areas, with special emphasis on the Gulf, the Middle East, and the horn of Africa.

Americans tend always to look at the Mediterranean in the classical terms they learned from Admiral Mahan, adapting the image of the "lifeline of the British Empire" and seeing the Mediterranean as an essential interior line through which the central position can project force to other areas. The first engagement of the Americans in the Mediterranean also had something to do with this problem, because they went there to fight against the Arab vessels that denied the free passage of American vessels to trade in the Mediterranean.

These coupled ideas of projection of force and freedom of access are essential. They were essential during the cold war for a certain type of threat; now it is even more essential to be able to project force to deal with a great number of possible conflicts and possible threats. The United States sees the Mediterranean corridor as essential to its power to assume effectively international responsibilities in the zone. It no longer seeks to have a presence in the Mediterranean because of the Soviet Union, but because of the new perception it has of its worldwide responsibilities.

Yet the diversity of Southern Europe makes it impossible to treat it as a uniform zone. Countries such as France, Spain, and Portugal will give priority to the problems of the western Mediterranean; Italy will always aspire to Mediterranean leadership in all directions; Greece and Turkey will concentrate more on relations with each other and with their other neighbors. Adding to this diversity of interests is the difficulty of establishing an intensive relationship with the Arab countries, especially when they fear being structurally weakened by such an opening. From the standpoint of a great power surveying the international scene, it may seem possible to see Southern Europe or the Mediterranean as a unit, as the Soviet Union did and as U.S. diplomacy appears to continue to do. However, the most profound reality is the existence of states strongly rooted in their autonomy or, perhaps, a group of subregions. Here again the end of the cold war has seen a reduction of the attracting force of the major common denominators.

International Organizations Look South

All of the international organizations have shifted their focus to the south, to pay more attention to Southern Europe, the Mediterranean, and North Africa. Analyze the United Nations, the Conference on Security and Cooperation in Europe, the European Community, NATO. In the strategic concepts of all these organizations one can find a shift toward the south.

The Conference on Security and Cooperation in Europe (CSCE), which institutionalized the East-West dialogue during the cold war period, made a strong contribution to the creation of a multilateral environment capable of addressing sensitive issues of security, human rights, and economic cooperation. The dissolution of the Warsaw Pact and the demise of the Soviet Union permitted the strengthening of this multilateral environment with the addition of other relevant issues in the areas of electoral processes; ethnic minorities; and linguistic, religious, and cultural identities. The CSCE—which is visibly becoming the regional forum for the United Nations in Europe—has accepted the challenge to resolve, through multilateral cooperation, a vast group of problems that have always been at the heart of

European conflicts. It is true that, in specific cases of enormous seriousness, such as Yugoslavia, the CSCE does not have the means to act with determination to prevent a crisis and deter a conflict. Nevertheless this does not mean that the CSCE is not an instrument of great usefulness and that conclusions cannot be drawn from it for Mediterranean security.

In 1991 when the "Five plus Five" dialogue began, a first step was made, inspired by the model of the CSCE, to deepen the cooperation between countries on opposing sides of the western Mediterranean, that is, between Southern Europe and the Maghreb. The scope of this dialogue ranges from diplomatic consulting and the exchange of points of view on the political level to financial problems, to the issue of migration, and to cooperation on the environment. For the first time it was possible, in an informal context, to establish a multilateral, subregional nexus of relations among these countries and to attempt to resolve the issues under debate in their respective areas.

It is no surprise that the notion developed that it was necessary to advance from the informal and colloquial level of the "Five plus Five" to a more formal and institutionalized level. The idea of a Conference on Security and Cooperation in the Mediterranean (CSCM) modeled on the CSCE thus began to acquire force. The existence of different cultural heritages (differences that do not compare in degree with the ideological differences that separated the members of the CSCE during the cold war) does not mean it is inappropriate to call for an intergovernmental conference on security and cooperation in the Mediterranean, with an agenda including, subject to necessary adaptation, the principles, main issues, and subjects that have governed the Helsinki process. A broad version of the CSCM (with all of the countries surrounding the Mediterranean and covering all of the points of the CSCE) is certainly not practical at the moment. But a version embracing the countries of the western Mediterranean that began the "Five plus Five" dialogue, one that would concentrate on some of the subjects of the CSCE (such as environmental and economic cooperation, confidence-building measures, and cultural and legal dialogue), is already realistically attainable.

The changes in the international situation have caused almost a reversal of what until now was the model of security and defense architecture. The central front has ceased to be the focus of attention and has become the periphery. The southern periphery has become the priority front, because of the new types of threats that have arisen there.

NATO's new strategic concept clearly reflects this type of concern. The new NATO force structure—especially as regards rapid deployment forces—takes into account the imperative need not to create gaps in security for the Alliance on its southern flank, since it is from this direction that some of the new risks come today. Although NATO has not yet, in this field, gone beyond mere assessments of risk or simple consultations, the truth is that the organization is structuring itself militarily to be in the position to respond satisfactorily to events in the region, namely being able to integrate operations to reestablish or maintain peace under the auspices of the UN and the CSCE and under the umbrella of the new allied philosophy for out-of-area intervention.

The facts that Spain and France do not participate in the integrated military structure, that relations between Turkey and Greece have never been good, and that the United States and Europe have not agreed entirely on a policy for the Mediterranean are factors that make a dynamic performance of NATO in the whole region somewhat difficult. Nonetheless the creation of the Standing Naval Force Mediterranean, the progress in the area of air defense, and the establishment of new land force structures for rapid deployment show NATO's clear concern to adjust its capabilities to the new realities and to give the southern flank a different focus from the one it has had up to now.

Indeed in this period of transition NATO must not hold back from developing relations with the South, but rather make the same effort to keep track of developments it has learned to make in relation to countries in central and Northern Europe, through a sort of North Atlantic Cooperation Council for the South or at least a kind of consultation with the Maghreb countries. A failure to do so would undermine the Alliance's dogma that security is indivisible.

The European Community—now the European Union—has also been paying increased attention to Southern European problems. From an internal perspective, the Community, by transferring greater financial resources to give the southern zone an adequate infrastructure, has made effective a policy of economic integration that itself is a true guarantee in the area of security. From an international standpoint, and with regard to the Mediterranean, the Community has acted in two complementary ways. It has, in a defense mode, adopted collective measures regarding border control, immigration policies, and the status of resident aliens, with obvious consequences for the North African peoples. On the other hand it has developed, through its Renewed Mediterranean Policy dating back to 1990, a more active role in the region, which includes a vast set of mechanisms for financial support and cooperation. The renegotiation of accords with the countries of the Maghreb aims at solidifying a "Maghrebian economic space," the aim also of the Arab Maghreb Union.

In reality if it cannot achieve economic cooperation in this area, Europe will be unlikely to be able to compete in the Mediterranean with the intensified influence represented by the American military presence (especially air and naval forces) in the region.

The adoption of common foreign and security policies, as provided for in the Maastricht Treaty, and the role attributed to the Western European Union (WEU) as the armed branch of the future European Union are factors that lead to the prediction of greater convergence of the EC member countries in Mediterranean policy and in its development not only in the area of internal control of migratory flows but also in economic aspects, as well as components of foreign policy, security, and defense. One of the critical tests for this new development will certainly be the Mediterranean, in view of its proximity and the importance that the region has for the countries of the Community. The impossibility of making the Mediterranean uniform will certainly lead to a continuation of a special identification with the Maghreb, despite the Libyan irritant. This will stimulate the existence of a partner on the other side of the Mediterranean with an integrated economy. The cooperation between organizations will be made easier.

At the same time the adoption of a Common Foreign and Security Policy will not make less important the need for a specific national foreign policy for each country in the whole region, in the north and in the south, taking into account the weight of the acquired notions of autonomy, liberty and the independence of the state, sovereignty, the historical roots of national decisions, and even nationalistic prejudices (which are not exclusive characteristics of the Arab states).

It is no surprise that international institutions and countries are making the necessary doctrinal and structural changes to deal with this new reality. This trend affects national policies and the sort of relationship that all these countries have with the United States.

A Continued Role for Bilateral Relations

However, the facts that international organizations are gradually extending their umbrella of influence to Southern Europe and that Southern Europe is now bound by the obligations of certain regional understandings do not mean that the states will not maintain their own identity; and it is on this basis, in the last analysis, that the substance of their foreign policies will be defined.

National foreign policy decisionmaking by the states of Southern Europe will not be banished in the next decade. There is an interaction with the growing role of international organizations, but clearly this type of intervention will not disappear. National states are very much the reality in this area today.

On the southern side of the Mediterranean the tendencies for any movement toward integration are very precarious and the Arab Maghreb Union itself is, in practical terms, a goal for the longer term. In the relations between Tunisia and Libya, Libya and Egypt or Algeria, Mauritania and Morocco, and Morocco and Algeria nationalism is dominant to the detriment of any multilateral solution.

Unilateralism on the northern side is obviously balanced by the practice of participating and the need to participate in a larger alliance for the sake of security, and by the fact that European integration has been and promises to be the source for assistance in economic and social development. However, the uprooting of the age-old roots that are at the basis of and reinforce the main lines of countries' respective foreign policies will not take place any time soon. The tenacity of established national positions has often been demonstrated when consensus has been sought, whether in the Atlantic Alliance or in the EC.

Basic perceptions in foreign policy will remain linked to the actual circumstances of the individual states, and it is unlikely that any movement toward convergence—which is certainly important for the affirmation of Europe internationally—will be converted into an automatic uniformity of positions. Who can imagine Portugal relinquishing its special relations with Africa or Brazil or its special care in dealing with questions related to Spain? Or Spain agreeing to end its presence in the Hispanic world and decreasing the importance it gives to issues affecting relations with France? Italy, Greece, and Turkey also have their particular national interests to defend. One can find, with respect to this national priority and to the unilateral policies, the basic elements of action for the Mediterranean countries in the field of international relations.

Yet the type of links the United States will have in the area cannot be built up with the idea of having the same sort of environment forever. It is in fact changing.

Let us, as an example, take up three cases—Italy, Spain, and Portugal—omitting the case of France because it is a very special one. In these three cases after World War II the United States built up different types of relations. In subsequent years these types were modified.

There was a purely bilateral model: the defense agreements with Spain, a purely bilateral relationship outside NATO and at times outside any European structure. With Italy and Portugal there was a different type of bilateral relationship, both bilateral and within NATO. This was a very special model that the United States developed for the area, in order not to have all its eggs in the same basket. As needed it used one or the other country platform to provide access for its moves in and across the area.

This was the model of the 1950s, subsequently modified. The modification was more significant in the case of Spain than in that of Portugal. In Italy it did not take place.

Spain joined NATO and the European Community, and these two connections have been used as balancing elements to reduce the bilateral aspect of the defense relationship with the United States. In the case of Portugal there has been a rebuilding of the defense agreement clearly oriented toward improving Portuguese national control of military facilities. At the same time Portuguese entry into the EC and the WEU introduced an allied element to balance the previous relationship.

This was the model for Portugal and Spain of the rebuilding of the defense relationship with the United States in the 1980s. It has not been the case in Italy, where the model is still that developed in the early post–World War II period and there has been no subsequent evolution. I think that Italy now is confronting all of its internal problems in a very special way; one cannot for the moment foresee all of its dimensions and implications. How can the type of relationship the United States has with Italy resist what is happening in Italy? This relationship must be submitted to very profound analysis from a diplomatic and geopolitical point of view.

Now we have come to another stage, the end of the cold war. Relationships must respond to the diversity of risks in the area and beyond. They must take account of a role for the CSCE and the UN. The Atlantic Treaty doctrine must be reconstructed on the basis of a clear recognition of the European defense identity. Even though the European defense identity needs further clarification beyond what is said in the Maastricht Treaty, the fact is that it exists and there is no going back; it needs and claims accommodation and cannot be denied a role in the future.

The new context of multilateralism—having an impact on this area through the CSCE and also the UN, and through the reconstruction of NATO in the sense of accommodating a European identity in a common foreign and security policy (in defense probably through the WEU)—raises the question of whether the model we have been using to define bilateral relations in the defense field with the United States is a sustainable model for the future. If not, how can that model be reshaped in order to incorporate all these new trends?

The worst temptation for U.S. diplomacy may well be to try to establish a special tie with Mediterranean Europe with the intention of fostering a division (decoupling) in the European integration process, instigating strategic differences in Western Europe, which NATO has denied over the decades in the formulation of its military doctrines.

The southern flank will also always be incomplete if the United States is suspicious with regard to any initiative that tries to establish a forum between the two sides of the Mediterranean for the discussion of security issues in a broader sense. The region, because of its heterogeneous aspects and its problems, demands foresighted diplomacy and the formulation of a set of proposals and initiatives that do not amount to the mere maintenance of the status quo. This new stage basically fits the bilateral actions of foreign policy and not those of multilateral association, especially in the regions where the actions of international organizations are not fully effective.

The United States continues to favor a global analysis of the world situation and the definition of global strategic objectives. It seeks thus on the one hand to integrate the attempt to stabilize and establish areas of influence, and on the other to affect the expansion of power necessary previously for the management of bipolarity and today for the affirmation of world leadership. This global approach often collides with the capacity to generate and maintain long-lasting relations, transforming them, in many instances, into intermittent bilateral relations, determined by the need for intervention in moments of crisis. With effective air-naval presence and empowered with significant bases, the United States is capable of establishing a corridor for multiple uses in the Mediterranean, not only on the northern side but also including Morocco and Egypt, through which its access for demonstration or intervention in a variety of conflicts is guaranteed. Despite the new world context and the priorities resulting from budget constraints, the truth is that reductions in the number of bases abroad have not affected the essential U.S. military capabilities in the region. These have adjusted to the nature of the new missions, whether they are of a type similar to Desert Storm or Restore Hope, or aimed at maintaining peace and justified by the need for international stability, or among the different contingency plans for Bosnia.

The Mediterranean policy of the United States does not always equally balance support for both sides of the sea, and it is not always devoid of friction with its allies to the north of the Mediterranean, whether Spain, France or Greece.

The American emphasis on Turkey is a good example of how its global approach, and its lack of care for the attitudes of its northern Mediterranean allies, can cause friction. This situation is sometimes not well understood or easily accepted by the other allies, whether they are Arabs or Europeans. Excessive endorsement by the United States of Turkish activism does not lead to a balanced role for the United States with respect to the region, and with time, taking into consideration the end of the cold war, would appear to risk eroding U.S. diplomatic capability vis-à-vis the Mediterranean countries.

Taking into account the specifics of the Turkish position vis-à-vis several different problems around its borders, the Americans are today emphasizing a Turkish platform. In the days of the cold war concept of a Mediterranean corridor, Portugal, Spain, and Morocco were essential for access through the corridor. Italy, when there was a northern threat, was essential as a "land-based aircraft carrier," if I may put it that way. Now—given the evolution of the situation in such areas as the Caucasus, Central Asia, the Middle East, and the horn of Africa—Turkey is, in the American concept, the platform, the land-based aircraft carrier.

This is an understandable product of a pure strategic, global vision. But it faces a very serious problem, because it is not clear that all the other European allies are in agreement with the United States in its evaluation of Turkey.

If Atlantic solidarity means being involved through NATO in the type of conflict that threatens Turkey, or the wider Turkish-speaking world, that means being involved in all the problems related to the disintegration of the Soviet empire. Furthermore it is not clear that all Western European countries would side with Turkey, if there is a positive evolution in Russia, in the case of a dispute between the former Russian and Ottoman empires—or rather between policies oriented by the spirit of empires that no longer exist, but that inspire political choices by national government officials and the political leadership in those countries.

All this is not at all clear; in any event, this problem remains in the future. The question is, how can we handle it?

There is another difficulty in relations between Southern Europe and the United States that has its origins in the cold war. The strategic environment of the cold war led the military area to be given a special status in the relationship between the United States and its allies in Southern Europe. The need to provide for the deterrence of the Soviet Union's power beyond its borders gave special importance to countries like Turkey, Greece, and Italy, which were positioned on the front line of the southern flank with regard to air and ground threats. Countries such as Spain and Portugal, clearly located in the rear, were still highly relevant for the activity of naval and naval air forces. The complex infrastructure of support for the U.S. Sixth Fleet shaped Washington's foreign policy over the years, aiming at assuring the fleet's freedom to act throughout the Mediterranean corridor. These activities were nominally carried out within NATO, but the diplomatic efforts were mostly bilateral. Thus the essence of U.S. relations with the Southern European countries was military. The militarization of bilateral relations had the result that, owing to laws restricting access to information in this area, the treaties in many instances only contained generic principles. The real details of the military links were covered by technical agreements, most of the time without the knowledge of the public and the respective countries' governmental and political representatives.

International developments after the end of the cold war necessitate a change of philosophy from the military-centered model of relationship with the United States. Bilateral relations need to be demilitarized and to reflect the current international system and the will of the respective players. This has been understood by those who—not just in the Mediterranean region—defend the growth of bilateral relations with the United States on a new diplomatic basis.

In this period in which bipolarity has ceased and the United States is seeking to reconstruct its international role through a reformulation of the role of the UN, while maintaining at the same time the essence of its traditional alliance (NATO), there is a desire that the countries of Southern Europe stimulate bilateral relations with the United States, but on a basis different from that of the confrontational period of the cold war.

The role of the United States as a world power is not limited today to military or economic aspects. Its performance in science and technology and in communications and culture, and its model of consumer behavior, are factors that tend today to reinforce its role on a global scale. For a region such as Southern Europe, which is undergoing development, the relationship with the United States is not, therefore, limited to military aspects. If the relationship is to be continued, and also brought up to date to reflect the new international reality, it is vital for these countries to improve their cooperation with the United States, in order to introduce a synergy into their growth process. Economic cooperation, in particular in the areas of finance, investment, and trade, is fundamental. Great importance must also be given to education and science because of their multiplier effects on society. The creative diversity of the United States in such significant areas as basic and applied research, computer science, production engineering, management, marketing, and communication, and the standards of excellence of some of its investments in this field, foster a special interest in obtaining access for students and experts from Southern European countries to U.S. universities, research institutions, and companies. The role of the English language in the world, the quality of cultural and artistic creation in the United States, and its dissemination by virtue of the global reach of the media—a process in which the United States plays a key role—are other relevant factors. It is perfectly clear that Southern Europe should not remain bound to a single model of relationship with the United States that is apparently outdated and that exists throughout several other countries from Asia to Central Europe, created or recreated after the demise of the Soviet Union.

Very alert to events following the dismantling of the Warsaw Pact and the demise of the Soviet Union, the United States certainly will not, from one day to the next, withdraw from Southern Europe. It will be interesting if the United States seeks to balance its presence in the region, making the same effort that it seems to be making regarding the reconstruction of central and Northern Europe—if, above all, it does not see Southern Europe solely as a springboard for access to areas in crisis, the result of a relationship dictated by military considerations and periodically reactivated according to the old model of the cold war. The need to establish the basis for U.S. diplomacy as more preventive than remedial or even surgical produces a demand for long-lasting bilateral relations, taking into account the specific needs of each country, its location in the Mediterranean region, and the fact that all the countries are a part of NATO and, with the exception of Turkey, of the European Union.

The need for a special relationship with the United States is clearly being stressed by all of the Southern European countries. They do not want to be totally unified by a common foreign and security policy in Europe that would emphasize a more Northern vision. That this is clearly the case was demonstrated by their reluctance to succumb to the pressure brought to bear by Germany for the recognition of Slovenia during the early stages of the Yugoslav conflict.

The Southern European countries also recognize the balancing role of the United States in the Mediterranean as regards our relationship with the other side of the Mediterranean. For that the balance and linkage provided by the United States will be seen as essential.

The Southern European countries' desire for an active relationship with the United States stems not only from the U.S. presence in the region, but also, and above all, from the U.S. role in the international system. Leaving aside France, which for reasons of organization of its defense and its foreign policy has positioned itself on a different level, the "entente" with the United States takes on a vital role for the remaining countries.

However, the content of specific defense agreements between those countries and the United States will inevitably be reviewed in accordance with the fact that those countries now belong to a larger and effective community, the European Union, which desires to play a role in the foreign policy, security, and defense fields. Obviously the content of the bilateral defense relationship will tend to be more balanced.

Portugal: A Case Study in Relations with the United States

Portugal is a country that is characterized by balance and linkage. Territorially located in the far west of Europe with its position on the Iberian Peninsula, it is at the same time geographically proximate to the United States: it opens to the Atlantic with its long coast and its island groups (Madeira and the Azores).

Orlando Ribeiro summed up its geostrategic qualities well, stating that Portugal was Atlantic by location and Mediterranean by vocation. Even though it does not border the Mediterranean, the truth is that the Mediterranean, in particular the western Mediterranean region, has a profound influence on the formulation of Portuguese foreign policy, especially security policy.

On the other hand the fact that Portugal has developed as a nation with interests directed toward emphasizing a Portuguese-speaking sphere in many continents fundamentally increases its attention to the Atlantic. Although it is certain that the Atlantic does not necessarily or exclusively mean the North Atlantic in this case—Brazil and Africa are to the south—it is no less certain that the preservation of Portuguese nationhood is connected to the North Atlantic area, above all if we take into consideration the historic importance of the British alliance for the strengthening of Portuguese autonomy in international relations. The conservation of Portuguese naval power, given support by that alliance, solidified its independence in the face of various plays for influence by European powers, liberated it from more risky involvements in European confrontations, and prevented the unification of the Iberian peninsula by the Castilian forces.

When the British Empire ceased to be a world power and the United Kingdom reshaped itself in a European role owing to the size of the United States and its international importance, it was the United States with which Portuguese diplomacy had to deal to develop a vital relationship—one that was not always easy, but thanks to which it reached a certain level of stability in the world context.

It was hard for Portugal to accept the fact that England was no longer the leading world power and that, since World War I, the United States had clearly emerged as the more dominant country internationally. As a result of Portugal's difficulty in perceiving this shift, until World War II Portuguese diplomacy tried to mediate its relationship with the United States on vital questions through British diplomacy.

The United States, however, had long been aware of the importance of Portugal's strategic position in the Atlantic, from the time when it had provided facilities to whaling fleets and to ocean transport between America's east and Pacific coasts. The naval facilities of World War I and the air facilities at the end of World War II were not structurally different from those earlier ones. The position the Azores assumed, as a consequence, was no more than that of a platform, justifying the development of a special diplomacy to organize relations between the United States and Portugal.

In general the United States needed the Portuguese facilities to expand its capability for deployment in a Europe that was threatened by Soviet pressure; in order to assure the freedom of the seas in a vital region of the Atlantic; and also to reach other areas in the Middle East, the Gulf region, southwest Asia, the Mediterranean, and Africa. The link with the Azores was vital for the reinforcement of Europe and the provision of support to U.S. and allied forces in West Germany. The use of facilities in the archipelago allowed particularly efficient monitoring of Soviet threats to the U.S. coast as well.

For Portugal the establishment of an accord with the United States in such a delicate matter gave an authoritarian regime legitimacy in the international arena after World War II and guaranteed it a passport to membership in NATO. In addition it received help in acquiring military supplies that could not possibly be entirely covered by the national budget. The value ascribed to the Azores by the United States was also important in influencing Washington's assessment of the Portuguese policy in Africa in the 1960s as well as the caution exercised in monitoring the disturbed period following the 1974 Portuguese revolution. The establishment of constitutional normality in the country contributed to a stabilization of relations between Portugal and the United States in the area of defense, within the international context of participation by both countries in a common alliance and the existence of a growing bipolarization of the world.

The end of the cold war, as was to be expected, modified a model of bilateral relations that had been in decline for some time. Various factors had contributed to this evolution prior to the disintegration of the Warsaw Pact, namely the economic and diplomatic impact of Portugal's entry into the European Common Market, marked by a decrease in trade between the two countries, and the adjustments introduced in the formulation of Portuguese foreign policy by the mechanisms of European political consultation.

On the other hand the end of the cold war led the United States to rearrange its military forces in Europe and in the Atlantic, a step that obviously had consequences for its base in the Azores. This led to a contraction—proportionate to the absence of a Soviet threat—in antisubmarine defense. At the same time the base's basic purpose was reformulated; it was now geared more to supporting airborne refueling, an operation likely to be more frequent, both for military interventions to reestablish or maintain peace and for rapid access to crisis areas.

The change in the nature of the threat, and the U.S. priority of cutting public expenditures, especially in the military area, also caused a decrease in the resources that the U.S. allocated to Portugal for the use of its facilities. The main beneficiaries of this funding had been the Portuguese armed forces and the budget of the Autonomous Region of the Azores, where most of the facilities are located. The end of the financial assistance transferred these burdens to the Portuguese budget, a change with special import for the new Military Program Act for 1993–97.

It is certain that the new policy is justified in Washington by the fact that Portugal today is part of a competing trade bloc, the European Union, and that it thus does not lack assistance. This change will affect the judgment that the beneficiaries made about maintaining a special relationship with the United States: they often placed maximizing specific advantages above overall national interests. A greater degree of self-financing of military expenses by Portugal will render its international posture more truly independent and remove its military and diplomatic system somewhat from the influence of the donor country.

These trends are developing concurrently with the European integration process, the institutionalization of a common foreign and security policy, and the deepening of European political cooperation. If the Maastricht Treaty yields concrete results in the area of common defense policy and common defense, it will not be easy for Portugal to ignore this context when the time comes to define the parameters of its military relationship with the United States. Portugal, like the other countries of the European Union having a bilateral defense relationship with the United States, will then find it very difficult to provide facilities to the United States for the use of force in an international conflict unless the American action is supported by a European consensus.

The fact that the United States today aspires to world leadership and the emphasis that it places on intensive interventionism by the UN are factors that Portuguese diplomacy will not fail to ponder. This will especially be the case when these moves involve distant geographic areas that are, from a Portuguese point of view, less important strategically, or when they may conflict with the normal perceptions and the consensus of Portuguese opinion concerning the involvement or noninvolvement of Portugal in international crises. The projection of Portugal onto stages of conflict to which it is traditionally alien will not have the support of public opinion. Opinion will also tend to be particularly sensitive to actions by the United States that do not achieve at least a minimum consensus within the European Union. Portuguese opinion will also be sensitive to whether the United States maintains uniform human rights standards, with particular reference to its stand regarding East Timor and the content and scope of its relations with Indonesia.

Today Portugal does not need to have its political regime legitimated, as was the case during the dictatorship or at the beginning of the political changes of the mid-1970s that led to the installation of a pluralistic democracy. The fact that the national budget finances military modernization, and that regional finances in the Azores have been receiving much more significant assistance from Brussels than from Washington, eliminates the possibility of subjecting Portuguese domestic choices to U.S. diplomatic arguments, especially when the U.S. intention is to negotiate from a position of superiority. If we add to that a greater degree of alienation of public opinion regarding the need for the American factor in international affairs—with the disappearance of its principal raison d'être, Soviet expansionism—do we then have to conclude that this is really the end of a diplomatic relationship on which Portuguese-American ties have been based since the last world war? Does its revitalization require not merely a reformulation of its pattern but instead a total reformulation of the reasons for a partnership to exist between the two allies? This partnership should be based on shared interests and should be a visibly two-way relationship.

The delay in arriving at agreement on a new accord between Portugal and the United States in the area of defense is indivisibly linked to the end of the treaty model on which their former agreement was based and the need to be more in line with the reality of modern times. In a context of increased multilateralization, there is a need to define with clarity the content of this understanding, and that is particularly true within the area of responsibility of the Atlantic Alliance, which after all is aimed at efforts in the military and defense field. There will be a need to identify those issues that are within the scope of responsibility of the Alliance. Then and only then can the issues be defined that will remain to be addressed bilaterally by the two countries, without overlapping those being addressed within the Alliance. Again, for bilateral relations to be effective, it is important that they be based on explicit interests and mutual advantages.

If we review the evolution of the Portuguese-American accords since 1951 we observe that although the U.S. diplomatic formulation is clearly couched offensively—that is, the Americans know exactly why they want the Lajes base—the Portuguese diplomatic formulation is predominantly defensive, based on subordinate interests (the acquisition of military supplies, regional development assistance); it does not have comprehensive national security and defense goals as a priority.

Although Portugal and the United States are both NATO members, the truth is that, in reality, the Lajes base does not function as a NATO base. To ensure the hybrid character of operation of this installation is in fact one of the main purposes for the U.S. negotiations.

When Portuguese diplomacy concentrated on seeking financial compensation or military aid, its negotiating capacity to demand a clear framework for the accords was, from the outset, limited by an erroneous formulation of purposes.

The 1983 negotiations between Portugal and the United States sought, under controlled circumstances, to limit the additional facilities requested by the American forces, especially by not accepting the stationing of offensive naval forces in the area of Portuguese jurisdiction. Portugal also attempted to deconcentrate the military relationship with the United States throughout its entire national territory.

At the same time, displaying foresight regarding the need to demilitarize relations between Portugal and the United States, the negotiations were directed toward enlarging the support for the regional development of the Azores and sought to obtain a useful instrument (the Luso-American Development Foundation) for the energizing of the scientific, technical, commercial, and cultural relations between the two countries, fulfilling interests on the part of researchers, professors, artists, students, technicians, and businessmen. The repositioning of the relations between Portugal and the United States within other parameters required additional efforts in areas vital for Portuguese development, and this was noted in an instrument drawn up with the necessary flexibility to implement such an important mission.

Writing a radically new accord was, therefore, not just a legal question. Rather there was an attempt to reinforce developments in new areas that had at that point started to justify special attention. Naturally the future evolution cannot be predicted—but the way has been opened for a new, wide reformulation of various diplomatic instruments signed between Portugal and the United States, namely the signing of a friendship and cooperation treaty capable of summing up the set of partial accords, giving them an overall focus.

One of the major disruptive elements in the relationship between Portugal and the United States results from the superficiality with which the issue itself is treated. From the American standpoint there is a resurgence of interest every time Portugal goes through serious convulsions (wars in Africa, changes in regime, decolonization). There is also a resurgent interest every time the United States has the need to use Portuguese facilities to deploy its military forces or any time that the Portuguese vote is useful for U.S. diplomacy in any type of international conflict. Later, however, when events return to normal, Portuguese affairs in Washington are reduced to the administrative level in the different agencies, in Congress, and even in the universities. On the Portuguese side, the alienation is no less; it is disguised by a superficial and many times rhetorical commitment that confuses intentions with realities and the superfluous with the essential, and almost invariably is not capable of implementing its declaratory objectives. The occasions on which numerous personalities from different walks of life express their support for the development of relations with the United States are frequent. However, the real record of accomplishment is poor: bilateral trade has decreased, and the same has happened to U.S. investments in Portugal; the number of Portuguese students with scholarships in

American universities is not proportionally comparable to that of students from other European countries; the transfer of knowledge and technology is insignificant; the exposure of Portuguese culture in the United States is almost nonexistent; and even military cooperation, excluding the transfer of some equipment, is very embryonic and has not produced the technically modernizing effects that might be expected in key areas of the Portuguese military and defense structure.

This difficulty on the part of Portugal in establishing a relationship with the leading world power has at times given rise to conduct that combines alternately extremely positive statements with an attitude of distrust, a lack of capacity to establish attainable objectives, and even a dose of resentment. We are therefore a step away from synthesizing positions according to which some faithfully maintain a preferential alliance to the United States in opposition to European integration, and others, favoring such integration, seek to avoid any sort of lasting relationship with the United States If we add to these attitudes a tendency toward simplification, one can observe how easy it is for a certain type of public debate to lean toward a view of the options chosen by Portuguese foreign policy that does not take into account nuances, complexity, or the less obvious points. This results in a serious risk for Portugal's foreign relations in this respect.

The change in the scenario of the international context produces changes in the strategic position of a country such as Portugal. The decline of Soviet pressure, namely its naval presence in the Atlantic and access to the Mediterranean Sea, is now counterbalanced by a new type of risk that confronts the area. Those risks of closer proximity affect the western Mediterranean even if risks are to be found spread along the length of the Mediterranean or are focused in the center or to the east, with the involvement of the Balkans, the Middle East, the Gulf, the Caucasus, Central Asia, and the horn of Africa. These are places in which disturbances will always affect the security of the North Atlantic Alliance's southern flank and the vital interests of U.S. foreign policy.

It is no surprise, therefore, that Portugal and Spain try to give priority in their military programs to the defense of the region, with special attention to air defense, the strengthening of naval capability, and the creation of programs aimed at giving their ground forces the highest level of air mobility. The defense of their own borders, which are now also common borders with the members of European Community, is another concern and requires significant changes in customs, fiscal, and border policies. Although Spain is not part of the military organization of NATO, its national programs, and the accords for coordination established with the allied command, point in the direction of an intensification of the security ties in the region, a concern that is also demonstrated by the new Portuguese military program act and by the recent measures adopted for the control of entry by aliens and the restructuring of customs, fiscal inspection, and immigration services.

By stressing the southern flank, the Atlantic Alliance shifted a part of the missions performed by the Portuguese armed forces from a significant role in antisubmarine warfare and in reinforcing the defense of the north of Italy to the defense of the region and to the capability to join the rapid deployment forces that AFSOUTH will have available to protect the southern flank and act, from Portugal to Turkey, to resolve crises and conflicts. The notion of the transatlantic link will have a less important role in the strategic function of Portugal, and missions of other kinds will be more salient in a scenario in which the actions of the United States toward Europe will no longer benefit from any privileged national link, but will instead be based on a division of tasks between the American and European pillars, both members of the same alliance. However, the facts that the ties of friendship between Spain and Portugal are still not capable of generating defense accords, that the dispute between Morocco and Spain over Ceuta and Melilla continues, and that the United Kingdom is not giving up its presence in Gibraltar all end up casting the United States in the role of mediator in the region. It is a very significant role, all the more so because Morocco has not seen its aspirations for a closer connection to the European Union come true.

With no historical problems with the United States, Portugal will, for a long time, be an important link in the chain of American foreign relations, and it is not certain that this prediction will be modified by the strengthening of the European political union, since such a policy would not be sufficiently uniform to abolish the freedom of countries to exercise foreign policy or an individualized defense. The fact that Portugal is not located in the Mediterranean—and therefore is quite protected from the repercussions that its acts may cause in that region—adds to its strategic position an appreciable advantage that places it from the start on extremely favorable ground to address the issue of special relations with the United States on several levels. Issues such as the new role of AFSOUTH within NATO, the reevaluation of the Supreme Allied Command Atlantic, or even the extension of certain CSCE mechanisms to the western Mediterranean are some points on which the Portuguese-American dialogue may contribute toward reaching mutually advantageous solutions.

Conclusion

Today, in terms of foreign policy, there is no purely bilateral or purely multilateral approach. The fact that multilateral diplomacy is expanding its scope and involving an increasing number of countries does not preempt the possibility of bilateral relationships, but it does mean that the characteristic style of bilateral negotiation prior to the proliferation of multinational institutions is changed. Similarly the relationship between international organizations is influenced by the bilateral relations that the participant countries continue to develop.

As we have seen, there is overlapping intervention in Southern Europe by multilateral institutions. The UN and, very specifically, the CSCE (with its possible extension to the southern margin of the Mediterranean) make themselves felt. NATO is reassessing the nature of its own mandate; it seems to demonstrate increased interest in restructuring the forces on the southern flank, taking into account new risks and possible threats. The effects of the Common Foreign and Security Policy of the European Union are also felt, with the prospect of future development pursuant to the Maastricht Treaty in defense policy and defense, and with the revitalization of the Western European Union, as both armed force of the European Union and European pillar of the Atlantic Alliance. In the areas of legal and cultural cooperation, the Council of Europe, which has contributed greatly to the spread of the model of a state based on law to emerging democracies on the European continent, continues its important work.

The coincident intervention of all these international organizations, shaping similar standards of conduct throughout Europe, has greatly strengthened convergence and minimized disparities. Their actions in the areas of security, defense, economics, law, politics, diplomacy, and culture have been synergistic and have brought about a significant reinforcement of stability and progress in this part of the world. Southern Europe would be completely different if the expanded authority of the international organizations did not include binding standards for the actions of these countries in the world arena.

The recent multilateralization of international relations will not, however, eclipse bilateral foreign policy. Numerous bilateral disputes persist in Southern Europe. The CSCE and NATO are important instruments for structuring the actions of the United States in the region. But they do not obviate an active bilateral policy that will take into account the interest of each participant—and on the Mediterranean side the countries are extremely differentiated and sometimes sharply competitive with their immediate neighbors.

These indispensable bilateral relations will reflect the fact that the United States is the partner of the European countries in organizations for security and defense (the CSCE and NATO) but will not be part of the European Union. The problems of compatibility between NATO and the WEU, so as not to disrupt the transatlantic link, will not be approached similarly by all the countries of Southern Europe. It will be possible to detect differences between the followers of a more classic Atlantic concept and the more intense followers of a European identity in foreign relations. The fact that the Mediterranean area today poses specific security problems that counsel preservation of constructive relations with the United States, suggests that the majority of the Southern European countries will favor a prudent approach to European unity with regard to security and defense issues, so as to preserve, although with necessary adjustments, the essential transatlantic solidarity.

The interaction between different foreign policy approaches will have effects throughout Southern Europe. Bilateral policy will survive and will begin to comprise issues other than those typical of classic diplomacy. Multilateral approaches will begin to incorporate some issues previously handled through bilateral policy. The specifics of bilateral relationships will have to take into consideration the multilateral framework. In some areas, such as human rights and security, multilateral relations will be important, but in areas such as defense or the core of foreign policy the bilateral will prevail, perhaps under the name "multiple bilateral." It is through an interaction of diplomatic approaches that Southern Europe and the Mediterranean region will participate in the international system and, consequently, handle their relations with the United States.

Part Four

THE UNITED STATES AND SOUTHERN EUROPE

ELEVEN

U.S. Interests and Policy Options

John W. Holmes

FOR FORTY YEARS U.S. policy toward Europe was dominated by two relationships. First, the U.S. responded to the power and threat of the former Soviet Union by according primacy to U.S.-Soviet relations. The second, and related, emphasis was on Western Europe, particularly as a military ally. The main channels of U.S. relations with Western Europe were the North Atlantic Treaty Organization (NATO) and bilateral links with Western Europe's major military powers: Germany, the United Kingdom, and France.

The end of the cold war has weakened the claims of these two relationships on American attention; in *relative* terms other foreign policy concerns have become more important. Among these are relations with the European states on the north side of the Mediterranean.

A discussion of U.S. policy toward Southern Europe and the Mediterranean must take into account two circumstances. The first is a perennial factor. The United States lacks an integrated view of the problems of the Mediterranean area.[1] One can argue that the Mediterranean is not a coherent subject for analysis or policy.[2] But to pretend that Europe and the Middle East and North Africa are in separate universes ignores the strong North-South interactions across the Mediterranean.

Second, the United States seems to be changing its basic approach to foreign involvement. The Bush administration, by 1992, appeared to stand for an effort to continue U.S. leadership in the world, while acknowledging the end of the cold war, and America's loss of economic dominance, by a more selective approach to intervention. Its choice of problems with which to deal seemed to be founded on "realism."

213

The new Clinton administration arrived carrying with it, some thought, a fundamentally different neo-Wilsonian approach stressing universal human values; Secretary of State Warren Christopher said that human rights were the cornerstone of the Clinton administration's foreign policy. That point, rephrased, continues to be stated; speaking to the World Conference on Human Rights in June 1993, Secretary Christopher called reinforcing democracy and human rights "a pillar of our foreign policy."[3]

However, it seems increasingly clear that the change from the Bush administration's policies is not as radical as had been expected. The Clinton administration came around to the view that intervention in Bosnia could be perilous, and bore little relation to U.S. national interests, whatever the humanitarian arguments. Secretary Christopher, in defense of U.S. inaction, said, "My job is to worry about American interests and I think we're pursuing American interests adequately there."[4] The extrication of American forces from Somalia and the avoidance of military intervention in Haiti are further signs that the new administration, like the old, will judge the wisdom of intervention by the standard of American interests, not on the basis of humanitarian concerns. President Clinton himself put it rather clearly in May 1994 when he listed Rwanda among the many world conflicts in which the interests at stake do not justify the use of American military power.[5]

However, there continues to be a gap between the risk-avoiding actions of the Clinton administration and its universalist rhetoric. (The latter is given its best presentation in National Security Advisor Tony Lake's September 1993 speech, "From Containment to Enlargement."[6])

There *is* an important discontinuity between the Clinton administration's foreign policy and that of its predecessors. There is a vanished middle between pursuing narrow national interests and proclaiming universal principles: acting in the interest of the Alliance.[7]

Finally, and possibly more important than the theoretical or practical details of the Clinton administration's foreign policy, it is generally accepted that foreign policy is not the priority of this administration. President Clinton's own interest is clearly focused on domestic issues. This emphasis is likely to continue throughout the four years of his term; health care reform, to take an important example, will take months if not years to enact, and years to phase in. President Clinton recognizes that some foreign problems must have his attention, at least sporadically: Russia is the main case in point. International economic issues are also stressed, because of their impact on the domestic economy. This domestic focus reflects the desires of a majority of Americans; limiting foreign involvement, even attention to foreign affairs, is seen as the price of attending to that which is much more urgent: focusing attention and resources on domestic needs.

It is this lack of attention and involvement at the top that permits the flowering of many and diverse foreign policy views at lower levels. This situation is different from the inflamed competition between the State and Defense departments, and the National Security Council in previous administrations. Those were struggles for the attention of the president and the power of his involvement. What we see and hear today smacks more of a genteel academic debate.

This is not to say that the United States will easily yield its primacy in world affairs. It continues to proclaim, rhetorically, its leadership. In more than one recent instance, it has seized on a development initiated or largely financed by others and insisted on presiding over it.[8] But this is leadership on the cheap.

In the discussion that follows I have tempered my judgments by my perceptions of the policy stance of the Clinton administration. I have done so in the belief that, whereas some of the particulars of the Clinton administration's approach to foreign policy are peculiar to it, pursuing a much more selective approach to foreign commitments reflects political reality in the United States, both at present and for the foreseeable future.

U.S. Interests

American interests in the nations of Southern Europe are partly direct, but they partly derive from the fact that these nations share a neighborhood—a rather rough neighborhood—with countries and movements that constitute a potential threat either to Southern Europe, to the United States, or to both. This neighborhood—the Mediterranean and the lands around it—is in fact one of the relatively few areas of the world where two conditions are met: the United States has important national interests and the circumstances of the area are such that what the United States does can make a big difference.

Our Interest in Southern Europe

Our *direct* interest derives from the fact that Southern Europe has developed, especially economically, and may continue to grow in importance. Although these countries were all, until quite recently, economically backward and politically undemocratic, they are now all democratically governed and have, for the most part, enjoyed exceptional rates of economic growth.[9] Italy, the first in the class in terms of both political and economic development, is now one of the world's major economic powers, and conceivably, when it emerges from its "second revolution," it may be a more assertive and important political actor. Collectively, as increasingly prosperous and mature democracies, the nations of Southern Europe count steadily for more in the world.

The European Union's (EU) progressive replacement of NATO as the most important European regional organization is contributing to the growth of the relative political weight of these states, compared to the traditional great powers of Northern Europe ("the warrior states").

That said, the progressive transfer of economic powers to the EU level reduces somewhat the importance of the United States' bilateral economic relations with all the individual governments of the EU. The dominance of the Union to date by the Paris-Bonn axis, and the persistent failure of the Southern European nations either to play individual leadership roles of note or to organize effective coalitions reduces the significance of these countries for an outside power like the United States. Yet this situation, too, could change. Spain, for a new member, has been a fast learner of the EU game; and Italy, which hitherto has played a relatively strong foreign policy hand weakly, even within the EU, may in the future demand a role more equal to its material strength.

This is the dominant, and brighter, side to the picture of Southern Europe. Coexisting with these happy developments and observations are some more worrisome facts and possibilities.

The relatively stable governments and leadership of several Southern European countries—with which the United States has found it easy to work—show signs of fragility. The political system in Italy is in the midst of changes that bear comparison with those in Japan, and, in terms of the displacement of a ruling group that has retained unbroken power for forty years, with Eastern Europe. The outcome is still uncertain even after the elections of March 1994, which brought a right-wing coalition to power for the first time in Italy's postwar history. At worst it may be found that the old Italian political system, corrupt and undemocratic though it was, performed better than its replacement. In any case the old political class has largely been replaced, and so may be the old style of governance. This change may increase the energy level of Italian foreign policy, but it could conceivably make Italy a less accommodating partner for the United States.[10]

At the other end of the Mediterranean, paths taken by recent govern-ments may change. In October 1993 Andreas Papandreou and his Pan-hellenic Socialist Movement (PASOK) party returned to power in Greece. The Mitsotakis government, which it replaced, had its failings, but it had made a serious effort to liberalize—and therefore modernize—the Greek economy. Like all Greek governments it was distracted by foreign affairs, but its priorities were properly elsewhere. PASOK returned to power bear-ing the burden of its demagogic past, at a time when troubles in the Balkans provide great and dangerous temptation. The death of Prime Minister Turgut Ozal in Turkey also left a void, and it is still too soon to know how, or whether, Prime Minister Tansu Ciller will fill it.

Despite these unknowns, the Southern European members of NATO are overall—as they almost never were in the past—a collection of liberal democracies in which the market economy predominates. The United States has material (as well as cultural and sentimental) interests in these countries. No serious conflict with them is likely: they now form part of the community of liberal states among which war is inconceivable. Francis Fukuyama might say they are at the end of history.

Our Interest in the Middle East

The story is very different when we turn to the other basis for U.S. interest in Southern Europe: its location in a part of the world where the threat of conflict is very real. Even Fukuyama allows for continuing conflict within the surviving historical world (the old third world, more or less) and between it and the posthistorical world (the liberal democracies). As Nadji Safir has already pointed out, Fukuyama's three axes "along which the two worlds will collide"—oil, migration, and "world order" issues (especially the transfer of sensitive, militarily significant technologies)—describe the situation, actual or potential, in and around the Mediterranean.[11]

The United States has strong national interests in part of this zone of conflict: the area at the eastern end of the Mediterranean. With the end of the cold war, the Middle East may in fact be the area of the world where U.S. interests are most actively engaged.

The stability of the Middle East will be important to the United States as long as it wishes to play the role of world power. Indeed an interruption in the flow of oil from the Persian Gulf or a threat to the survival of Israel would probably elicit a response even from an America that in other respects had abdicated that role. We could not escape the international economic impact of a massive cutoff of oil, and our domestic politics would prevent us from ignoring a vital threat to Israel. Southern Europe also has important interests in the Eastern Mediterranean and the Gulf. Although historically there has been backbiting about specifics, European-American cooperation has increased in recent years. This is fortunate from an American point of view. Events as recent as the Gulf War of 1991 have reinforced the U.S. view that the pursuit of its interests in the Middle East requires a secure corridor through the Mediterranean, which in turn requires Southern European cooperation.

At one time the U.S. role in the Middle East was justified by the threat of communist (or Soviet) expansionism. That threat, for the moment, no longer exists. But the underlying material ground for interest in the Middle East, access to oil at a reasonable price, remains.

The United States has only rarely engaged in direct military action to protect this interest. More typically we have employed aid to and cooperation with friendly governments; sometimes we have even looked benevolently on oil price increases as the price we pay for the stability of friendly producers.

These methods may have their uses in the future. However, particularly since the Iranian revolution, indirect means have been less effective in preserving the Persian Gulf balance of power. If, as Graham Fuller suggests, Iraq were to disintegrate, a tolerable regional balance might be very hard to achieve: there would be a threat of Iranian hegemony.[12] Under these circumstances, more than ever, the United States, for its own interests and those of its allies, must continue to play at least a balancing role in the Middle East.[13] This role requires secure access through the Mediterranean: the analogy is with the British lifeline to India in the days of the Empire.

There are two principal arguments for a more detached approach to the question of oil access. The first is that it does not matter very much; the oil, somehow or other, at some price or other, will flow. But it is the price effect that counts. It is probably excessive to see the first oil price crisis of 1973–74 as the cause of the distinct inflection in the trend line of Western economic growth, although the temporal coincidence is striking. What is not in doubt is that the Yom Kippur crisis, and the second oil crisis at the end of the same decade, shocked the world economy and caused significant losses in income for consumer countries (as well as adding fuel to inflation).[14] According to one expert, if Iraq had gained control over Middle Eastern oil prices in 1990–91, "the long-term price of oil would have been as much as 50–100 percent higher than it would be with oil resources under the control of regimes friendly to the existing world order."[15]

The other way to avoid involvement is to reduce dependence on Persian Gulf oil. One could exploit oil resources outside that area. The most promising zone is the former Soviet Union. But realization of its potential will depend on foreign investment and technology, and these in turn depend on internal political stability—a prerequisite that to date is far from a sure thing. Even if there is a substantial increase in exports from the former Soviet Union, the Middle East will still be the main source of additional oil supply over the next decade.[16]

One could also practice oil conservation. Judging from the tiny increase in transport fuel prices enacted in the United States in 1993, despite the most favorable of circumstances (a major effort to reduce the government deficit and low oil prices), this is a road that will not be taken.[17] (It may be that maintaining the threat of military intervention is a cheaper option— particularly if, as in the war against Iraq, we can "tax" other consumers for the surge cost of actual war.)

Therefore, taking a cold-eyed view, active U.S. involvement in the Middle East to preserve reasonable access to oil seems likely, and given the current lack of alternatives, it has a certain bounded rationality.

The other major U.S. interest in the Eastern Mediterranean, the security of Israel, may, on the other hand, be greatly affected by a recent development: the understanding reached in September 1993 between Israel and the Palestine Liberation Organization (PLO). If this development leads to a general and durable peace between Israelis and Palestinians, the threat to Israel from the Arab world would dwindle.

That development in turn would change the nature of the U.S. interest in Israel and its immediate neighbors. It is hard to imagine America's ceasing to have strong personal and economic ties with Israel, but the relationship would be different from that in the past. Furthermore, we would not have quite the same interest in maintaining the goodwill of certain other states.

The most important case, from every point of view, is Egypt, which has received heavy American assistance since the Camp David accords. It would, if the Palestinian issue is resolved, cease to have the same priority for U.S. assistance, and U.S. political support for its government might become less unconditional. The degree and rapidity of these shifts should not be exaggerated. It may be decades before relations between Israel and its Arab neighbors are truly normalized; until then Egypt, the only Arab country capable of threatening Israel militarily, is vital to U.S. policy relating to Israel. Egypt is also important for access to the Persian

Gulf area. If Egypt were to fall under radical Islamist domination, it would be more difficult to resist that movement elsewhere.

Nevertheless a *lasting* settlement of the Palestinian question would permit, and probably produce, a reduced U.S. commitment to the eastern Mediterranean.

Other Mediterranean Interests

Migration is largely a regional problem. Although the United States is playing host to a number of immigrants, legal and illegal, from the Islamic world, the bulk of our immigrants come from Latin America; Europe is the target for migration from the arc running from Turkey to Morocco and extending even beyond the Sahara.

Similarly the threats posed, for example, by the proliferation of missile technology to unstable and potentially unfriendly nations on the Southern Rim, are threats to Europe (mainly Southern Europe) as well as within the Southern Rim, but not to the United States.

This is not to say that the United States has no interest in what may happen. Developments that would harm Southern Europe would have some impact on the United States, even if they did not threaten our more clearly vital interest in access to the eastern Mediterranean. It is true that our ability to influence the socioeconomic conditions in Southern Rim countries that are the soil in which these threats may grow is limited. However, as Antonio Badini argues,[18] the United States is not only a global military power, it is also a global trading power. The idea of a vertical division of the world, with the United States concentrating only on its supposed economic bloc in the Americas, runs counter to the existing patterns of trade and investment.

Taking a still broader, more political, point of view, the United States should take an interest in avoiding a clash of civilizations between "the West" and the Islamic world. A failed relationship between Western Europe and the Maghreb might be the flash point for such a clash, but it would spread and affect U.S. interests in a much broader area, starting with but not limited to the eastern Mediterranean and the Persian Gulf.[19] The American effort in 1994 to persuade the Algerian government to enter into a dialogue with the more moderate elements in the Islamist opposition suggests that that point has been taken.

The need for U.S. involvement in limiting the transfer of sensitive technologies to unfriendly nations is evident. The United States is both one of the great sources of these technologies and the power most able to coax or coerce other potential suppliers into controlling such flows. Furthermore, this objective forms part, as Fukuyama notes, of a complex of "world order" issues. The United States has a generalized interest in achieving multilateral discipline on such issues, not just for humanitarian reasons but also because this would reduce the calls on the United States to be the world's policeman.

Greece and Turkey

All of the interests I have discussed are ones that have survived the end of the cold war. But the cold war has left some orphans, particularly Greece and Turkey.

The American military involvement in these countries dates from the early post–World War II days when both of them were on the front line of what, at least in the case of Greece, was more than just a cold war. Unlike other Southern European countries, these countries continue to be recipients of American military assistance. We are also witnessing a very significant build-up in these countries' stocks of modern military hardware by purchase and even more by virtue of the provisions of the Conventional Forces in Europe treaty. (Other NATO countries are permitted to transfer modern equipment to Greece and Turkey; they destroy equivalent obsolete equipment, but the effect is a radical modernization and improvement in capability.[20])

Over the years the military threat from the Soviet Union became less acute, but regrettably Greece and Turkey renewed a hostility to each other that had been submerged in the early days of the cold war. The United States was trapped: it could not tailor its military assistance to these countries to the outside threat but had to limit the natural imbalance between them by applying the famous 10:7 ratio to assistance to Turkey and Greece.

The end of the Soviet threat has had an uneven effect on the U.S. interest in these two countries. For the moment the Russian threat is nonexistent. But Turkey is seen in Washington as a potential ally or agent in the traditional Middle East, and much more arguably in the "new Middle East," Central Asia.

Turkey is unhappy that the United States has not clarified its view of Turkey's post–cold war role. It feels that it was misled, perhaps let down, when it did not receive American financial support for its efforts in Central Asia. It is also uneasy about what is seen as U.S. support for Russia in the latter's apparent efforts to reassert dominance in the areas that were once part of the Soviet Union.[21]

Despite these differences it is generally agreed in the United States that there is a case for bolstering Turkish capabilities, even if there is some vagueness about the purpose thereof.[22]

Greece is a different case. Greece obviously has strong ethnic and cultural links to the United States. It feels threatened, at least potentially, by Turkey. It looks to the United States to play the role of subregional balancer. But its geostrategic significance for America has largely been exhausted with the end of the cold war. Greece, like Turkey, could be a base for potential U.S. military actions in the Middle East. Some investments are being made in the remaining U.S. bases in Greece (principally the air and naval facilities at Souda Bay); agitation against the bases seems to be dormant. However, Souda Bay is viewed as useful but not crucial.

Greece's present claim on American attention derives from the possibility of Greek involvement in a Balkan war. There may, therefore, be actions that the United States will want to take to maintain some influence over Greece. But the intrinsic interest of Greece for American foreign policy has changed radically.

There is, in fact, some thinking in Washington about phasing out military assistance to both Greece and Turkey (it would be impossible to end it for Greece alone). This step would at least get the United States out of the position of contributing to a threat of military conflict.

U.S. Policy Options

The new American administration wishes to limit, not deepen, foreign involvement, with a view to focusing attention and resources on domestic needs. The Mediterranean–Southern Europe area may not escape the effect of the diminished U.S. interest in the world. Action in the Persian Gulf and reactivation of the Middle East peace process may have been the end of a chapter, rather than developments that will continue or be repeated. Just as the United States has tried to view Eastern Europe and Yugoslavia as fundamentally European problems, it could reduce its involvement in this area. If the American military drawdown goes beyond the 1995–96 target of 100,000 Europe-based military personnel (mostly army and air), the Sixth Fleet could be vulnerable even though it has a separate justification.

All of this has to be said. But it needs to be balanced by some arguments for the likelihood of an active U.S. policy in this area.

Some of the U.S. interests in this area are perceived as truly national interests; this is most obviously true of our commitment to Israel, but it also applies to our interest in the free flow of Persian Gulf oil. These interests therefore should not be subject to the "Yugoslav precedent"—that is, to the growing U.S. unwillingness to act on the basis of collective interests in cases in which the narrowly conceived U.S. national interest is not important.

Furthermore, our military role is seen as effective, within our resources, and hard to replace. Proportionally, the U.S. military drawdown in the Mediterranean area has been far smaller than that in central and Northern Europe. No other power or combination thereof is capable of substituting for us in the sort of action we led against Iraq, and our military capabilities are tailored for such a challenge. This contrasts with the U.S. military commitment to East Asia, for example.[23]

Finally the rather strong universalist streak in American thinking, of which Lake and others in the Clinton administration are exemplars, could conduce to a grasp of the importance of bridging the gap between the West and Islam.

What Should We Try to Do?

Put very broadly, the United States should aim to avoid the shocks to the world economy (and to its own) that would result if the oil resources of the Persian Gulf fell into unfriendly hands. It should also seek to create a situation of cooperation and friendship among the countries of the Southern Rim of the Mediterranean (including Israel) and between them and the developed world, especially Europe and America. Finally, although it is now only a distant threat, we would not want a revived Russia (the only other outside force of consequence in this area) to imperil either the independence of the countries of the region or the economic benefits we derive from it.

These are objectives that should gain general assent on both sides of the Atlantic. But the agreement fades on specifics.

Take the special, but important, case of Turkey. Turkey is important for its strategic location and for the example it sets for the Islamic world. The United States, to its credit, recognizes this. Unfortunately the United States cannot provide what Turkey needs most if it is to remain attached to and increasingly incorporated in the world of the liberal democracies: a market for its goods and people. Geography dictates that the European Union is the natural economic partner for Turkey. And the EU up to now has not been willing to accept Turkey fully, but has indefinitely postponed its application for membership for a combination of cultural and economic reasons.

Western Europe seems to be telling the United States, "Turkey is your problem." It does not say this with regard to the Maghreb. Yet its response to the challenge it recognizes in the Maghreb—repeatedly described as a "time bomb"[24]—reminds one of its casual attitude toward Turkey. The response is strikingly incommensurate with the size of the problem. European government assistance has been feeble compared to the effort recently mounted on behalf of Eastern Europe.[25] Private investment there has also been weak.[26] Faced with a situation similar to but more serious than that with which the United States has dealt in its relationship with Mexico, Europe has been dysfunctionally unimaginative. Aside from EU politics—a point on which I shall touch shortly—the explanation seems to be partly cultural, a sense that the Islamic peoples of North Africa are the "wholly other." Unless and until Europe can escape from this frame of mind, it is likely to follow Huntington's script. The United States, which generally has stood aloof from this problem, will share in the bitter harvest.

How Should We Do It?

How should we deal with these problems: bilaterally, via the EU, through new multilateral arrangements, or by modifying old ones like NATO?

DIVIDING THE LABOR WITH THE EU. The Bush administration began, with Yugoslavia, to attempt a division of labor. The United States welcomed the signs that the European Community wanted to take primary responsibility for this problem, which did not seem to impinge directly on American interests. Letting the Europeans do it seemed appropriate as part of a general strategy of selective intervention.

In the event the Community was incapable of dealing with the situation; its failure has had considerable impact on the self-confidence of that institution (at a time when much else was going wrong for it) and has created new grounds for transatlantic recrimination.

In the Mediterranean the same policy is being pursued de facto; it may be that the results will be comparably poor. The United States has been dominant in the eastern Mediterranean; Europe has been left the lead in the western Mediterranean. This arrangement is tidy and it reduces friction, but it is not a perfect solution. For one thing it does not reflect interests and capabilities accurately.

It may be natural for the United States to take the lead in the eastern Mediterranean. The United States is the only power capable of massive power projection; it has developed and maintained strong special relationships with certain key states, especially Israel, Egypt, and Saudi Arabia.

Yet it needs the cooperation of others, mainly the nations of Western Europe. It was encouraging that the EU was willing to put so much into the Palestinian development effort; it was an act of hubris for the United States to seek to deprive the Union of the lead in monitoring that effort. If the countries of the eastern Mediterranean—like the rest of the Southern Rim—are to have a more prosperous and, one hopes, a more peaceful and democratic future, it must be through enhanced economic integration with Europe.

The United States may also need military cooperation. Although it is capable of fighting another Iraq-type war by itself, it could not do so in terms of American political reality. (Recall the narrow vote in favor of military action against Iraq in the U.S. Senate, even when we were assured of allies.)

Leaving the western Mediterranean to the Europeans is also too simple an option. As noted, the European Union has been delinquent in addressing the problems adequately, and the United States will not escape the impact of negative consequences should that time bomb blow up.

The notion of a mutually agreed-upon division of labor is not intrinsically wrong, as long as the "nonleader" is willing to lend a hand. But the United States finds it somewhere between uncomfortable and impossible to be junior partner in enterprises it joins. And Europe is betwixt and between: no single European power is willing (or capable) of shouldering major external responsibilities by itself, and the European powers collectively have so far not been able to get beyond rhetoric in their professed progress toward a Common Foreign and Security Policy (CFSP).

The likeliest future for the EU may still be one in which political union is achieved along Maastricht lines. However, if this goal is achieved, it is not likely to be reached in this century, nor perhaps early in the next.

The EU's recent troubles should not blind us to its present importance and its great potential. The United States, for broad reasons of transatlantic and international economic policy, should now seek to reach a grand accord with the EU.[27] It should furthermore encourage the development of a European defense capability, as it did at the January 1994 NATO summit.

But for the remainder of this decade dealing with the EU is not likely to be an entirely satisfactory way of coordinating Mediterranean policy, because of both the incomplete development of the CFSP and the inadequate attention the EU currently gives to Mediterranean problems. The latter problem is not attributable to the inadequate development of the security aspect of the EU. The Union already has most of the means necessary to make an impact on the socioeconomic situation on the Southern Rim of the Mediterranean. The problem lies in the inadequate efforts of the Southern European countries to fix the EU's attention on the Mediterranean, and the even more inadequate results of these efforts.

Antonio Badini is entirely right in saying that, although the EU may not have the capability of playing a worldwide role, it can and should be a regional power, and the areas to the south and east of the Mediterranean are a proper focus for it.[28] When the Union realizes this and acts on this agenda, a division of labor with it will be possible and desirable.

MODIFYING NATO. What of cooperation in and through NATO? Over the last few years, as a senior Defense Department official remarked to me, most of NATO's activity has been south of the Alps. For months, as a result of the continuing strife in the former Yugoslavia, air bases such as that at Aviano have been jammed with aircraft from NATO countries. A permanent, integrated NATO naval force has been organized in the Mediterranean. Planning for southern contingencies has preoccupied NATO staffs.

NATO has been the beneficiary of the failures of other organizations. The blunting of the spears of the Conference on Security and Cooperation in Europe (CSCE), the UN, and the EC on the Yugoslav catastrophe has left NATO almost alone in the ring as a possible agency of collective action. But its credibility could also be diminished by Yugoslavia as a result of the reluctance of NATO's member countries (the United States included), despite bellicose statements, to do much more through NATO than the members of the other organizations were willing to do through them.

Furthermore, NATO has had and continues to have a number of problems dealing with the "southern flank":

—The area never has formed a coherent whole in the way the old central front did. Each of its countries had quite distinct interests and felt little involvement with those of the others; the main connection was not with other Southern European countries but with the United States. Much more than north of the Alps, "NATO" tended to be the cover for bilateral relationships with the United States. Since the end of the cold war on the one hand there has been some increased cooperation, but on the other the one agreed-upon threat—the Soviet Union—has been lost.

—The southern flank, furthermore, has suffered and suffers from the fact, unique in NATO, that two of its countries, Greece and Turkey, are as much adversaries as allies. The "security community" that includes most of Western Europe does not include them.

—Beginning with the Gulf War, NATO has displayed some operational flexibility about operating "out-of-area," with its logistical and staff capabilities being put to use first in Iraq and now with regard to the former Yugoslavia. But there has not as yet been a clear decision to address out-of-area activity as a matter of open and accepted practice, with the arguable exception of Yugoslavia. Even when NATO figures like the late Secretary General Manfred Wörner talked about NATO's future being out-of-area, the reference seemed to be to Yugoslavia and possibly other Eastern European areas, not to the Mediterranean.

—Somewhat similarly, the debate regarding the expansion of NATO that is going on within the U.S. government, and which occupied the NATO summit of January 1994, has to do with its expansion to the east.[29] In other words, the one major political change in NATO that has been proposed has nothing to do with the area to the south of Europe.

—I would not want to discount the potential military threat from the Southern Rim.[30] However, in the short to medium term, the "threat" from the South is not military; it is of a wave of new migrants landing on Europe's shores as a result of socioeconomic conditions and political explosions. The means to avoid this threat are nonmilitary, and, if they work, may also limit the long-term threat. NATO, although showing remarkable flexibility and adaptability on its military side, has not given any evidence of becoming a significant agency for political-economic purposes.

All of the above points should not be taken as an argument for getting rid of NATO. NATO has its distinct strengths, and for certain purposes it has no substitute. But its capabilities, present and prospective, do not closely match the problems that the United States and Southern Europe confront in the Mediterranean area.

NEW FORMS OF COOPERATION. The Italo-Spanish proposal for a Conference on Security and Cooperation (CSCM) in the Mediterranean did not get very far. The diversion of Gianni De Michelis's attention by Italy's internal political crisis is a sufficient explanation, but the CSCM proposal faced many other obstacles. Notably, until the Israeli-Palestinian dispute is resolved, trans-Mediterranean cooperation on a grand scale is inconceivable; on this score there has been progress, but so far not enough to change the prognosis.

The American opposition, which persists, exists for the wrong reasons. The United States is opposed to any country participating in more than one regional organization—unless that country is the United States.[31] This hub-and-spoke conception of the world is part of the reluctance of the United States to abandon the trappings of universal leadership, even when it wants to relieve itself of the responsibilities of that role.[32] (Underlying this formalist position once lay a fear that U.S. freedom to act in the Mediterranean area would be constrained by some sort of unholy alliance within the CSCM.[33])

In any case the second coming of the CSCM does not appear imminent. What seems more feasible is something less ambitious. Antonio Badini makes a number of interesting suggestions in chapter 6, which deserve consideration. Where American participation is requested and would be useful, we should take part. But at least in the short term, these schemes for cooperation are at best a partial answer to the needs of American policy in the area.

THE SHORT-TERM SOLUTION. The absence of ways of transferring or dividing responsibility for U.S. interests in the Mediterranean suggests that for the time being—perhaps for the remainder of this decade—U.S. policy will be put into effect by a combination of unilateral and bilateral means.

The United States by itself must, as a deterrent to those countries or movements that would threaten either access to Persian Gulf oil or the security of Israel, retain a substantial military force in the Mediterranean, plus the capability of reinforcing that force in case of need.

This same force, incidentally, will serve, at least psychologically, as a defense of Southern Europe from a military threat (or the fear of a military threat) from the South.[34] Without the Sixth Fleet and some other American military forces, Southern European countries might justly feel themselves naked to their neighbors; Northern European countries seem less willing to extend military protection than the United States.[35]

The United States should also continue—in its own and in the collective world interest—its efforts to achieve a settlement in the Arab-Israeli dispute. The new climate created by the war against Iraq and by the U.S.-sponsored Middle East peace talks that began in Madrid in October 1991 certainly constitutes a large part of the explanation for the opening and successful conclusion of talks between Israel and the PLO. Although those talks show that the United States does not have to be present for progress to be made, it is far too soon to let the United States exit from the scene: we are nearer the beginning than the end of the peace process, and U.S. influence is one of the keys to its ultimate success.

But the United States cannot act in the Middle East without cooperation, and some of that cooperation must be sought elsewhere. The use of bases and prepositioning in some of the Persian Gulf countries themselves is important. So is continued access to military facilities in Germany and elsewhere.[36] But the cooperation of Southern European countries is vital.

The United States has slimmed down its inventory of bases in this area. Some of this reduction has been carried out under pressure from host governments, notably in Spain and Greece, but some has been for reasons of economy. There may be some further winnowing out. The United States has a strong interest, for example, in only one base in Turkey: the one at Incirlik, because of its potential for usefulness in actions in the Middle East.

Although NATO cover continues to have some usefulness, base rights will, even more than in the past, be a matter essentially for bilateral negotiation with the several host countries. But this negotiation will be conducted on a different basis from the past. Portugal is now being added to the list of countries that receive nothing for their bases, even implicitly. Greece and Turkey could be put in a similar position in the future. Host countries will all grant rights, as many do already, on the basis of shared interests rather than "rent." There is enough redundancy in the base inventory so that the reluctance of one or two countries to do this would not be threatening to U.S. interests—a fact that reduces the bargaining power of the remaining aided hosts.

Nevertheless it is unwise to tie base arrangements solely to military requirements. It is far better to embed them in a general pattern of relations—of cooperative relations. The current Portuguese base negotiations have set an example for this approach.

Indeed the loosening of the traditional NATO framework argues for a deepening of the bilateral relationship between the United States and the several Southern European countries.

No one who knows the past of those relationships would deny that there has existed between the United States and the Southern European countries a special relationship. Even today a Turkish, or even an Italian, prime minister goes to Washington with different desires and expectations than the leaders of Northern Europe. Unfortunately the interest Southern Europeans bring to their relations with the United States has not been reciprocated. What former ambassador Morton Abramowitz says with regard to Turkey is true generally. The United States has a major stake in these countries. "But preserving that stake will demand more concentrated and sympathetic attention than senior U.S. officials have usually been willing to devote to their long-time ally."[37]

With at least some of the Southern European countries our relationship has lacked breadth and depth; as another former U.S. ambassador, Monteagle Stearns, says with regard to Greece and Turkey, "despite the intimacy of our relations since 1947, our prior relationship was superficial, leaving little foundation of shared interest and understanding to cushion the shocks to which intimate relations can be more subject than casual ones."[38]

The task of enriching bilateral relations is one that the United States and the Southern European countries can and should share. It would be useful if the United States and the Southern Europeans could work together on another objective that they should share: avoiding a cultural-political clash with the Islamic world.

The ingredients of this cooperation, in an ideal world, seem clear. We could work together to remedy the socioeconomic backwardness of the Mediterranean's Southern Rim; we could seek to reduce cultural misunderstandings; we could work together politically to encourage democratic development in the Mediterranean's south; we could seek to work together even on migration issues (where Europe has much to learn from the American example). But there are two problems with this approach in the real world.

The first is that the United States, for reasons of geography and economics, is bound to be the junior partner in the effort—and the United States continues to be unwilling to be on a team unless it is the captain. This must change.

The second is that the tools of policy in the areas in question—including trade, aid, economic policy, and migration—have largely been ceded by the Southern European countries to the European Union. This is not necessarily a negative development. Conceptually it could lead to more resources being available for these purposes. So far, however, Southern European countries have displayed neither the insight nor the bureaucratic political skills necessary to focus the EU's attention on what should for it be *the* priority area of foreign involvement. This too must change if all of our interests are to be served.[39]

The bilateral stress of this discussion may displease some; but at this time, and in the absence of alternatives, it is dictated by realism.[40] Our bilateral efforts cannot, of course, be limited to Southern European nations, even if the geographic area in question is contiguous to them. Military efforts of a certain scale almost always require consultation with and, it is to be hoped, cooperation by the major military powers of Northern Europe. Assistance to the Palestinians, as part of the effort to bring an end to the Arab-Israeli dispute, involves contributions from all of Europe, not just the more contiguous nations. But even in such efforts it would help to have the Southern Europeans in agreement.

The Longer Term

The longer-term prospects for U.S. relations with Southern European countries are dependent on developments in at least three areas:

—The stability, in the longer term, of the area to the south and east of the Mediterranean depends on whether its economies, and also its political systems, develop favorably. Even if Europe and the United States do what they can to aid the development process, the results are unpredictable.[41] Not many of the countries in the area are likely to become stable and prosperous democracies during the next generation. Thus trouble, both internal and international, remains very probable, and Persian Gulf oil, to take a specific, will continue to be at risk.

—What will happen to the European Union, politically and economically? Will it develop institutionally to the point of being a capable and responsible regional power (one with which the United States could divide responsibilities, perhaps leaving it most of the responsibility for the Mediterranean)? Will its economy get back on track? If not it is likely to be, for example, unreceptive to immigrants, regardless of the political consequences.[42]

—Will the United States retreat even from its current limited willingness to involve itself internationally? It too could be pushed in an inward-looking direction by continued economic difficulties. It could also be pushed in that direction by a perceived lack of cooperation by the outside world, and especially by the part of the outside world it counts on most, Western Europe. It is true that the interests of the United States in the Mediterranean are closer to bedrock than those that underlie American involvement in most parts of the world; but it is not incredible that the United States would retreat from them over the next generation. Regrettably that retreat is likeliest if the United States does not receive cooperation from its erstwhile allies; in that case, it could produce a power vacuum.

The United States is not likely to pull out of the Mediterranean soon, but it will probably try to limit its involvement. A continued (if diminished) U.S. presence and interest would be of value to Southern European countries, and they should try to preserve it. But at the same time they might well begin taking out insurance for a possible U.S. withdrawal. As of now—even after its post-Maastricht disasters—the European Union seems to be the only good alternative to continued dependence on the United States: re-nationalization of security is not an attractive option for the Southern European countries. They consequently have a strong interest in turning the EU into an effective political entity. With some luck, in this longer time frame, the United States and the European Union can work together on what will surely still be a lengthy Mediterranean agenda.

Notes

1. Ellen Laipson, "Thinking about the Mediterranean," *Mediterranean Quarterly,* vol. 1, no. 1 (Winter 1990), pp. 50–65. The discussion of this point is on pp. 63–65.

2. One could go a step further and note that while the Southern European countries share some problems, they sometimes seem to share little else.

3. Elaine Sciolino, "Despite Heat, Christopher Has 'the Time of My Life,'" *New York Times,* June 1, 1993, p. A3; "Democracy and Human Rights: Where America Stands," *U.S. Department of State Dispatch,* vol. 4, no. 25 (June 21, 1993), p. 441.

4. Interview with Robert McNeill, "McNeill-Lehrer News Hour," PBS, June 1, 1993.

5. In a speech at the Naval Academy on May 25. See Paul Lewis, "Boutros-Ghali Angrily Condemns All Sides for Not Saving Rwanda," *New York Times,* May 26, 1994, p. A1.

6. *U.S. Department of State Dispatch,* vol. 4, no. 39 (September 17, 1993), pp. 658–64. Lake said, "The successor to a doctrine of containment must be a strategy of enlargement—enlargement of the world's free community of market democracies." Perhaps more revelatory of the administration's operational thinking was Under Secretary of State Peter Tarnoff's off-the-record speech of May 1993, in which he argued for selective engagement.

7. A senior State Department official told me that when an attempt was made in September 1993 to draft a comprehensive foreign policy speech for Secretary Christopher, language referring to acting in the interest of the Alliance was carefully stripped out. (In the event it proved impossible to draft such a speech; he spoke instead about the Palestinian donors conference.) The discontinuity should not be exaggerated; the Bush administration, in its approach to Yugoslavia, could be seen as heading in the same direction.

8. This was true of the Israeli-Palestinian agreement brokered by the Norwegians. Less usefully the United States provoked an unnecessary dispute with the European Community, insisting on being in charge of monitoring the distribution of aid to the Palestinians, despite the fact that the European financial contribution was much larger. (One good effect of this dispute was that the United States suddenly increased its contribution.) Mary Curtius, "US, EC viewed at odds over monitoring of aid to Mideast," *Boston Globe,* October 1, 1993, p. 12. A similar

attitude underlies the continuing U.S. government hostility to a Conference on Security and Cooperation in the Mediterranean.

9. France is obviously in part a Southern European country, and it is a very important player in the Mediterranean game. But my focus is on the countries traditionally considered part of the southern flank: Portugal, Spain, Italy, Greece, and Turkey.

10. The troubles of the Spanish socialists of the Partido Socialista Obrero Español (PSOE), hit by accusations of corruption, are reminiscent of the disintegration of the Italian Socialist Party in the early 1990s. However, there are apparent differences between the situations. The PSOE leader, Prime Minister Felipe Gonzalez, does not seem personally to be suspected of illegal activity; and whereas the Italian electorate came to reject all the "ins" of the last forty years, opprobrium in Spain seems to be limited to the PSOE.

11. See chapter 4 in this volume. See also Francis Fukuyama, *The End of History and the Last Man* (New York: Avon, 1993), pp. 276–78.

12. See chapter 5 in this volume. Iran is, of course, basically the most powerful state bordering on the Gulf; even an undivided Iraq would not, under normal circumstances, balance it. However, one should not conclude that Iraq's division would necessarily create an easy situation for Iran. Indeed the division of Iraq can be seen as a threat, not an opportunity, for Iran. Iran's current borders include several non-Persian, non–Farsi-speaking ethnic groups that might seek to follow the Iraqi example. Perhaps for this reason, Iran has not given the support to the Shi'ites in southern Iraq that it could have.

13. Some of the states in the area also want us to play a balancing role. See Terry L. Deibel, "Strategies Before Containment," *International Security,* vol. 16, no. 4 (Spring 1992), p. 86.

14. Yergin estimated that the G-7 industrialized nations alone lost $1.2 trillion in economic growth as a result of the two oil shocks. See Daniel Yergin, "Crisis and Adjustment: An Overview," in Daniel Yergin and Martin Hillenbrand, eds., *Global Insecurity: A Strategy for Energy and Economic Renewal* (Boston: Houghton Mifflin, 1982), p. 5. The indebtedness of less-developed countries, which racked their economies and societies during the 1980s and early 1990s, was partly due to these "temporary" oil price shocks. See Robert Lieber, "Oil and Power," *International Security,* vol. 17, no. 1 (Summer 1992), p. 172.

15. Edward N. Krapels, "The commanding heights: international oil in a changed world," *International Affairs,* vol. 69 (January 1993), p. 72.

16. See Joseph Stanislaw and Daniel Yergin, "The Oil Shocks to Come," *Foreign Affairs,* vol. 72 (September-October 1993), pp. 81–93.

17. See Lieber, "Oil and Power," pp. 174–76.

18. See chapter 6 in this volume.

19. Samuel P. Huntington's widely read essay is useful for calling attention to a potential problem but not for its basic approach nor for its sense of inevitable conflict. See "The Clash of Civilizations?" *Foreign Affairs,* vol. 72, no. 3 (Summer 1993), pp. 22–49. What is good in Lake's contrasting approach (see note 6) is the idea of incorporating more and more of the world into the democratic community, a concern for the projection of American values abroad that is one of the three perennial categories of the American national interest (the others being physical security and economic prosperity). See Deibel, "Strategies Before Containment," pp. 82–83.

20. See William Drozdiak, "Greece, Turkey Amassing Arms: Some Fear They Will Be Used in Balkan Wars," *Washington Post,* September 30, 1993, p. A14.

21. Based on a discussion with a Turkish source regarding topics to be raised by Prime Minister Ciller during her mid-October 1993 visit to Washington. For a discussion of recent U.S.-Turkish relations (and missed connections), see Morton L. Abramowitz, "Dateline Ankara: Turkey After Ozal," *Foreign Policy,* no. 91 (Summer 1993), pp. 178–80.

22. There are, in fact, some extreme Turkophiles in Washington who advocate giving Turkey a role that is almost certainly beyond its capabilities and desires.

23. See Paul Bracken, "The Military After Next," *Washington Quarterly,* vol. 16, no. 4 (Autumn 1993), p. 169.

24. For example by the Spanish Foreign Ministry: "L'Europe et le Maghreb: Rapport," Madrid, February 26, 1992. I am indebted to Nadji Safir for this citation.

25. See, for example, Yves Boyer, "Europe and Its Southern Neighbors," *Washington Quarterly,* vol. 16, no. 4 (Autumn 1993), p. 151.

26. See the figures cited by Safir in chapter 4.

27. This strategy is argued for in the study chaired by Robert B. Zoellick: Mark M. Nelson, *Atlantic Frontiers: A New Agenda for U.S.-EC Relations* (Washington: Carnegie Endowment for International Peace, 1993).

28. See chapter 6 in this volume.

29. An argument for this expansion, which attracted much attention, is found in Ronald D. Asmus, Richard L. Kugler, and F. Stephen Larrabee, "Building a New NATO," *Foreign Affairs,* vol. 72 (September-October 1993), pp. 28–40. The permanent bureaucracies in the State Department and the Defense Department were opposed, partly because this expansion would dilute NATO and partly for fear of the Russian reaction. The latter fear was seemingly confirmed by a letter from Russian President Boris Yeltsin to Clinton, Mitterrand, Kohl, and Major. See Roger Cohen, "Yeltsin Opposes Expansion of NATO in Eastern Europe," *New York Times,* October 2, 1993, p. 4.

30. For a succinct discussion, see Boyer, "Europe and Its Southern Neighbors," pp. 147–49.

31. The potential European members of the CSCM are, of course, already members of the CSCE.

32. The United States has abandoned its opposition to the creation of a regional security organization in East Asia (formerly it wanted no such organization, but only bilateral arrangements with the United States, to exist). But this organization does not transgress the principle of nonduplicative membership.

33. For example, that the riparian states might agree to a form of naval arms control that would exclude the fleets of outside powers, both Soviet and American.

34. The point I am trying to make is akin to that in Michael Howard's 1982 discussion of NATO's reassurance, as opposed to its deterrent, function. See Michael Howard, "Reassurance and Deterrence," in his *The Causes of Wars* (London: Temple Smith, 1983), pp. 246–64. The same article appeared in the Winter 1982–83 issue of *Foreign Affairs.*

35. The United States might also encourage Southern European countries to acquire antimissile defenses.

36. One of the unspoken, or at most whispered, reasons for continued U.S. commitment to NATO is that it provides cover, in the inelegant phrase used in some

U.S. military circles, for the garaging of U.S. forces to be used outside the NATO area.

37. Abramowitz, "Turkey After Ozal," p. 181.

38. Monteagle Stearns, *Entangled Allies: U.S. Policy Toward Greece, Turkey, and Cyprus* (New York: Council on Foreign Relations Press, 1992), p. 5.

39. One of the most important steps the European Union could take to smudge the all-too-sharp boundary between "the West" and "Islam" would be to admit Turkey to membership. Southern European countries, although not the main obstacles, have not exactly been advocates of this step.

40. Stearns, for example, argues for a growing NATO political role in the Mediterranean area, specifically in resolving the several Greco-Turkish disputes. Regrettably, this does not seem to be a practical option. The United States, exploiting continuing dependencies, may be the only outside force able to prevent or limit a potential conflict between Greece and Turkey. See Stearns, *Entangled Allies,* especially pp. 145–50.

41. Paul Kennedy writes, "In the 1960s, South Korea had a per capita GNP exactly the same as Ghana's . . . whereas today it is ten to twelve times more prosperous." See "Preparing for the 21st Century: Winners and Losers," *New York Review of Books,* February 11, 1993, p. 32. One would guess that the cultural-political climate for economic growth in the Southern Rim countries is somewhere between the East Asian and the African levels.

42. Although the European resistance to Islamic immigrants is primarily based on cultural-ethnic motives, economic conditions also contribute to it. See Myron Weiner, "Security, Stability, and International Migration," *International Security,* vol. 17, no. 3 (Winter 1992–93), p. 105.

Contributors

Roberto Aliboni is director of studies of the Italian Institute for International Affairs and has edited numerous books on Mediterranean affairs.

Antonio Badini, now Italian ambassador to Norway, has been personal representative for the G-7 Summit, diplomatic advisor to the Italian prime minister, and ambassador to Algeria.

Dimitri Constas is chancellor of Panteios University in Athens and the editor of *The Greek-Turkish Conflict in the 1990s.*

Graham E. Fuller, formerly national intelligence officer for the Middle East, now with RAND, is the author of several books, including *Iran: The Center of the Universe.*

Jaime Gama, a member of the Portuguese Parliament, was formerly Portugal's Foreign Minister.

John W. Holmes, a former U.S. diplomat who served for many years in Italy, most recently as deputy chief of mission in Rome, was a senior associate of the World Peace Foundation.

Ian O. Lesser is a Mediterranean specialist with RAND and the author of several books, including *Mediterranean Security.*

Andrés Ortega, now director of the Spanish Prime Minister's policy planning staff, has been a journalist; he is the author of two books, including *La razón de Europa.*

Fernando Rodrigo is deputy director of the Spanish Center for International Relations and has contributed to several books on European affairs.

Nadji Safir is professor of sociology at the University of Algiers.

Index

239

MAELSTROM